Keep this book. You will need it and use it throughout your career.

MANAGING QUALITY SERVICES

Educational Institute Books

MANAGING QUALITY SERVICES

Stephen J. Shriver, CHA

EDUCATIONAL INSTITUTE
of the American Hotel & Motel Association

Disclaimer

This publication is designed to provide accurate and authoritative information in regard to the subject matter covered. It is sold with the understanding that the publisher is not engaged in rendering legal, accounting, or other professional service. If legal advice or other expert assistance is required, the services of a competent professional person should be sought.

—From the Declaration of Principles jointly adopted by the American Bar Association and a Committee of Publishers and Associations

The author, Stephen J. Shriver, is solely responsible for the contents of this publication. All views expressed herein are solely those of the author and do not necessarily reflect the views of the Educational Institute of the American Hotel & Motel Association (the Institute) or the American Hotel & Motel Association (AH&MA).

Nothing contained in this publication shall constitute a standard, an endorsement, or a recommendation of the Institute or AH&MA. The Institute and AH&MA disclaim any liability with respect to the use of any information, procedure, or product, or reliance thereon by any member of the hospitality industry.

Library of Congress Cataloging-in-Publication Data
Shriver, Stephen J.
Managing quality services.

1. Hotel management. 2. Motel management
3. Food service management.
I. American Hotel & Motel Association. Educational
Institute. II. Title.
TX911.3.M279S49   1988   647'.94'068—dc19   88-11153
ISBN 0–86612–040–8

Editor: George Glazer

Contents

Part III
Problem-Solving Teams

Part IV
Performance Standards

Preface

This book defines quality assurance as a management system that ensures the consistent delivery of products and services. Quality assurance enables managers, supervisors, and employees to increase the profitability and productivity of a hospitality operation by solving problems and developing performance standards.

Part I introduces three major components of quality assurance: strategic planning for operations, problem-solving teams, and performance standards. Chapter 1 provides brief examples of these components and describes the kind of organizational environment and management support necessary to successfully implement them. Chapter 2 presents more details about these components of quality assurance and stresses the need for top management executives to adapt them to the unique needs and characteristics of their organizations.

The quality assurance system presented in this book is not a turnkey system. Quality assurance is a dynamic, ongoing process. While there are basic similarities among successful quality assurance systems in the hospitality industry, each system is recognizably unique. The components of quality assurance presented in this book are not rigid, inflexible processes. They can and should be changed to meet the specific needs of individual hospitality operations.

Part II examines strategic planning for operations in great detail and provides hospitality operators with practical tools with which to conduct strategic planning sessions. These tools include step-by-step suggestions for how to conduct each session, along with sample meeting agendas, sample meeting procedures, and sample flip chart sheets. Part II also alerts the organizer of the strategic planning process to the information which must be processed after each meeting in order to ensure an efficient and successful strategic planning process.

Part III provides hospitality operators with basic tools with which they can develop problem-solving teams at their properties. These tools include:

- A specific problem-solving process which has been used with success in a number of hospitality operations

- A detailed example of a problem-solving team in action

- Materials that can be used to train managers, supervisors, and employees to function as productive members of problem-solving teams

- Methods for tracking the progress of problem-solving teams and their overall success at improving quality at the property

Part IV examines performance standards but does not set standards for the hospitality industry. Performance standards are required levels of performance that are established by individual hospitality organizations. Although standards will vary from property to property, every property can ensure the consistent delivery of products and services by demanding 100% conformity to the standards established by their organizations.

I would like to thank the people who were involved in the crisis and opportunity of writing this book. On the crisis side, I thank my wife, Denise, for her understanding, and our preschool sons, Matthew and Andrew, for their lack of it. I also thank George Glazer, a hard-working magician, for transforming the manuscript into this book.

On the opportunity side, I would like to thank John Dawson and Pam Donner for initiating and supporting the quality assurance process presented in this book. Their daily involvement in the process has contributed to the continuing success of quality assurance at The Dawson Companies. I thank Pat Pierson and Jeff Brown for their pioneering spirit and the hours they spent contributing and commenting on sections of the book. I also thank Jeni Miller, who years ago wrote the employee survey that appears in Chapter 3.

A debt of gratitude is owned to Judy King, Manager of Quality Assurance, Opryland Hotel, Nashville, Tennessee; James Hart, CHA, Vice President Human Resources, Mississippi Management Inc., Jackson, Mississippi; and, Stevenson W. Fletcher III, Hotel, Restaurant, and Travel Administration, University of Massachusetts, Amherst, Massachusetts. They invested substantial amounts of time and effort in reviewing the manuscript with the express purpose of making it a more valuable resource for the hospitality industry.

I thank the members of the American Hotel & Motel Association's Quality Assurance Committee who, over the years, have contributed significantly to the development of quality assurance in the lodging industry.

Last, but not least, I thank all the members of The Dawson Companies, past and present, for helping to develop the quality assurance process presented in this book, and for proving that it works.

Stephen J. Shriver, CHA
Vice President of Organizational
    Development and Quality
    Assurance
The Dawson Companies, Limited
Scottsdale, Arizona

Part I
An Introduction to Quality Assurance

1

An Overview of Quality Assurance

One of the greatest challenges facing the hospitality industry today is managing the human resources within the industry to provide quality products and services to guests. Quality assurance is a management system that can help each hospitality operation meet this challenge.

This book defines quality assurance as a management system that ensures the consistent delivery of products and services. Quality assurance enables managers, supervisors, and employees to increase the profitability and productivity of a hospitality operation by solving problems and developing performance standards. Three major components of quality assurance examined in this book are:

- Strategic planning for operations
- Problem-solving teams
- Performance standards

This introductory chapter begins with a brief history of quality assurance in the hospitality industry. Early studies on how to provide quality services to guests revealed widespread confusion about the meaning of the term "quality." Many hospitality owners and operators felt that quality was a subjective evaluation of the intangible aspects of service. Few thought that quality could be measured objectively, or that the term could apply to any type or size of hospitality property. The opening sections of this chapter attempt to correct these misconceptions by defining quality as the consistent delivery of products and services to guests. This definition enables individual properties to define what quality means for their particular operations by establishing consensus on standards. Standards are defined as required levels of performance. Many common industry problems can be solved through the cooperative efforts of managers, supervisors, and employees in developing, implementing, and managing performance standards.

The next section of this chapter provides an overview of recent quality assurance efforts in the areas of problem-solving teams and strategic planning for operations. Brief examples are presented to show how these components of quality assurance solve problems that affect the profitability, productivity, and performance of a hospitality operation.

The final sections of this chapter describe the kind of organizational environment and management support necessary to successfully implement the three components of quality assurance. The chapter closes with two stories. The first story describes an organizational environment in which quality assurance efforts fail because of a lack of management support. The second story describes an environment in which quality assurance efforts thrive because of the commitment of perceptive managers.

Early Quality Assurance Efforts

Since the 1970s, manufacturing industries in America have faced a crisis in quality. New competitors began capturing significant shares of world and domestic markets with products that were perceptibly *better* than those manufactured in the United States. In 1981, Douglass Fontaine, then Chairman of the American Hotel & Motel Association (AH&MA), began efforts to avoid a similar crisis in quality within the hospitality industry. The task of exploring the nature of quality services was directed to Kenneth Hine, and, in 1982, AH&MA's Quality Assurance Committee was formed. AH&MA's Quality Assurance Committee worked closely with the consulting firm of Collins Hall Associates to assess the needs of the hospitality industry in relation to the delivery of quality services to guests.

Misconceptions about Quality

The AH&MA *Quest for Quality* field inventory report by Collins Hall Associates surveyed almost 400 properties and revealed widespread misconceptions about quality. Many hospitality operators believed that quality applied only to properties with high room rates, or that quality was a subjective evaluation of the services provided by properties throughout the industry. Few survey respondents thought that the idea of quality could apply to every property in the industry, regardless of size, room rates, or the number of services provided. Even fewer respondents believed that quality could be quantified and measured.

Thirty-four percent of the respondents defined quality in terms of superlatives such as "best," "highest level," and "finest." While the term quality carries a connotation of excellence, definitions of quality that rely on superlatives are always subjective, making quality difficult to measure.

Twenty percent of the respondents defined quality in terms of a price/value relationship. These responses included phrases such as "fair exchange of values" and "getting value for your dollar." While there is an unmistakable price/value component to quality, this component cannot be the sole basis for a workable definition, because price/value relationships vary from individual to individual. Also, there is the question of who sets the price/value relationship: the hospitality manager or the guest?

Eighteen percent of the respondents applied the concept of quality to limited functional areas within a property, such as at the front desk or in the dining room. Quality certainly relates to service, but not only to service. Quality applies to housekeeping and the kitchen just as much as it applies to the front desk and the dining room. Friendly check-in and a dirty room, or fine dining service and poor food, do not add up to a quality guest experience.

Fourteen percent of the respondents defined quality in terms of offering a unique guest experience such as an "escape from everyday life," or in terms of viewing their own properties as unique among all others in the industry. Definitions of quality that focus on uniqueness are ultimately subjective, making quality difficult to measure in terms of day-to-day operations.

Five percent of the respondents defined quality in terms of constantly exceeding guest expectations. The problem with this definition is that properties cannot constantly exceed guest expectations. The "bonuses" that guests receive today will become part of their expectations tomorrow.

Only nine percent of those responding to the survey defined quality in relation to standards established by a hospitality organization.

Standards: Required Levels of Performance

AH&MA's Quality Assurance Committee strongly felt that if properties established a consensus on standards within their operations many common industry problems could be avoided. Exhibit 1.1 lists common industry problems compiled by the consulting firm of Collins Hall Associates.

The work of the Quality Assurance Committee and the results of the *Quest for Quality* study prompted AH&MA to promote quality assurance in the hospitality industry by urging individual properties to:

1. Develop standards by obtaining consensus among managers, supervisors, and employees on the required levels of performance for their positions within the organization

Exhibit 1.1 Common Industry Problems

Front Desk

1. The guest arrives with a confirmed reservation but no rooms are available.

2. The guest arrives with a confirmed reservation but the hotel cannot find a record of the reservation.

3. The desk clerk is impolite.

4. The guest, or the bellperson, is given the wrong key or a key that doesn't work and must return to the front desk.

5. Check-in and/or check-out lines are too long, resulting in a long wait.

6. The type or location of the room requested is not available when the guest arrives.

7. The front desk clerk fails to deliver a "hold for arrival" message or guest mail.

8. The guest arrives at the assigned room and finds that it is not ready for occupancy.

9. Proper identification is not made and the guest gives the wrong name. The bill is not collectible.

10. Guest credit is not verified and the bill is not collectible.

11. The guest's personal data on reservation and registration forms is not legible and the billing process is difficult.

12. The guest's luggage is sent to the wrong room.

13. Reservations are not properly controlled and overbooking results.

14. The guest's key is not collected at the time of check-out, and the guest returns to the room and makes a phone call or uses the room for other purposes.

Bell Service

15. The bellperson fails to inform the guest of the services offered by the property (e.g., laundry, restaurant, room service, recreational facilities, etc.).

16. The bellperson fails to demonstrate to the guest how to operate mechanical items in the guestroom (e.g., air conditioning, television, heating equipment, remote controls, etc.).

Housekeeping

17. Rooms are not properly cleaned.

18. Towels, wash cloths, soap, and amenities are not placed in the rooms.

Exhibit 1.1 (continued)

19. Room attendants fail to report maintenance problems (e.g., showers not working properly, plugged drains, out-of-order televisions, etc.).

Food and Beverage

20. The guest is served the wrong items because the order was taken or prepared incorrectly.

21. The guest is not asked whether he/she wants a cocktail before the meal, or whether he/she wants another round during the meal.

22. The guest's restaurant reservation is not recorded.

23. Foreign material is found in the guest's food.

24. The guest is not advised of the menu items that are out of supply and the server must return to retake the guest's order.

25. Tables are set up with dirty glasses, dishware, and/or silverware.

26. The food server fails to ask if the guest would like wine with the meal.

27. Items ordered and served are not entered on the guest check and the guest is not charged.

28. Buspersons fail to service tables properly (e.g., refilling water glasses, serving breads, clearing tables, etc.).

29. Service is slow.

30. Room service is slow.

31. Food preparation personnel are not properly advised of changes in banquet/catering function counts.

32. In clearing tables, silverware and linen are not properly separated and are thrown out with the garbage or trash.

Engineering

33. Maintenance is slow to respond to a guest service call.

34. Maintenance is not properly informed about meeting/conference needs (e.g., equipment is not ready when needed, such as meeting room sound systems, projection equipment, etc.).

35. The incorrect room number is listed on a maintenance request form resulting in slow service or no service at all.

36. Guestroom air conditioning and heating filters are not kept clean.

37. Inadequate energy conservation exists because of poor communication across departments (e.g., room attendants neglect to reset heating or air conditioning controls when guests check out, etc.).

Exhibit 1.1 (continued)

Sales and Marketing

38. The sales representative fails to follow up on a prospective function and loses the business to the competition.

39. Sales representatives make promises they cannot keep (e.g., promising additional services without additional charges, etc.).

40. There is inadequate communication across departments concerning function requirements.

General Problems

41. Remote charges are not posted until after the guest checks out (e.g., a late restaurant charge must be billed to the guest after he/she has already checked out and left the property, etc.).

42. The guest's signature is not secured on charge vouchers.

43. Employees are not aware of the range of services offered by the property and guests are not properly informed about room service, laundry, valet, and limousine services.

44. Employees are distant from and aloof around guests.

45. The room rates quoted by travel agents do not conform with the rates for accommodations when the guests arrive.

46. Vending machines do not work properly.

47. Guests' cars are not delivered as requested.

48. Guest laundry and/or valet service items are not returned as requested.

49. Wake-up calls are not made as promised.

50. Guest messages are not delivered.

2. Implement standards by training managers, supervisors, and employees to perform according to the agreed-upon levels of performance

3. Manage standards by monitoring performance and insisting upon 100% conformity to standards

AH&MA's Quality Assurance Committee partially funded the work of Collins Hall Associates as the firm helped seven pilot properties to adapt these fundamental features of a quality assurance system to the needs of their organizations. Chapter 2 provides an overview of how performance standards continue to serve as an important component of a quality assurance system.

Recent Quality Assurance Efforts

In the past several years, quality assurance efforts in the hospitality industry have built upon the early foundation of developing, implementing, and managing performance standards. Problem-solving teams and strategic planning for operations are now recognized as effective ways by which to resolve service problems in the hospitality industry and to increase the profitability, productivity, and performance of individual operations. The following sections provide brief introductions to problem-solving teams and strategic planning for operations. More details on these important components of quality assurance are presented in Chapter 2.

Problem-Solving Teams: Questions and Answers

Implementing problem-solving teams as part of a quality assurance system enables individuals to work together as a team in solving work-related problems. The following section answers some of the most frequently asked questions about problem-solving teams.

Question: What do problem-solving teams do?

Answer: They identify and solve problems that affect the profitability and productivity of their organization.

Question: Are there different kinds of problem-solving teams?

Answer: Yes. There are basically three kinds of teams: teams of department managers, teams of supervisors, and teams of employees.

Question: How many members should there be on a problem-solving team?

Answer: A team may be composed of five to seven individuals from the same department or from related departments or functional areas within the property.

Question: How does someone become a member of a problem-solving team?

Answer: Individuals volunteer to become members of a problem-solving team. However, before participating as members of a team, individuals are trained in the problem-solving process adopted by the property.

Question: How often do problem-solving teams meet?

Answer: Problem-solving teams meet for one hour each week.

Question: Are members of problem-solving teams paid to attend meetings?

Answer: Individuals are paid for the time they spend in training and in attending team meetings.

Question: At what level of the organization are problem-solving teams first formed?

Answer: Problem-solving teams are formed at the management level first. When teams of department managers successfully solve problems and receive the necessary support from their managers, teams can be formed at the supervisory level. When teams of supervisors successfully solve problems and receive the necessary support from their managers, employee problem-solving teams can be formed.

The following examples briefly describe the efforts of several problem-solving teams at different hospitality properties. These examples suggest the types of problems that teams may choose to solve.

Example #1: The New Telephone System. Months after the new telephone system had been installed, few employees remembered how to use the telephone intercom system to transfer an incoming call directly to the appropriate person in another department. As a result, some incoming calls were channeled from one extension to another until someone happened to make the correct transfer. This created poor first impressions on prospective guests. In addition, meeting planners wondered, "How are they going to help me put this function together when they can't even transfer my call properly?"

A newly formed problem-solving team of administration employees, called "The Administrative Angels," came to the rescue. The Angels conducted training sessions on all aspects of the new telephone system, coached employees in telephone etiquette, and made sure that all departments received updated lists of telephone extension numbers. The training provided by the Angels enabled employees to transfer calls directly to the appropriate person. Callers now get "one-stop service," and their first impression of the property is more likely to be one that is appreciative of the staff's friendliness and efficiency.

Example #2: Group Reservation and Rooms Records. Whenever guests stopped at the front desk for information about their group's reservations and/or room assignments, front desk agents had to retrieve the appropriate files from the group reservationist's office. If the group reservationist was not immediately available, they had to sift through the piles of paper on the reservationist's desk or ransack the file cabinets. Meanwhile, bewildered guests waited impatiently at the front desk for answers to what they thought were very simple questions.

A newly formed front office problem-solving team, "The Sellouts," tackled this as one of their first problems. When investigating the problem, the team discovered that, with the proper training, they could access information in group reservation files by using the computer terminals at the front desk. The computer system's operating manuals were finally put to use and front office agents were soon answering questions about group reservations without scurrying back to the reservations office. Groups at the property are now likely to be impressed by the staff's competent use of modern technology.

Example #3: Collecting for Emergency Paid-Outs. Employees were purchasing emergency items to meet guests' needs. However, getting reimbursed for their efforts to please guests was like fighting City Hall. First, employees had to track down their department managers to get their signatures on paid-out slips. Next, they had to "walk the paid-outs" through the front office. At the front office, they were frequently told that the paid-out slip was improperly coded, or that more details were needed before the paid-out could be processed. Employees had to return to their departments for the correct coding or for the appropriate details. Understandably frustrated, employees began shying away from meeting guests' needs that involved emergency paid-outs.

The accounting department's problem-solving team, which called itself "Accountants Have Better Figures," addressed the problem of reimbursing employees for emergency paid-outs. The team designated one position in the accounting department to process all paid-out slips, and made sure the position was staffed so that employees could be quickly repaid whenever they went out of their way to accommodate guests. Today, employees no longer have to "fight City Hall" to get reimbursed, and they no longer avoid purchasing items to meet guests' needs.

Example #4: Will the Real Las Vegas Style Please Set Up? A meeting planner requested a Las Vegas style banquet setup. The catering manager informed the setup crew, and thought that all was well. The banquet manager inspected the room and was appalled. "This is not a Las Vegas seating!" he exclaimed. The setup was changed. Later, the catering manager inspected the rearranged setup and cried, "This is not Las Vegas style!"

Communication problems brought a problem-solving team together consisting of the executive chef, the director of catering, the executive steward, the banquet manager, and the supervisor of the setup crew. They agreed that banquet event orders contained information that was often incomplete and vague, and sometimes wrong. The team held brainstorming sessions and eventually reached a consensus on every type of banquet setup and the proper terminology that should be used. Next, the team diagramed each type of banquet setup and distributed copies to every department involved in the sale or service of banquet functions. It soon became much easier for these departments to communicate effectively with one another.

Distributing the setup diagrams to prospective banquet customers completed the last link in the chain of communication and helped to ensure that hotel employees and prospective guests were speaking the same language. This eliminated unwelcome surprises and assured prospective guests that their needs would be met.

Example #5: Housekeeping and Maintenance Finally Get Together. Housekeeping inspectresses were frustrated by the lack of response to work orders which they submitted to the maintenance department. They often had to send two or three requests for each guestroom repair. The inspectresses felt that maintenance not only failed to respond to work orders quickly enough, but, more important, they failed to understand how prompt repair work significantly increased guest satisfaction with the housekeeping department and with the entire property.

A problem-solving team was formed, consisting of inspectresses from the housekeeping department and employees from the maintenance department. The first problem the team tackled was the maintenance department's alleged slow response to repair requests from housekeeping. At their team meetings, each department finally got the opportunity to hear the other side of the story. The team agreed on priorities for handling the different work order requests. The team also instituted a reply system by which maintenance could keep housekeeping informed on the current status of work orders, and on the status of parts or furniture that had to be ordered. The housekeeping and maintenance departments are no longer at odds with each other because the problem-solving team opened the communication channels.

These examples indicate the types of problems that teams choose to solve and the results of their problem-solving efforts. However, the examples do not convey the systematic process by which the teams identified the problems, developed solutions, completed cost/benefit analyses, and presented their solution proposals to management. Chapter 2 provides an overview of these stages in the problem-solving process and explains how problem-solving teams serve as an important component of a quality assurance system.

Strategic Planning for Operations

The primary objective of strategic planning for operations is to enhance the profitability of the hospitality business by increasing the productivity of managers, supervisors, and employees. More details on this important component of quality assurance are presented in Chapter 2. The following example of strategic planning for operations focuses on the activity of a single planning group, consisting of representatives from the stewards department of a large resort.

The stewards department claimed that it never received adequate advance notice from food and beverage outlets about their needs for china, glassware, and silverware. The current procedure required captains or managers to inform a specific steward of their outlet's needs. But, in practice, individual servers made requests (for example, for soup spoons) to anyone they could find in the stewards department. When the stewards department was late in responding to these needs, servers or captains from one food and beverage outlet would "borrow" supplies from other outlets. At times, one banquet room would end up with as many as 300 extra soup spoons, while other banquet rooms were left with embarrassing shortages.

The planning group eventually solved this problem by determining par levels and suggesting that each food and beverage outlet maintain its own inventory. After the food and beverage director and the controller approved the plan, the maintenance department created the necessary inventory storage areas, and, within a few weeks, the accounting department began processing inventory orders from each food and beverage outlet.

Organizational Change

Adapting a quality assurance system to the needs of an organization often means making significant changes in the working environment. Changing the working environment within an organization is seldom easy and never quick. Any kind of change often threatens people and provokes resistance. Imagine the kinds of resistance which could arise in departments when changes are forced upon the staff, such as new procedures for:

- Making beds
- Computer operations at the front desk
- Logging maintenance repairs
- Reporting calls in the sales office

These kinds of changes are small when compared to the changes that a quality assurance system may bring about in the working environment of an organization.

Quality assurance is a management system that brings a new philosophy of doing business into an organization. For some departments, this may mean fundamental changes in managing human resources. Shifting to a quality assurance management system requires careful, systematic planning. The following sections describe a process for directing systematic change. Steps in this process are diagramed in Exhibit 1.2.

Awareness

Directing systematic change begins with raising awareness within the organization that there is a need for change. This is accomplished by identifying current problems. For example, in the case of equipment needs, this means demonstrating to everyone in a department that the existing equipment (or lack of equipment) is a problem.

The problem should not be defined one way for managers and another way for employees. The need for equipment will certainly have different consequences for different positions within a department. However, it is important that everyone be aware of all aspects of the problem. Otherwise, people will have a limited awareness of the need for change. In any situation involving change, people will ask: "What's in it for me?" Answering this question is important, but addressing all the consequences of a problem educates people beyond the narrowness of their own perspectives and suggests that the more appropriate question to ask is always: "What's in it for *everyone*?"

Understanding

Only after people become aware that a problem exists can they begin to understand what the proposed change is all about. If the "awareness" step of introducing the need for equipment educates everyone about the many problems that new equipment will solve, people will understand the proposed change in a way that achieves consensus throughout the organization. This consensus forms the foundation for solving the problem and also helps overcome resistance to future changes.

The early efforts of those implementing a quality assurance system should attempt to prevent resistance by systematically preparing each level of the organization for change. Planned, systematic change involves educating and training everyone in the organization in quality assurance concepts and activities. This may seem to be a slow process, but it is the most effective. Memos, directives, and fiats provoke resistance. Educating the people that the change affects will have a much better chance of producing an informed, willing acceptance.

Acceptance

Awareness and understanding form the basis not only for accepting change, but also for accepting responsibility for carrying out that change effectively.

Exhibit 1.2 Steps in Directing Systematic Change

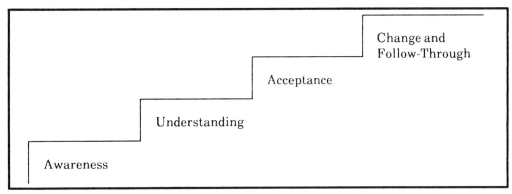

When acceptance is built upon awareness and understanding, managers and supervisors no longer need to reach into a bag of tricks to motivate the employees in their departments. An informed consensus among people within a department leads them to accept responsibility for implementing change. This willing acceptance of responsibility is the only kind of motivation that ever truly lasts and actually gets things done.

Change and Follow-Through

With awareness and understanding of problems, and with acceptance of proposed solutions to those problems, people become ready to change. The degree to which change succeeds depends on efforts to follow through. In terms of our example of equipment needs, follow-through means actually doing it: reaching consensus on the type of equipment needed and how it will be used and maintained. As people follow through, they adopt the change as part of their everyday working environment. People like to do things that are their own ideas. Involving people in each step of change ensures successful, meaningful, and consistent progress.

Management Support

Management support is the key to successfully adapting a quality assurance system to the needs of an individual property. Quality assurance can exist only when top management executives accept responsibility for making quality a reality within their organizations.

Exhibit 1.3 shows the sequence for implementing any or all of the components of quality assurance. Exhibit 1.3 also indicates that the success of the quality assurance effort pivots on the commitment with which the highest organizational level actively supports and monitors all other levels.

Exhibit 1.3 Implementation Sequence and Support Structure

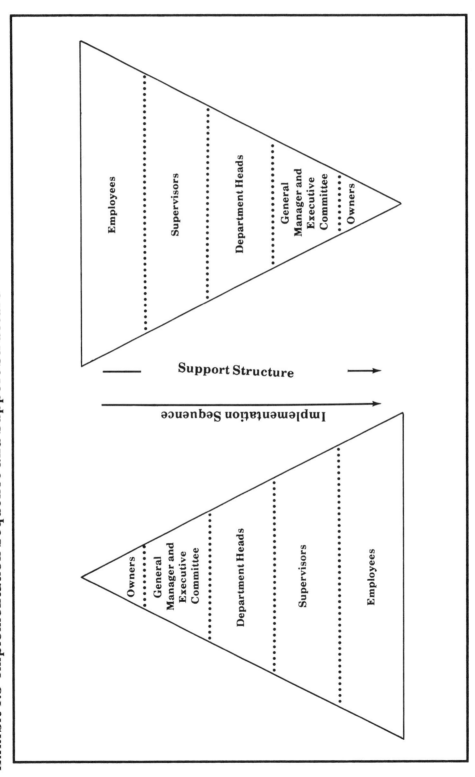

Implementation starts at the top level of the organization. The owners (or management company), corporate executives, the general manager, and members of the executive committee must all be aware of, understand, and accept responsibility for the organization's quality assurance efforts. After support is obtained from the organization's top levels, the commitment to quality assurance must be communicated to department managers. Department managers must all be aware of, understand, and accept responsibility for their department's quality assurance efforts. Their commitment must be communicated to the supervisors within their departments. Supervisors, in kind, must all be aware of, understand, and accept responsibility before employees become involved in the quality assurance process.

Some top management executives tried to implement a quality assurance system at their properties without their full commitment to the process. They showed up at management meetings and talked up the quality assurance efforts, but never followed up by keeping the day-to-day commitments that would give direction to the process. This approach failed. In order for quality assurance to work, department managers, supervisors, and employees must all know that the chain of command within the organization has become a chain of commitment to quality assurance.

Two Stories

This chapter closes with two stories. The first story describes an organizational environment in which a single individual's quality assurance efforts fail. The story makes the point that quality assurance must be a team effort that is fully supported by management. The second story describes an environment in which quality assurance thrives because of the team spirit within the organization and the commitment and dedication of managers to the quality assurance process.

The Player Without a Team

After graduating from high school, Andrew Smith started taking classes at the local community college. He needed to support himself while going to school, and one of the counselors at the community college informed him about an opening in the housekeeping department of a hotel in town. Andrew applied for the job and was hired as a houseman.

Andrew hadn't decided what profession to pursue at school, but his talks with Milly Jones, the afternoon housekeeping supervisor, made him think seriously about a career in the hospitality industry. Milly always took the time to get to know her new employees. She spent about an hour a day with Andrew during his first few weeks on the job.

Milly considered the time they spent together as Andrew's training program.

After a month on the job, Andrew went to Milly with a problem and a solution. The problem was the time wasted because of the vacuum cleaner situation. Room attendants constantly complained that their vacuum cleaners didn't work properly. Andrew spent over an hour each day exchanging "broken" vacuum cleaners from room attendants with "repaired" vacuum cleaners from the maintenance department. He made so many trips that the maintenance manager finally just gave him a key to the maintenance shop so that Andrew could exchange the vacuum cleaners without constantly bothering the maintenance workers. The problem was getting out of hand, because half the time room attendants complained that the replacement vacuum cleaners were just as bad as the machines they had used to begin with.

Andrew told Milly that he was tired of being in the middle of the problem, and he suggested the following solution:

1. Number all vacuum cleaners.
2. Assign the same vacuum cleaner to the same room attendant every day.
3. Create a maintenance log to track repairs on each vacuum cleaner.
4. Track the time maintenance takes to repair the vacuum cleaners.

Milly thought Andrew had a good idea. She told him that she didn't have the authority to set policy, but that she'd try to get approval from Mary, the executive housekeeper. Andrew felt great and thought that working in the hotel business might be an interesting career after all.

The next day Andrew went to work early because he was eager to hear from Milly about whether or not his proposal had been accepted. He didn't mind waiting until Milly arrived at the beginning of the afternoon shift. He thought over his proposal and still felt great. As soon as he saw Milly, he asked her what the executive housekeeper thought about his idea.

"She didn't like it," Milly answered coldly.

"Why not?" asked Andrew.

"She said they tried it at a hotel she worked at before and it didn't solve the problem."

"How come?" asked Andrew.

"Beats me. Then she chewed me out for interrupting a meeting she was having with an inspectress. She told me I should think these things out better before asking her to change current policy."

"What should we do now?" asked Andrew.

"You'd better get to work," said Milly. "It's going to be a busy night."

Andrew felt like someone had let the air out of his balloon. To top it off, he had to spend two hours that night running back and forth with vacuum cleaners. After work, he had a soda with one of the maintenance workers in the lunchroom. The maintenance worker told Andrew that the room attendants broke the machines on purpose so they wouldn't have to vacuum the rooms. He said that half the time the vacuum cleaners broke down because the room attendants were too lazy to empty the bags. He also made it clear to Andrew that the people in maintenance had many more important things to do than fix vacuum cleaners. Andrew asked if it was very difficult to fix the vacuum cleaners. The maintenance worker said that it would only take 30 minutes to teach Andrew all he needed to know about fixing a vacuum cleaner.

The next day Andrew asked Milly if he could come to work early every day to repair vacuum cleaners himself. Milly's reaction to Andrew's new idea was not positive. She told him that the maintenance department didn't know enough about vacuum cleaners to teach him anything. Andrew said that the father of one of his friends was a vacuum cleaner distributor. Andrew thought he could get an appointment to talk with him about what was involved with vacuum cleaner repairs. Milly replied that what he did on his own time was his own business. She also said that Andrew should quit thinking about it at work and concentrate on getting the soiled linen to the laundry faster.

Two days later, Andrew met with Mr. Henderson, the vacuum cleaner distributor. Mr. Henderson gave him a repair manual and spent two hours explaining how to repair vacuum cleaners. Andrew had the next day off. He spent most of the day in the community college library drafting a maintenance log for vacuum cleaner repairs. He tracked the time he'd spent picking up and delivering vacuum cleaners. He concluded that he could spend the first 45 minutes of his shift repairing vacuum cleaners and so increase his speed in delivering the soiled linen by 25%. At the end of the day he felt like he'd completed his first real business proposal. He couldn't wait to get to work the next day.

The next day he went directly to Milly's office. He told her that he had the vacuum cleaner problem all figured out. He said that this time there was no way that Mary, the executive housekeeper, would reject his idea.

Milly told Andrew that she'd had enough of this vacuum cleaner talk. She said there was no way she was going to get chewed out again on his account. She reminded Andrew that she had told him to forget about the vacuum cleaners. Milly's closing remark was that Andrew probably would make a better dishmachine operator than a houseman.

Andrew was shocked. He worked in a daze for the rest of the shift. The next day he visited his college counselor. He told the counselor that he would be interested in any job as long as it had nothing to do with the hospitality industry. That day Andrew got a job in a grocery store. He called Mary, the executive housekeeper, and told her that he wouldn't be back to work. When the executive housekeeper informed Milly, her reply was, "Andrew was more trouble than he was worth anyway."

The Team Recruits a Player

Matthew Jones never finished high school. He was a quiet kid and hung around with a group of other kids who dropped out of school. Matthew had been fired from three different gas stations and was having trouble finding another job. His mother saw an ad for a dishmachine operator at a local hotel. She insisted that Matthew apply for the job.

Matthew was surprised that he had to interview with three different people. First he talked to Randy Dotts, the chef. Randy told Matthew that two other people in the kitchen hadn't finished high school when they were hired. Both people started as dishmachine operators. One of them, Mike, was now a line cook; the other one, Tom, became a server in the restaurant.

The second person Matthew interviewed with was Cindy McClure, the dining room manager. She interviewed him in the restaurant. She ordered coffee and talked Matthew into having a soda. Cindy told him that the dishmachine operator was just as important to the restaurant as her position was. It surprised him when Cindy said she had been trained to operate the dishmachine. Matthew didn't think that restaurant managers did that kind of work.

Pat Rolsen, the food and beverage director, was the third person to interview Matthew. Pat informed him that Randy and Cindy thought he should be hired. He said that he only wanted to tell Matthew two things: "First, welcome to the hotel. Second, my door is open whenever you have any problems or would like to talk."

Pat introduced Matthew to the general manager, the executive secretary, the front office manager, and the controller. Then he escorted him back to the chef's office. Once there, Matthew said he would like the job.

Randy congratulated Matthew for accepting the job, handed him a training manual to read, and asked him to report to work at 5:30 the next morning. Matthew left in a daze. He didn't think he'd get the job when he walked in, and he couldn't remember meeting that many people in one day in a long time.

He went home and told his mother that the dishwasher was a pretty important job at that hotel. He told her there were high school dropouts working as servers and cooks. He said that they had even given him a book to read. His mother told him he had better stay home and read it. When she left for work, Matthew went out with his friends.

His friends told him that the last thing in the world they would ever do was wash dishes for a living. That night Matthew didn't read the training manual. In fact, he wouldn't even have gone to work the next day if his mother hadn't dropped him off at the kitchen door.

Randy, the chef, was waiting in his office with Mike, the line cook.

"Hi, Matthew! How are you this morning?" said Randy.

"Okay," said Matthew.

"This is Mike. He's going to be your trainer. You guys can sit in my office and go over the training manual."

Randy left and Mike introduced himself to Matthew.

"Did you read the training manual last night?" Mike asked.

"No, I didn't get a chance to."

"I didn't read mine before I started either," said Mike.

"Did you finish high school?" asked Matthew.

"You bet," said Mike. "I dropped out after my junior year. But I finished after I started working here. The hotel paid for my G.E.D. training."

This was a surprise to Matthew. They spent the rest of the morning going over the training manual, and Matthew started washing dishes that afternoon.

Mike worked with Matthew off and on for the first week. Matthew's performance improved every day. At the end of the first week, Cindy and Pat had lunch with Matthew in the employee lunch room. Over the next month, Matthew began to open up and got to know a lot of the employees. With more and more positive reinforcement from his supervisors, Matthew began to think of himself as a professional.

About six weeks after Matthew started work, Pat Rolsen called a meeting of the entire kitchen and restaurant staff. He complimented the staff on the last month's business, and reviewed the forecasted business for the next month. He then announced that Mike, the line cook, had been elected employee of the month. Pat reviewed Mike's history of employment at the hotel. Pat and Mike both smiled when Pat mentioned that Mike's attitude toward work when he first started didn't make anyone think he'd end up being employee of the month. Pat reminded everyone that Mike was the first employee to complete his G.E.D. under the hotel's education program. He continued by describing Mike's progress from dishmachine operator to prep cook to line cook. Mike received a standing ovation from the employees at the meeting and returned to his seat next to Matthew.

Matthew was proud of Mike and also felt challenged by Mike's achievements. Mike had mentioned the hotel's education program a few times in casual conversation, but Matthew hadn't paid much attention. He didn't feel confident to participate in it himself.

Pat continued the meeting by citing a few problems that were occurring in the restaurant. One of the problems was water spots on the silverware. Pat asked Cindy to select three employees to help her solve the problem and report at the meeting next month. Cindy selected Mike, Matthew, and Tom. She asked them to stay after the meeting.

Matthew was surprised that Cindy selected him. As the people were leaving the meeting, he mentioned to Mike that he didn't understand why he was selected. Mike said they'd ask Cindy about it.

"Cindy," Mike said, "Matthew wants to know why he got selected."

"I selected the three of you because you all have experience with the dishmachine. I've been trained on it, Mike and Tom used to do it, but you do it now, Matthew. We think you know more about the problem than we do because you're at the dishmachine every day."

They began to discuss the problem. They went into the kitchen and walked the silverware step by step through the process. Cindy said she would call and have the chemical salesperson meet with them the following week.

Matthew didn't know Tom very well because Tom worked the afternoon shift. On their way to the time clock, Matthew discovered that he and Tom had attended the same high school. They talked about school and found that they had had some of the same teachers. Matthew said that he respected both Tom and Mike for getting their G.E.D.'s, but that he didn't think he learned enough in school to make it even worth trying. Tom said that he felt the same way, but it had turned out to be easier than he thought.

The next week Cindy, Mike, Tom, and Matthew met with the chemical salesperson. They concluded that the silverware was spotted because it wasn't being pre-soaked. Buspersons were dumping all the china, glasses, and silver together in the same bus tubs, and Matthew was breaking the contents of the tubs into racks and sending the racks through the machine.

Matthew volunteered to separate all the dishes and pre-soak the silverware for 30 minutes. The group decided to try this for a week. It was a frustrating week for Matthew. His work slowed down because of the extra sorting and the silverware wasn't getting through on time. Tom suggested that Matthew set up a system so that the buspersons would do the sorting. Cindy thought this was a good idea. They tried it for a week. The system worked great. Cindy asked Matthew to present the results at the monthly meeting.

This time Matthew received the standing ovation at the monthly meeting. On the way to the time clock, he asked Tom and Mike if they would coach him through the process of getting his G.E.D. Matthew decided that there might be a good career in the hotel business.

2

Components of Quality Assurance

The previous chapter defined quality assurance as a management system that ensures the consistent delivery of products and services. This chapter provides a brief overview of three components of a quality assurance system. These components are: strategic planning for operations, problem-solving teams, and performance standards. Separate parts of this book examine each of these components in great detail.

This chapter also stresses the need for top management executives to adapt quality assurance components to the unique needs and characteristics of their organizations. The quality assurance system presented in this book is *not* a turnkey system. Owners, general managers, and top company executives should not expect to find every aspect of each component of the system presented here to be appropriate for their hospitality organizations. Likewise, implementation strategies will vary among hospitality organizations. Small properties, such as hotels and motels with less than one hundred rooms, may find that problem-solving teams and performance standards are the only components they need to ensure the consistent delivery of products and services. Large properties may find that strategic planning for operations can solve many of the communication problems that arise simply because of the size and scope of their organizations.

Quality assurance is a dynamic, ongoing process. While there are basic similarities among successful quality assurance systems in the hospitality industry, each system is recognizably unique. The components of quality assurance presented in this book are not rigid, inflexible processes. They can and should be changed to meet the specific needs of individual hospitality operations.

For example, there are many ways to implement and conduct strategic planning for operations. In fact, there are probably as many methods of strategic planning as there are consultants who teach them. Not all of these methods are appropriate to the needs of every hospitality organization, and not all focus on problems related to day-to-day operations. Top management executives must adapt, not adopt, the strategic planning process that best fits their overall business plans and can be easily integrated with their current budget planning, strategic marketing planning, and long-range planning processes.

Likewise, the problem-solving process described in this book is not the only process that problem-solving teams can use to function effectively. Top management executives may wish to contract the services of professional consultants who can design a unique problem-solving system to meet the special needs of their hospitality operation. However, consultants cannot be expected to do everything. Top management executives must be ready to adapt the problem-solving process in response to new company objectives, new personnel, and new quality assurance methods and problem-solving techniques.

The performance standards component of quality assurance discussed in this book does not set standards for the hospitality industry. Performance standards are required levels of performance that are established by individual hospitality organizations. Although standards will vary from property to property, every property can ensure the consistent delivery of products and services by demanding 100% conformity to the standards established by their organizations. As pointed out in the previous chapter, this book focuses on ways to help individual properties to:

- Develop standards by obtaining consensus among managers, supervisors, and employees on the required levels of performance for their positions within the organization

- Implement standards by training managers, supervisors, and employees to perform according to the agreed-upon levels of performance

- Manage standards by monitoring performance and insisting upon 100% conformity to standards

After a brief discussion of strategic planning for operations, problem-solving teams, and performance standards, this chapter identifies pitfalls to avoid when starting a quality assurance system. The most important pitfall to avoid is failing to conduct manager/supervisor and employee surveys. Conducting these surveys is the necessary first step in starting a quality assurance system. Chapter 3 presents sample surveys that have been used with success in a variety of hospitality organizations. However, like other procedures and processes connected with a quality assurance system, top management executives should consider revising the statements and questions of these sample surveys to yield important information that may be unique to their organizations. To guide management's revision of the surveys, Chapter 3 presents a five-step method of survey construction.

Strategic Planning for Operations

The primary objective of strategic planning for operations is to enhance the profitability of the hospitality business by increasing the productivity of managers, supervisors, and employees. The strategic planning process accomplishes this objective by:

- Aligning all levels within the organization around a common vision of what the hospitality business stands for or strives to create

- Engaging managers, supervisors, and employees in a planning process that challenges them to think beyond the demands of day-to-day activities

- Increasing communication within and among the diverse departments and functional areas that make up the organization

- Identifying and solving problems that affect the quality of products and services delivered by the organization

Strategic planning for operations involves setting up a steering committee and several planning groups. The steering committee should include the general manager and selected division directors and/or department managers. Individuals selected to serve on the steering committee should be systematic thinkers capable of analyzing current operations and identifying factors which may affect the property's future. Planning groups may work best with five to six members. The composition of these groups depends on the size of the property and the number of departments. If there are eight or fewer departments, planning groups may be formed for each department. The number and sequence of strategic planning meetings may vary in relation to the needs of individual hospitality properties.

The steering committee and the planning groups meet separately but follow the same sequence of planning activities. Strategic planning activities include:

1. Writing mission statements
2. Collecting data
3. Determining objectives
4. Developing action plans
5. Assembling the annual strategic plan for operations
6. Reviewing the plan and monitoring results

Both the steering committee and planning groups follow this sequence of planning activities. The efforts of the steering committee are directed toward areas of the operation that are generally considered beyond the scope of individual departments. In addition, the steering committee selects and approves objectives and action plans developed by all planning groups. The steering committee also performs many tasks which are necessary for an effective and efficient planning process.

Part II of this book examines strategic planning for operations in great detail and provides hospitality operators with practical tools with which to conduct strategic planning sessions. These tools include step-by-step suggestions for how to conduct each session, along with sample meeting agendas, sample meeting procedures, and sample flip chart sheets. Part II also alerts the organizer of the strategic planning process to the information which must be processed after each meeting in order to ensure an efficient and successful strategic planning process.

Problem-Solving Teams

The purpose of the problem-solving process is to enable individuals to work together as a team in solving work-related problems. Problem-solving teams are groups of managers, supervisors, or employees that meet on a voluntary basis for one hour each week to identify and solve problems. A team may be composed of five to seven individuals from the same department or from related departments or functional areas within a property. Individuals are paid for the time they spend attending team meetings, and they should be rewarded for successfully solving problems that affect the productivity and overall performance of the hospitality operation.

Problem-solving teams are formed at the management level first. When teams of department managers successfully solve problems and receive the necessary support from their managers, teams can then be formed at the supervisory level. When teams of supervisors successfully solve problems and receive the necessary support from their managers, employee problem-solving teams can be formed.

Upper management support is absolutely crucial to the success of the problem-solving process. This support must be more than mere lip service; it must be a real commitment to the problem-solving process as a way of doing business. This commitment must be made crystal clear to all division directors, department managers, and supervisors before any employee teams are formed.

Top management commitment means a substantial investment of time, expertise, and funds in the problem-solving process. It may take from six months to a year before a significant return on this investment is reflected in the financial statements of the business. However, more immediate returns will appear as increased communication within the property, higher employee morale, more teamwork within and between departments, and more positive employee attitudes. These more immediate returns eventually become long-term benefits in the form of lower employee turnover, higher guest satisfaction, and substantial increases in repeat business. As problem-solving teams become self-sufficient, revenue should increase and expenses should decrease, resulting in greater profits for the business.

Part III of this book examines problem-solving teams and provides hospitality operators with basic tools with which they can develop problem-solving teams at their properties. These tools include:

- A specific problem-solving process which has been used with success in a number of hospitality operations

- A detailed example of a problem-solving team in action

- Materials that can be used to train managers, supervisors, and employees to function as productive members of problem-solving teams

- Methods for tracking the progress of problem-solving teams and their overall success at improving quality at the property

Performance Standards

The primary objective of a quality assurance system is to ensure the consistent delivery of products and services to guests. Important keys to consistency are the standards which a property develops, communicates, and manages. Standards are required levels of performance. When performance standards are not properly developed, effectively communicated, and consistently managed, productivity suffers because people in the organization spend most of their time reacting to crises and putting out fires.

Standards are properly developed when the expectations of guests, managers, and employees are coordinated into agreed-upon levels of performance for every position within the organization. The most important aspect of developing standards is gaining consensus on how jobs should be performed.

Standards are communicated through management development and employee skills training programs. The most important aspect of communicating standards is top management's commitment to developing and training people in the organization.

Managing standards means ensuring conformity to the standards which have been developed on the basis of consensus and communicated through development and training programs. The most important aspect of managing standards is following up performance evaluations with specific coaching and retraining. This ensures that managers, supervisors, and employees throughout the organization consistently deliver quality services in the form of agreed-upon standards.

Part IV of this book examines how individual properties can develop performance standards within their operations, implement those standards in the form of in-house management development and employee skill training programs, and manage those standards to ensure 100% conformity to required levels of performance.

Pitfalls to Avoid

As pointed out in Chapter 1, it takes careful, systematic planning to successfully implement a quality assurance system. The components of quality assurance discussed in this book cannot be implemented overnight. It takes time to plan the scope and direction of each component, prepare people for change, and provide the appropriate training. The following sections describe pitfalls to avoid when starting a quality assurance system.

Skipping the Surveys. Those in charge of starting a quality assurance system at a property are often filled with excitement and high expectations. This high energy phase is normal and helps lead to a successful implementation of the process. However, people can get carried away with their enthusiasm and be in such a hurry to get the process going that they skip the surveys. This can lead to disaster.

Manager/supervisor surveys and employee surveys must be conducted before any of the components of the quality assurance system can be successfully implemented. When the surveys are properly constructed and administered, their results indicate what must be done before starting any of the components. The results also suggest where within the hospitality organization to begin each component. In addition, the survey results provide benchmarks against which the future success of each component of the quality assurance system can be measured.

Failing to Prepare People for Change. Most people, especially managers, like change. Good managers are eager to change things for the better and they seem to thrive on new challenges and opportunities. What people resist most is not so much change itself, but the methods used to implement it.

If people within an organization are not properly informed about why the organization is changing to a quality assurance system, they will feel that the system is being forced on them. When this happens, people will feel threatened by the system and resist change. Ignoring people's resistance to change will only aggravate the problem.

Preparing people for change means selling the concept of quality assurance in such a way that the people within the organization buy into the system. The "buy-in" not only reduces resistance to change, but may even transform resistance into enthusiasm. Successful salespeople are masters at this technique. They deal with customers' resistance to change every day. They overcome this resistance not by pushing products at customers but by helping customers make decisions to buy. Successful salespeople know that customers are more likely to buy a product if they feel that it is their own idea to buy it in the first place.

People like to do things that are their own ideas. Prepare people for change by selling quality assurance in such a way that people make it their own idea to buy into the system.

Failing to Develop a Quality Assurance Plan. Each component of quality assurance entails developing and implementing a plan. There is a strategic plan for operations, action plans of problem-solving teams, and standards-based training plans. The entire quality assurance effort also needs a plan.

The overall quality assurance plan should list objectives, time frames for achieving them, and expected costs of implementing the system. Sample first-year objectives are:

- Conduct manager/supervisor surveys and employee surveys
- Organize strategic planning sessions
- Train and manage six problem-solving teams
- Develop, implement, and manage performance standards in every department

The quality assurance plan should also identify what actions should be taken if, after a period of time, achievements fall short of the plan's objectives. The general manager and top company executives should help formulate the plan, identify obstacles which may block implementation of it, and determine strategies to overcome these obstacles should they materialize.

Never Changing the Property's Quality Assurance Plan. Quality assurance must be as dynamic as the organization within which it functions. A property's quality assurance plan must be flexible enough to change in response to new company objectives, new personnel, and new quality assurance methods and problem-solving techniques.

Placing the Position of Quality Assurance Manager Too Low in the Organization. The individual appointed as quality assurance manager is usually involved in each component of the quality assurance system and, therefore, must be able to communicate effectively with people at all levels within the organization. The quality assurance manager often organizes strategic planning for operations by conducting the meetings, helping the steering committee to assemble the strategic plan, and monitoring the progress of departments in achieving the plan's objectives. The quality assurance manager also oversees the activity of all problem-solving teams and generates the necessary support for their success. In addition, the quality assurance manager may guide the efforts of each department in developing, implementing, and managing performance standards.

Given the range of possible responsibilities, the position of quality assurance manager should be at least equivalent to that of a department manager. Placing the position too low in the organization endangers the success of the quality assurance effort by giving the impression that top management is not really serious about quality assurance. For example, when disagreements arise about aspects of the quality assurance process, a division manager may find it difficult to accept advice from a quality assurance manager whose position is equivalent to that of an assistant manager in the human resources department.

Selecting the Wrong Person as the Quality Assurance Manager.
The individual appointed as quality assurance manager must be accepted by his or her peers and have a reputation for fairness. A good candidate for the position is an individual with work experience as a department manager, a supervisor, and as a line employee. If the person appointed as quality assurance manager cannot speak and understand the language of supervisors and line employees, the quality assurance system will never get off the ground.

It is always better to select someone from within the organization than to recruit someone new who is unfamiliar with the hospitality organization and the people who work there. A successful department manager who has already developed a team spirit among the supervisors and employees of his or her department is often the best candidate for the position.

Like everyone else connected with the problem-solving process, the individual selected to serve as the quality assurance manager must receive specific training. The general manager should assume some of these training responsibilities. For example, the general manager should ensure that the individual selected to serve as the quality assurance manager is given the opportunity to acquire a good working knowledge of the various departments and functional areas within the hospitality organization. In addition, the general manager should act as a mentor and instruct the quality assurance manager how to communicate effectively with division directors, department managers, supervisors, and employees.

Training in specific areas of quality assurance can be made available by top management contracting the services of specialized consulting firms which serve the hospitality industry. In addition, many universities and community colleges offer courses in participative management and workshops in the areas of job training, group dynamics, and problem-solving techniques. One of the best ways that a newly appointed quality assurance manager can learn the specifics about his or her job is by visiting hospitality properties that have successfully implemented a quality assurance system. The American Hotel & Motel Association's Quality Assurance Committee meets every six months and presents an excellent opportunity for new quality assurance managers to establish industry contacts and learn how other properties have adapted quality assurance components to the unique needs of their organizations. The Quality Assurance Committee also sponsors an annual Quality Assurance Conference hosted by organizations with successful quality assurance systems.

Trying to Do Too Much Too Soon. Owners and top management executives are often tempted to push the quality assurance system to do too much too soon. Since the quality assurance system begins by identifying problems, it is only natural for owners and executives to want these problems solved as soon as possible. However, doing too much too soon can create problems where they did not exist before.

If too many changes take place simultaneously in many different areas of a hospitality operation, the quality assurance process can collapse under its own weight. Internal resources can become stretched to the point where administrators and managers cannot provide the support that the system requires. It is vital to the success of the quality assurance effort that management sets realistic goals for each component of the system. It may take several months to test, evaluate, and refine the system to meet the unique needs of the organization. While all the problems identified by the system may not be solved immediately, quality will constantly improve within the organization as some problems are solved as completely as possible.

Never Measuring Results of Quality Assurance Efforts. Owners, general managers, and top company executives expect the organization's investment in quality assurance to increase overall performance and productivity, to increase revenue and decrease expenses, and, most of all, to increase profits. In order to maintain the support of owners, general managers, and top company executives, the quality assurance manager must be able to demonstrate how the organization's quality assurance efforts meet these expectations. This can only be accomplished by quantifying results and monitoring the progress of the quality assurance system. It is not enough to measure results with general statements such as: "Morale is higher than ever before," or "Harry is treating his staff much better these days." If these statements are true, it must be possible to quantify them in terms of changes in absenteeism, turnover, overtime pay, productivity, guest feedback, operating expenses, and profits.

Forgetting Middle Management. Owners and top management executives often want to start the quality assurance system at the line employee level of their organizations because they believe that is where the system will produce the fastest results. However, if department managers are passed over in the early stages of implementation, they may feel threatened by the system and disrupt the problem-solving efforts of their employees.

The idea of employees meeting regularly to identify and solve problems is completely new to most department managers. If department managers do not understand the problem-solving process, they may see the activity of problem-solving teams as direct criticism of the way they have been managing their departments. When this happens, department managers may disrupt and even sabotage the process. They may feel that they have to compete against their employees to solve problems before the employees can. They may claim that the employees take too long to solve problems, or that the employees choose to solve the wrong problems. Some department managers may not actually prevent employee teams from developing and implementing solutions, but they may create obstacles by withholding the kind of support, advice, and direction that the employee problem-solving team often needs.

The problem-solving process must begin with department managers. They must participate in the process, use the same problem-solving methods, and learn firsthand the kind of support that problem-solving teams need in order to function effectively. When teams of department managers successfully solve problems and receive the necessary support from their managers, teams can be formed at the supervisory level. When teams of supervisors successfully solve problems and receive the necessary support from their managers, employee problem-solving teams can be formed.

Not Allowing the Degree of Autonomy Necessary for Standards Groups and Problem-Solving Teams to Function Effectively. One of the primary assumptions of quality assurance is that if managers want to know what employees need to perform their jobs properly, they should begin by asking the employees who actually do the work. If employees are excluded from standards groups, management loses not only the expertise that employees can bring to the process of developing performance standards, but they also lose the "buy-in" to the process that consensus on standards creates. Without this buy-in secured through employees participating in the process, employees may resist management's efforts to implement and manage performance standards.

People like to do things that are their own ideas. It is crucial to the success of the problem-solving process that employee teams be permitted to select their own problems. These problems may not always be those which management would select. However, it is only natural for employees to want to solve the problems that bother them the most. If management selects the problems and directs the employee teams to solve them, employees will feel management's lack of confidence in their abilities and the process will eventually fail.

Not Allowing Employee Problem-Solving Teams to Present Their Solutions to Management. People like to get credit for their own ideas and to be recognized for putting their ideas into action. The problem-solving process should give employees credit for their own ideas and provide opportunities for management to recognize and praise their efforts. Not allowing employee problem-solving teams to present their solutions to management takes away management's most important opportunity to recognize and praise the efforts of employee problem-solving teams.

During the problem-solving process, managers and supervisors provide support, advice, and direction for the problem-solving teams in their departments. Also, throughout the process, a problem-solving team communicates its efforts to managers and supervisors whose departments are affected by the problem the team is attempting to solve. There is so much communication during the problem-solving process that management may consider a team's solution proposal to be anticlimactic and, therefore, unnecessary. This is not the case for members of problem-solving teams. To them, the presentation to management crowns their achievement and motivates them to continue their efforts on the next problem they select to solve.

Not Communicating the Success of the Quality Assurance System. Before starting a quality assurance system, people within an organization must be educated about quality assurance objectives and techniques. After a system is implemented, people within the organization must be kept informed about the progress and success of quality assurance efforts throughout the property.

Poor communication about the progress of the quality assurance system deprives participants of recognition and may make those who are not directly involved in strategic planning groups, problem-solving teams, or standards groups feel excluded from the quality assurance effort. No one likes to be kept in the dark about changes that affect his or her working environment. One of the best means of communicating the organization's commitment to quality assurance and the objectives and progress of the system is with a monthly quality assurance newsletter.

The first issues of the newsletter can contain letters from the owner and general manager which briefly explain the quality assurance system, communicate their commitment to the system, and inform staff that management will eventually offer everyone the opportunity to participate in the organization's quality assurance efforts. Later issues of the newsletter can contain sections devoted to each quality assurance component. One section can communicate statistics on increased productivity by showing each department's progress in developing, implementing, and managing performance standards. Another section can be used to recognize departments as they achieve objectives set forth in the property's strategic plan for operations. A team leader section of the newsletter can contain articles describing each problem-solving team's progress during the month.

3
Conducting Surveys

Manager/supervisor surveys and employee surveys must be conducted before any of the components of the quality assurance system can be successfully implemented. When the surveys are properly constructed and administered, their results provide an informative picture of important operational features of a hospitality operation. Specifically, the surveys provide the following information:

- Areas of concern that must be addressed before the quality assurance system can be successfully implemented

- Departments within the hospitality organization in which individual components of the quality assurance system should be implemented first

- Benchmarks against which the future success of each component of the quality assurance system can be measured

This chapter presents a manager/supervisor survey and an employee survey, both of which have been used with success in a variety of hospitality organizations. The chapter examines the structure of these surveys, suggests procedures for administering them, and indicates how their results can be interpreted to yield information necessary for the successful implementation of a quality assurance system.

Since the needs and requirements of hospitality organizations vary, management may consider revising some of the questions contained in the sample surveys. Or, in order to address particular areas of concern that may affect a property's unique implementation of the quality assurance system, management may find that entirely different surveys are needed. In either case, the five-step method of survey construction presented in the final section of this chapter may serve as a useful guide.

The Manager/Supervisor Survey

Exhibit 3.1 presents a sample manager/supervisor survey that can be administered to top company executives, department managers, and supervisors. The survey asks respondents to circle a number indicating whether they strongly agree, agree, somewhat agree, somewhat disagree, or strongly disagree with the statements presented. The survey is designed to collect specific information about areas that directly affect the success of the quality assurance system. Areas covered by the survey (and the specific sections, or topics, within each area) are as follows:

Relationships
    Owner/management company
    Department managers
    Supervisors
    Networks

Support
    Owner/management company
    General manager

Information
    Information flow
    Development and evaluation systems

Operations
    Decision-making
    Opportunities
    Benefits
    Strategic planning

The following sections discuss how to tabulate the results of the sample manager/supervisor survey, and how to interpret the results as a guide to implementing a quality assurance system.

Tabulating Survey Results

Exhibit 3.2 presents the score sheet which is used to manually record and tabulate the results of the manager/supervisor survey. All responses to each survey statement are recorded on the score sheet by making tally marks under the appropriate column headings. The tally marks within each column are multiplied by the number of the column heading; the resulting figures are then added together to arrive at a point total for each survey statement. An average score for each statement is computed by dividing the statement's total points by the number of individual respondents.

The score sheet in Exhibit 3.2 indicates which statements apply to specific topics within each general area addressed by the survey. The topics form sections on the score sheet and each section receives a score. The section score is computed by dividing each section's total points by the number of statements in the section, and then by the number of individual respondents.

Exhibit 3.1 Sample Manager/Supervisor Survey

Instructions: Please respond to this survey by circling a number indicating whether you strongly agree (5), agree (4), somewhat agree (3), somewhat disagree (2), or strongly disagree (1) with the following statements.

Strongly Agree   *Agree*   *Somewhat Agree*   *Somewhat Disagree*   *Strongly Disagree*

1. Top management seeks feedback from all levels within the organization.   5   4   3   2   1

2. The management style of top management is more democratic than dictatorial.   5   4   3   2   1

3. Top management is more likely to cut costs by increasing productivity than by laying off employees.   5   4   3   2   1

4. Top management encourages new ideas from managers and supervisors.   5   4   3   2   1

5. The management style of department managers is more democratic than dictatorial.   5   4   3   2   1

6. Department managers seek feedback from members of their departments.   5   4   3   2   1

7. Department managers encourage new ideas from members of their departments.   5   4   3   2   1

8. Department managers have been trained in management techniques.   5   4   3   2   1

9. The management style of supervisors is more democratic than dictatorial.   5   4   3   2   1

10. Supervisors seek feedback from employees within their departments.   5   4   3   2   1

11. Supervisors encourage employees to develop new ideas.   5   4   3   2   1

12. Supervisors have been trained in management techniques.   5   4   3   2   1

13. The organization requires members of different departments to work together on joint projects.   5   4   3   2   1

14. Power within the organization is distributed fairly among department managers.   5   4   3   2   1

15. Power within departments is distributed fairly among managers and supervisors.   5   4   3   2   1

16. The human resources department communicates effectively with other departments.   5   4   3   2   1

17. The organization has the resources to publicize the property's quality assurance system.   5   4   3   2   1

18. The owner (or management company) supports the idea of developing employee problem-solving groups.   5   4   3   2   1

19. The owner (or management company) will publicly support the property's quality assurance system.   5   4   3   2   1

Exhibit 3.1 Continued

	Strongly Agree	Agree	Somewhat Agree	Somewhat Disagree	Strongly Disagree
20. The owner (or management company) will supply the time, expertise, and funds to implement and maintain the quality assurance system.	5	4	3	2	1
21. If the quality assurance system is successful on the department manager level, the owner (or management company) will implement the system at all levels within the organization.	5	4	3	2	1
22. The owner (or management company) will wait one to three years for a significant return on investment in the quality assurance system.	5	4	3	2	1
23. The owner (or management company) will fund job training programs.	5	4	3	2	1
24. The general manager will wait one year before evaluating the success of the quality assurance system.	5	4	3	2	1
25. Within specified limitations, the general manager will allow employee problem-solving groups to select and solve problems which they identify.	5	4	3	2	1
26. The general manager is receptive to new ideas from staff members.	5	4	3	2	1
27. The policies of the owner (or management company) are known throughout the organization.	5	4	3	2	1
28. The policies of the general manager are consistent with the policies of the owner (or management company).	5	4	3	2	1
29. The general manager keeps department managers informed on matters concerning the property.	5	4	3	2	1
30. Department managers keep supervisors informed on matters concerning the property.	5	4	3	2	1
31. Step-by-step job breakdowns have been written for positions within the organization.	5	4	3	2	1
32. Supervisors understand their responsibilities and what is expected of them.	5	4	3	2	1
33. Employees understand their responsibilities and what is expected of them.	5	4	3	2	1
34. The property's policy regarding salaries and wages is clearly defined.	5	4	3	2	1
35. Managers and supervisors use established criteria to evaluate the job performance of employees.	5	4	3	2	1
36. Managers, supervisors, and employees are satisfied with the amount of information which they receive.	5	4	3	2	1
37. The organization has a history of effective job training programs.	5	4	3	2	1
38. The organization currently provides training for managers and supervisors.	5	4	3	2	1

Exhibit 3.1 Continued

		Strongly Agree	Agree	Somewhat Agree	Somewhat Disagree	Strongly Disagree
39.	The organization offers an educational benefits program that pays for job-related instruction.	5	4	3	2	1
40.	The property consistently evaluates productivity, absenteeism, turnover, and guest feedback.	5	4	3	2	1
41.	Managers, supervisors, and employees within the organization have the ability to identify and solve problems relating to their work areas.	5	4	3	2	1
42.	Corporate headquarters defines the basic goals of the property.	5	4	3	2	1
43.	All levels within the organization are free to determine their own means to reach the goals of the property.	5	4	3	2	1
44.	Management strives to balance short-term results and long-term goals.	5	4	3	2	1
45.	Managers encourage employees to participate in making decisions.	5	4	3	2	1
46.	Department managers actively participate in making upper management decisions.	5	4	3	2	1
47.	Supervisors and employees establish and document work methods and goals.	5	4	3	2	1
48.	Departments within the property can successfully develop employee problem-solving groups.	5	4	3	2	1
49.	There are informal leaders within the organization that do not occupy management positions.	5	4	3	2	1
50.	The property responds well to change.	5	4	3	2	1
51.	Recognition systems within the property are tailor-made to suit employee needs.	5	4	3	2	1
52.	An employee suggestion system is used effectively at the property.	5	4	3	2	1
53.	There is an employee awards program at the property.	5	4	3	2	1
54.	The property produces a monthly newsletter.	5	4	3	2	1
55.	The property offers an employee recreation and fitness program.	5	4	3	2	1
56.	The property provides an employee lunch room and an employee meeting room.	5	4	3	2	1
57.	There are set procedures by which to communicate the goals of the property to all levels within the organization.	5	4	3	2	1
58.	Management consistently measures how well the property accomplishes its goals.	5	4	3	2	1
59.	Employees understand the mission statement of the organization.	5	4	3	2	1

Exhibit 3.2 Manager Supervisor Survey Score Sheet

I. RELATIONSHIPS

Owner/Management Company

	5	4	3	2	1	Total Points	Number of Individuals	Average Score*
1.								
2.								
3.								
4.								

Total Section Points

Section Score** = _____

Department Managers

	5	4	3	2	1	Total Points	Number of Individuals	Average Score
5.								
6.								
7.								
8.								

Total Section Points

Section Score = _____

Supervisors

	5	4	3	2	1	Total Points	Number of Individuals	Average Score
9.								
10.								
11.								
12.								

Total Section Points

Section Score = _____

Exhibit 3.2 Continued

Networks

	5	4	3	2	1	Total Points	Number of Individuals	Average Score
13.								
14.								
15.								
16.								

Total Section Points

Section Score = _____

RELATIONSHIPS SCORE*** = _____

II. SUPPORT

Owner/Management Company

	5	4	3	2	1	Total Points	Number of Individuals	Average Score
17.								
18.								
19.								
20.								
21.								
22.								
23.								

Total Section Points

Section Score = _____

General Manager

	5	4	3	2	1	Total Points	Number of Individuals	Average Score
24.								
25.								
26.								

Total Section Points

Section Score = _____

SUPPORT SCORE = _____

Exhibit 3.2 Continued

III. INFORMATION

Information Flow

	5	4	3	2	1	Total Points	Number of Individuals	Average Score
27.								
28.								
29.								
30.								

Total Section Points [   ]

Section Score = _____

Development and Evaluation Systems

	5	4	3	2	1	Total Points	Number of Individuals	Average Score
31.								
32.								
33.								
34.								
35.								
36.								
37.								
38.								
39.								
40.								
41.								

Total Section Points [   ]

Section Score = _____

INFORMATION SCORE = _____

Exhibit 3.2 Continued

IV. OPERATIONS

Decision-Making

	5	4	3	2	1	Total Points	Number of Individuals	Average Score
42.								
43.								
44.								
45.								
46.								
47.								

Total Section Points [   ]

Section Score = _____

Opportunities

	5	4	3	2	1	Total Points	Number of Individuals	Average Score
48.								
49.								
50.								

Total Section Points [   ]

Section Score = _____

Benefits

	5	4	3	2	1	Total Points	Number of Individuals	Average Score
51.								
52.								
53.								
54.								
55.								
56.								

Total Section Points [   ]

Section Score = _____

Exhibit 3.2 Continued

Strategic Planning

	5	4	3	2	1	Total Points	Number of Individuals	Average Score
57.								
58.								
59.								

Total Section Points _____

Section Score = _____

OPERATIONS SCORE = _____

SURVEY SUMMARY SCORES

RELATIONSHIPS = _____

SUPPORT = _____

INFORMATION = _____

OPERATIONS = _____

TOTAL SURVEY SCORE = Total Points ÷ Number of Statements ÷ Number of Individuals

= _____

*   The average score for a statement is computed by dividing the total points by the number of individuals responding to the statement.

**   The section score is computed by dividing the total points for the section by the number of statements in the section and by the number of individuals responding to the statements.

***   The part score is computed by dividing the total points for the part by the number of statements in the part and by the number of individuals responding to the statements.

Each general area addressed by the survey also receives a score. These part scores are computed by dividing each part's total points by the number of statements in the part, and then by the number of individual respondents.

Analyzing the Survey Results

The average score for each statement, section, and part can be evaluated according to the following table:

Score	Grade	Condition Indicated
5.0-4.3	A	Excellent
4.2-3.5	B	Positive
3.4-2.8	C	Area Needs Attention
2.7 and below	D	Major Problems Exist

Individual survey statements should be categorized by grade and typed as a summary report. Survey responses grouped into A or B categories indicate excellent or positive conditions for implementing a quality assurance system. These high scores should be sources of positive feedback to department managers and supervisors. Statements grouped into the C category may help to identify problems that are costing the organization time and money. The quality assurance system should be able to solve many of these problems over time. Therefore, the problems indicated by survey statements listed in the C category could be used to generate the kind of strong management support that is necessary for successfully implementing a quality assurance system. Statements grouped into the D category indicate serious problems that must be resolved *before* implementing a quality assurance system.

Relationships. Responses to statements covered by the first three topics within the area of relationships supply information about the management styles and the pattern of interaction among top management (owners or management company, general manager, and members of the executive committee), department managers, and supervisors. The fourth section, networks, addresses relationships among departments and throughout the hospitality organization. Scores below 3.5 in any of these four sections indicate critical problems which must be resolved *before* implementing a quality assurance system. The system will not work with dictatorial managers who resist change and discourage new ideas from members of their staff.

Support. Without top management support, a quality assurance system is doomed to fail. The type of management support required depends on the structure of the hospitality organization. Generally, support is needed from top management officials who have the authority to make things happen. Support from the owners (or management company) and the general manager is absolutely essential. If *both* of these section scores are 3.5 or above, the probability of successfully implementing a quality assurance system is high. If *either* of these section scores is below 3.5, the system should not be implemented until support is obtained and clearly communicated to department managers and supervisors. If department managers and supervisors believe that the general manager does not genuinely support the quality assurance system, they will approach it as just another passing fad.

Information. High section scores in this area of the survey are not as crucial to the success of a quality assurance system as are high scores in the area of support. In fact, high section scores in the area of information indicate that a hospitality organization has already institutionalized some aspects of quality assurance.

However, the survey results of most hospitality properties do not generally produce high scores for the section on development and evaluation systems. Scores below 3.5 indicate that standards for measuring performance throughout the property are not well-developed. A successful quality assurance system should steadily increase scores in this area.

Operations. High section scores in the area of operations are not required before a quality assurance system is implemented. Scores in the decision-making and opportunities sections should increase over time once the quality assurance system is implemented. However, a score below 2.8 in the benefits section may indicate that certain issues should be addressed before implementing the system. Finally, a high score in the strategic planning section is not required before implementing the system; however, scores should improve after implementation.

The Employee Survey

Exhibit 3.3 presents a sample employee survey that is constructed with open-ended questions. Responses to this survey are not as easily quantified as are responses to the manager/supervisor survey; therefore, the results cannot be tabulated as quickly, and analysis may be more time-consuming. However, the survey's open-ended questions permit employees to address issues in their own terms and from their own frames of reference.

The results of an open-ended employee survey can be adequately interpreted by simply reading the responses and applying a little

Exhibit 3.3 Sample Employee Survey

Please read and answer each question completely and thoroughly. Your answers will be kept confidential. Thank you for your cooperation.

1. What do you need to do your job with pride and to the best of your ability?

2. As a member of the (insert name of department) crew, what exactly do you do at your job?

3. What are your overall goals as a professional in your job?

4. What do you hope to gain by working in (insert name of department) at the (insert name of hospitality property)?

5. What are the obstacles that keep you from performing your job to the best of your ability?

6. What would make you proud and enthusiastic about your job?

7. Can you communicate with your supervisor? If not, why not?

8. Do you feel important at your job?

9. Is better communication needed among the employees of (insert name of department)? If so, what can we do to improve communication?

10. When do you look forward to coming to work?

11. When do you feel a sense of accomplishment at your job?

12. What can we do to make (insert name of department) run more efficiently?

Additional comments:

Exhibit 3.4 Sample Responses to the Employee Survey

Question #1
Results from the Restaurant

1. *What do you need to do your job with pride and to the best of your ability?*

"Compatible co-workers, caring supervisors, **ample supplies.**"

"**A cooler uniform for the summer.** A fuller, more dependable busperson staff to help the restaurant run more efficiently."

"The respect of my co-workers to know that they can come to me if needed and for them to know they can count on me."

"A full competent staff to work with."

"Need to have **good working conditions, supplies.**"

"**Enough supplies, cooperation and communication** between fellow employees and those departments with which we work closely and are linked to."

"**A pleasant working atmosphere.**"

"Need guests in restaurant, **supplies**, cooks (good), buspersons (good)."

"**Support from staff.** It's nice to hear 'You're doing a good job' once in a while. Not that they never say it, or not that I want to be told I'm wonderful, but some servers never say anything, otherwise, everything else is great."

Question #2
Results from the Laundry

2. *As a member of the laundry crew, what exactly do you do at your job?*

"Almost everything like folding sheets, run the towel folder and the presser."

"Fold sheets, towels and table linen."

"Fold sheets, towels and table linen."

"Work with the washers and dryers."

"Folding sheets, ironing table linen and folding towels."

"I will work in different areas of the laundry and not one duty. Feed linen, fold sheets, load and unload machine and occasionally supervise."

Exhibit 3.4 Continued

"I am a washman, which entails separating linen, loading washers, dryers, folding sheets, also helping laundry manager any way I can."

"Fold linen, towels, sheets, table linen, keep the room clean and organized."

Question #3
Results from the Maintenance Department

3. *What are your overall goals as a professional in your job?*

"To try to keep this place clean, and **do the best job I can.**"

"**Do the very best at my job**; get paid for my abilities."

"To move up the ladder (i.e., financially)."

"I would like to **know a little more in the area of air conditioning and electrical work.**"

"**Do the job efficiently.**"

"**To work fast with a high standard.**"

"**Develop an inventory system.**"

"**To please the guest and management.**"

"To do the job to the best of my ability, and to **get training to be more proficient.**"

"Do the job to the best of my ability and be rewarded properly."

"**To do the job to the best of my ability.**"

Question #4
Results from the Front Office Department

4. *What do you hope to gain by working in the front office of the hotel?*

"**Experience to further my individual course into hotel management.**"

"**To make my job and someone else's easier.** To help guests as much as my ability allows and possible advancement."

"**More sense of confidence and leadership.** The knowledge of new skills and a better knowledge of communication and human behavior."

"The experience of meeting different people and **learning how to deal with each individual.**"

Exhibit 3.4 Continued

"Experience, knowledge and understanding of service/hospitality industry. (What makes it work.)"

Question #5
Results from the Sales Department

5. *What are the obstacles that keep you from performing your job to the best of your ability?*

"When we do not have proper collateral material to represent the resort in other cities and most importantly, if **a meeting gets ruined because of lack of service** due to our departments, then it is difficult to re-book that group or others as a result."

"Some days **rushed with too many priorities.** Phone interrupting work thoughts, mailing processing."

"The **telephone interruptions during the day.** A mailing and processing department."

"Walk-in clients, clients without an appointment, playing 'phone-tag' with clients. No major obstacles regarding the resort; the resort sells itself."

"**Not being able to get answers to questions right away.**"

"**Inconsistency in procedures, lack of follow-through from other departments,** inexperienced meeting planners, verbal agreements to clients not documented in contract or file."

"**Lack of communication between departments, people not being trained in their area or not taking responsibility for their job. Policies and procedures not always defined or followed by everyone or they keep changing everyday. Lack of team work to certain extent, time lapse in receiving information.**"

Question #6
Results from the Housekeeping Department

6. *What would make you proud and enthusiastic about your job?*

"That I am **rewarded for my work.**"

"That **they approve of my work.**"

"**When my work is approved.**"

"To learn English. I would feel better and would have no doubts from not knowing the language."

Exhibit 3.4 Continued

"To gain the faith and satisfaction of the guests."

"That they **let us know they appreciate one's work.**"

"**The confidence and satisfaction of the guests and all my supervisors.**"

"**Improve my work.**"

"That they tell me **they like my work and that I do it clean and good.**"

"**That the boss treats us like a person.**"

"Have good **communication.**"

"That everyone is totally equal and amiable."

"**Improve and go up in my job.**"

"That I get a raise, as they are happy with my work."

"That there should be more **working together by all the employees in my department.**"

"That they give me a raise; it depends on how well one works."

Question #7
Results from the Banquets Department

7. *Can you communicate with your supervisor? If not, why not?*

"Yes, most of the time. **The problem comes in when they disagree with each other and it takes time to come up with an answer.**"

"Most of them. **Some of them are either unwilling to listen or uninterested in what others have to say.**"

"Sometimes."

"Yes."

"No; personality."

"No, they don't seem to really be interested."

"Occasionally; **they are pressed for time a lot and don't have time to answer questions without getting mad.**"

"No, **some of them are opinionated and I feel it would hinder future working relationships should I disagree.**"

"No, **they are closed-minded, egotistical and not respected by those who try hard to perform their duties with pride.**"

"Yes."

Exhibit 3.4 Continued

Question #8
Results from the Kitchen Area

8. *Do you feel important at your job?*

   "Yes."

   "To some extent."

   "**No.**"

   "**No.**"

   "Partially."

   "Yes."

Question #9
Results from the Accounting Department

9. *Is better communication needed among the employees of the accounting department? If so, what can we do to improve communication?*

   "No."

   "Yes, **we are kept in the dark on some things.** Meetings might help."

   "Yes. I think **we all need to have a better understanding of our jobs**; what is expected from superiors and how our jobs affect the others within our own department. Job descriptions and guidance from superiors."

   "Communication in accounting works smoothly, but everything stops at accounting. We are the end of the line after everything happens in all the other departments and that is where we are faced with communication problems. **The departments we deal with need to better their communications so we are able to do our job better.**"

Question #10
Results from the Security Department

10. *When do you look forward to coming to work?*

    "Always."

    "Sometimes; sometimes not. My work is important to me, I genuinely like many of my co-workers, so coming to work is often enjoyable. But, as always, there are days I shouldn't have gotten out of bed, much less come to work."

Exhibit 3.4 Continued

"Quite frequently."

"Daily."

"All times in the evening before my shift starts."

"Most of the time. I enjoy the people I work with and the atmosphere."

Question #11
Results from Room Service

11. *When do you feel a sense of accomplishment at your job?*

"When I leave in the evening I feel as if I have done the best possible job."

"At the end of the shift. It makes me feel good to know I did the best I could."

"When it was a challenge, the challenge was met and I was rewarded."

"After doing a good setup with a bar or a large dinner order, and being complimented on it."

"If we have been busy and I have had to carry a lot of weight, I feel like if everything goes smooth we are a good department."

"After a hectic day and a good job is acknowledged by my superiors."

"When everyone works as a team."

Question #12
Results from Landscaping

12. *What can we do to make landscaping run more efficiently?*

"Know the handling of all the tools."

"Buy the necessary tools."

"Delegate jobs to employees in sections."

"To have all adequate tools."

"Pay more attention to the Department Head."

"Prepare people to do the job necessary."

"More hours to work."

common sense. Exhibit 3.4 presents actual employee responses to questions from the sample survey shown in Exhibit 3.3. Responses indicating problems that could be resolved within the structure of a quality assurance system appear in boldface type.

How to Administer the Surveys

Three important aspects involved with the administration of the manager/supervisor survey and the employee survey are:

- Planning the sequence and timing of the surveys
- Ensuring the confidentiality of survey responses
- Providing feedback to respondents about survey results

The following sections discuss these aspects in detail. However, it is important to stress here that, before the surveys are conducted, top management must decide on the type of feedback that will be provided to respondents about the survey results. If department managers, supervisors, or employees feel that no one truly cares about the survey results, they will not take the survey seriously. Also, asking for information implies action. If there are areas in which top management is not prepared to make changes, they should not be covered in the survey.

Planning the Sequence and Timing of the Surveys. The surveys should be conducted in the same order in which the quality assurance process is implemented. This order of implementation is as follows:

1. Top management
2. Department managers
3. Supervisors
4. Employees

If, after administering the manager/supervisor survey to top management executives, the results indicate a lack of support for the quality assurance system, there is little to be gained by subsequently administering the survey to department managers. Clearly stated support from the owners (or management company) and the general manager must be effectively communicated to the entire organization before the survey is administered to department managers.

Selecting an appropriate time for conducting the surveys is important. Surveys should not be conducted when managers, supervisors, or employees feel unsettled, such as when the organization (or a specific department) is undergoing staff changes or radical restructuring. Nor should the surveys be conducted when people in the organization may be experiencing attitude extremes, whether positive or negative, such as during the new year holidays or when business is particularly slow.

Ensuring the Confidentiality of Survey Responses. Confidentiality affects the validity of survey results. Respondents should never have to put their names on the survey forms. Without an assurance of anonymity, respondents may fear recrimination and offer only safe responses to the survey questions. To ensure confidentiality, surveys may be processed by an outside agency. These agencies normally destroy the original survey forms after tabulating the results.

Problems relating to the confidentiality of survey responses may arise in connection with the specific categories by which the survey results are broken down. For example, in order to evaluate relationships within a hospitality organization, it is important to break down the results of the manager/supervisor survey in relation to top management, department managers, and supervisors. This breakdown does not affect the anonymity of respondents. However, if a breakdown pairs the responses of a department manager with those of the supervisors within the same department, the supervisors may feel threatened. Although their names do not appear on the survey forms, some may feel that they can be identified by their responses. Once supervisors sense a lack of confidentiality, their responses may be practically useless.

This problem may be even greater in relation to the breakdown of the results of the employee survey. If the breakdown does not ensure anonymity for employees, supervisors and department managers will be able to identify how specific employees responded to the survey questions. Before completing the survey, employees should be assured that management is seeking their honest and thoughtful replies, and that great care has been taken to enforce the confidentiality of all responses. Employees should be told how confidentiality will be secured. At the very least, employees should be informed that no one in their department will see the actual survey forms with the handwritten responses.

The atmosphere in which employee surveys are administered can significantly affect the validity of responses. The presence of a domineering department manager or supervisor may instill fear within employees that their responses will be used against them. A person not employed within the department (such as the human resources director, the quality assurance manager, or a representative from an outside agency) should conduct and collect the surveys.

Providing Feedback to Respondents about Survey Results. The general manager and members of the executive committee should receive the tabulated results of the manager/supervisor survey and the employee survey. They must decide how to communicate the results of the surveys to the respondents. The results of the employee survey should be communicated to department managers and supervisors without any finger-pointing or other actions that may make them defensive. No manager or supervisor should fear the survey results or feel threatened by them.

It is important that department managers and supervisors realize that *feelings are facts.* If employees *feel* that they are not considered important to top management or to other departments, this is a *fact*–regardless of how top management or other departments actually regard them. If employees *feel* that they will be terminated if they ask for raises, this is a *fact*–regardless of current company policy. If employees *feel* that managers do not listen to their ideas, then this is a *fact*–regardless of whether or not managers listen to their ideas.

In some instances, the general manager and executive committee members may consider having department managers and supervisors complete the same survey as their employees. They may be asked to fill out the survey in the way that they think their employees will fill it out. A comparison of the results may highlight discrepancies between what department managers and supervisors think is going on in their departments and what is actually happening.

Distributing survey results to employees must avoid fanning any fires that may be smoldering within departments. The general manager and executive committee members may consider it appropriate to feed back only selected results. However, if no information, or only insignificant information, is communicated to employees, they will quickly sense that management never valued their thoughts and opinions in the first place.

Five Steps in Survey Construction

Since the needs and requirements of hospitality organizations vary, management may consider revising the sample surveys presented in this chapter. Questions can be added, deleted, or changed in order to address particular concerns which may affect a property's unique implementation of the quality assurance process.

In rare cases, it may be necessary to construct entirely different surveys. In these situations, top management should consider contracting the professional services of consultants who are experienced in the area of survey construction *and* are familiar with the components of the quality assurance system. However, consultants will not be able to do everything. Top management and others within the hospitality organization must provide direction and important input during the process of survey construction.

If top management decides to have in-house staff members revise the sample surveys or construct different surveys, the following five-step method of survey construction may serve as a useful guide:

1. Identify the areas that the survey should address.
2. Choose the type of survey questions.
3. Write the survey questions.
4. Pretest the survey with selected respondents.
5. Finalize the survey and specify procedures for its use.

The sections which follow examine each of these steps in some detail. The information presented may guide the efforts of in-house staff members in the construction of surveys, and alert top management to the kind of direction and input they should provide if professional consultants are used.

Identify the Areas that the Survey Should Address

The starting point for developing a survey is to identify the areas that the survey should address. The primary areas covered in the sample surveys are essential in securing the information necessary for implementing a quality assurance process and for monitoring its success.

The primary areas addressed in the sample manager/supervisor survey are:

- Relationships
- Support
- Information
- Operations

These primary areas can be broken down in a number of different ways. Top management can use the breakdown within the sample survey score sheet as a guide in determining additional topics that should be addressed by surveys at their properties.

The primary areas addressed in the sample employee survey are:

- Professional goals
- Department communication
- Job satisfaction
- Obstacles to job performance
- Suggestions for work improvement

Although top management may wish to specify additional areas to include in a property's employee survey, these primary areas must be covered in order to secure the necessary information for properly implementing a quality assurance system and monitoring its success.

Once the areas are identified, careful consideration should be given to the order of the areas within the survey and the sequence of the topics within each area. The best sequence is not always the most logical sequence. Often, the best sequence is a psychological sequence which takes into account the backgrounds and experiences of the respondents.

Choose the Type of Survey Questions

There are essentially two types of survey questions: closed questions and open-ended questions. A survey with closed questions limits responses to stated alternatives. These alternatives may be simply "Yes" and "No," or they may consist of a series of replies from which the respondents choose. The alternatives may allow for various degrees of agreement and disagreement. Sometimes space is provided at the end of these surveys for individual comments. The sample manager/supervisor survey presented in this chapter is constructed with closed questions which allow respondents to indicate varying degrees of agreement or disagreement.

Since surveys constructed with closed questions elicit responses which can be easily quantified, results can be tabulated quickly. In some cases, relatively inexpensive computer software programs can be used to tabulate and partially analyze the results.

A survey with open-ended questions is designed to permit free responses rather than responses which are limited to stated alternatives. An open-ended question simply raises an issue; it does not provide, or even suggest, any structure for the respondent's reply. The sample employee survey presented in this chapter is constructed with open-ended questions.

Responses to open-ended questions are not as easily quantified as responses to closed questions. Therefore, the results cannot be tabulated as quickly and the analysis may be more time-consuming. The advantage of constructing an employee survey with open-ended questions is that employees can address issues in their own terms and from their own frames of reference.

Write the Survey Questions

The questions used in the sample surveys should prove very helpful to those responsible for constructing surveys which meet the unique needs and requirements of a particular hospitality organization. Even if the sample surveys seem adequate, the questions should be reviewed carefully from time to time and improved or replaced as necessary.

Those responsible for writing survey questions may find it helpful to test the effectiveness of their work by answering the following series of questions:

1. Is the form of response easy, definite, uniform, and adequate for the purpose?

2. Is the question necessary? What useful information will answers provide?

3. Are several questions needed on a topic currently covered by one question?

4. Can the question be misunderstood? Does it contain difficult or unclear words and phrases?

5. Is the question misleading because of unstated assumptions or hidden implications?

6. Is the wording biased? Is it emotionally loaded or slanted toward a particular kind of answer?

7. Would a more personalized or less personalized wording of the question produce better results?

8. Is the answer to the question likely to be influenced by the content of earlier questions?

9. Is the question in the best psychological order which takes into account the backgrounds and experiences of the respondents?

The number of open-ended questions may vary from 8 to 15 in one survey. Too many open-ended questions may prove too cumbersome for analysis. The number of closed questions may vary from 20 to 100. However, sixty questions are usually sufficient for identifying significant trends.

As the sample surveys indicate, several specific questions covering different topics within the same area may obtain more precise and useful information than a single general question. If top management desires some way of measuring the consistency of individual responses, the survey may include a few extra questions. For example, responses to roughly equivalent or closely related questions (well separated in the survey) may indicate the consistency with which individuals respond to the entire survey.

Pretest the Survey with Selected Respondents

A pretest is a tryout of the questions to see how well they work and whether changes are necessary before administering the surveys. The pretest provides a means of identifying and solving unforeseen problems such as the phrasing and sequencing of the questions, or perhaps even the survey's length. A pretest may indicate the need for additional questions or the elimination of others.

Finalize the Survey and Specify Procedures

After the questions have been revised according to feedback received through the pretest, the format for administering the survey should be established. Directions for administering the survey and for answering the survey questions should be as clear as possible. Suggested procedures addressed earlier in this chapter covered such areas as the sequence and timing of conducting the surveys, ensuring the confidentiality of survey responses, and providing feedback to respondents about survey results.

Part II
Strategic Planning for Operations

4

An Overview of Strategic Planning for Operations

For many years hotels have prepared annual financial forecasts projecting potential revenue, expenses, and probable profits. This data is used to prepare budgets and develop a general business plan for the upcoming fiscal year. Recently, hospitality businesses have seriously adopted strategic planning processes for specialized areas of business, such as financial management, company growth and expansion, and marketing. This chapter presents a strategic planning process specifically designed for the area of hospitality operations. However, in order to be effective, strategic planning for operations should be integrated with an organization's current budget planning, strategic marketing planning, and long-range planning processes.

The primary objective of strategic planning for operations is to enhance the profitability of the hospitality business by increasing the productivity of managers, supervisors, and employees. The strategic planning process accomplishes this objective by:

- Aligning all levels within the organization around a common vision of what the hospitality business stands for or strives to create

- Engaging managers, supervisors, and employees in a planning process that challenges them to think beyond the demands of day-to-day activities

- Increasing communication within and among the diverse departments and functional areas that make up the organization

- Identifying and solving problems that affect the quality of products and services delivered by the organization

In order for today's managers to adopt the kind of perspective necessary for effective strategic planning, they must be able to step back from the pressures and demands of day-to-day activities. This is not an easy step for many managers to take because they are used to handling the seemingly endless demands of operating a hospitality business 365 days a year. These demands range from carrying out routine operational responsibilities to handling unique situations that may arise during the course of a business day. Some of the more frustrating situations that may occur include:

- Unproductive management meetings
- Fewer employees showing up for work than were scheduled
- More guests arriving than were forecasted
- Accounting reports that fail to match figures kept by the department
- Hiring and firing employees
- Computer crashes

Given the immediacy of routine responsibilities and unique situations, it is not surprising that many managers in the hospitality industry focus almost exclusively on short-term results. This shortsightedness is often reinforced by the kind of information that managers receive about the hospitality business. For example, data typically made available to hospitality managers by accounting and management information systems suggest problems or inefficiencies; but, for the most part, data fail to draw attention to the specifics of any single problem or emerging opportunity.

To overcome the natural tendency of managers to focus on short-term results at the expense of long-range goals, some hospitality organizations are formally incorporating a process of strategic planning into the structure of their business operations, thus engaging their managers in some form of long-range thinking. But what does "long-range" mean to department managers in the hospitality industry? Is "long-range" three years? one year? six months? one week?

Managers must be able to relate the planning process to the immediacies of everyday operations. Therefore, depending upon the size and needs of a property, strategic planning for operations may best be conducted annually. This time span is long enough for managers to feel that they are engaging in a form of strategic planning, and it is short enough for managers to recognize the plan's connection to daily operations. If strategic planning for operations extends too far into the future, managers may consider the planning activities a waste of time.

Strategic planning for operations involves setting up a steering committee and several planning groups. The steering committee and the planning groups meet separately but follow the same sequence of planning activities. Before defining these planning activities in detail, the chapter will discuss the composition and function of the steering committee and planning groups.

The Steering Committee and Planning Groups

The strategic planning steering committee should include the general manager and selected division directors and/or department managers. Individuals selected to serve on the steering committee should be systematic thinkers capable of analyzing current hotel operations and identifying factors which may affect the property's future. Members of the steering committee must be able to concentrate on the "big picture" rather than on the details of any one problem or single area of operations. Individuals who can't see the forest for the trees should not be invited to attend. Members also need to be tolerant and open-minded enough to recognize the worth of opposing viewpoints regarding the future of the business. Questions to consider before selecting steering committee members include:

- Who should attend because of their positions within the organization?

- Who should attend because of the political roles they play in daily business operations?

- Who should attend because of their skills in strategic thinking?

- What will the individuals who are not asked to be members be told?

Planning groups may work best with five or six members. The composition of these groups depends upon the size of the hospitality property. If there are eight or fewer departments, a planning group may be formed for each department. Exhibit 4.1 lists sample planning groups and identifies members in terms of positions within departments of a hotel. The positions named in the exhibit are meant only as examples of the composition of planning groups. Members of these groups should be selected according to the same criteria used in selecting steering committee members. It is important that the ranking manager within each group does not stifle or inhibit the other members.

If there are more than eight departments in a hotel, departments can be combined so that strategic planning groups are set up on the basis of functional relationships. For example, individuals from the accounting and data processing departments could combine to form a single planning group. Other departments that could be combined into single planning groups are banquets and catering, sales and

Exhibit 4.1 Sample Planning Groups

<table>
<tr><td>

Administration
Controller
Security director
Data processing supervisor
Payroll supervisor
Night audit supervisor
Accounts payable clerk

Sales
Sales manager
Sales secretary
Sales account executive
Convention services manager
Convention coordinator

Front Office
Front desk manager
Reservationist
Front desk clerk (a.m.)
Front desk clerk (p.m.)
Bellperson

Housekeeping
Executive housekeeper
Laundry supervisor
Inspectress
Room attendant
Public area attendant
Laundry worker

</td><td>

Maintenance
Chief engineer
Assistant engineer
Maintenance person
Maintenance person
Pool attendant

Dining Room
Dining room manager
Dining room supervisor (a.m.)
Dining room supervisor (p.m.)
Server
Server
Busperson

Lounge
Lounge manager
Bartender
Bartender
Cocktail server
Cocktail server

Kitchen
Chef
Sous chef
Line cook
Baker
Dishmachine operator

</td></tr>
</table>

convention services, housekeeping and laundry, dining rooms and room service, and so on.

The number and sequence of strategic planning meetings may vary in relation to the needs and requirements of individual hospitality properties. Exhibit 4.2 shows the sequence of meetings that will be used in this book to explain the process of strategic planning for operations. Detailed information about how to conduct these strategic planning meetings is presented in the next chapter.

Strategic Planning Activities

The following sections describe each strategic planning activity and define the roles played by the steering committee and planning groups.

Exhibit 4.2 Sequence of Annual Strategic Planning Meetings

MEETINGS	TIMES
Planning Groups Meeting #1	4 hours each
Steering Committee Meeting #1	8 hours
Planning Groups Meeting #2	4 hours each
Steering Committee Meeting #2	8 hours
Planning Groups Meeting #3	4 hours each
Steering Committee Meeting #3	8 hours
Steering Committee Quarterly Reviews	4 hours each

Strategic planning activities include:

1. Writing mission statements
2. Collecting data
3. Determining objectives
4. Developing action plans
5. Assembling the annual strategic plan for operations
6. Reviewing the plan and monitoring results

The efforts of the steering committee are directed toward areas of operations that are generally considered beyond the scope of individual departments. In addition, the steering committee selects and approves objectives and action plans developed by all planning groups. Exhibit 4.3 diagrams the interaction between planning groups and the steering committee. The steering committee also performs many administrative tasks which are necessary for an effective and efficient planning process.

Writing Mission Statements

Strategic planning for operations begins with the preparation of a mission statement for each department and for the organization as a whole. Mission statements answer basic questions about operations, such as:

- What do we do?
- How do we do it?
- For whom do we do it?

Exhibit 4.3 Strategic Planning Activities

A planning group's mission statement conveys the basic function of a particular department or area of operations. For example, the following mission statement conveys the basic function of one resort's front office department:

We serve as a communications/information center for the resort. Our professionalism and high standards provide comfort and ensure a memorable experience for our guests.

The mission statement for the entire resort may read as follows:

The Guest comes first at the ABC Resort. We provide a luxurious resort experience, state-of-the-art convention facilities, and consistent, friendly, professional service.

When the organization's mission statement includes its "distinctive competencies" (its particular business strengths or resources), it can serve as a basis for determining how to allocate present resources and how to identify directions for future growth. A mission statement also serves as a screening mechanism that keeps management's attention focused on only those opportunities that clearly mesh with the company's business purpose. Mission statements also give a clear direction to everyone working in the organization because they:

- Foster common basic goals

- Serve as a basis for communication

- Assert a philosophy of doing business

- Provide a basis for evaluating individual departments and the entire organization

In the strategic planning process, mission statements are written by consensus. Planning groups write mission statements for their departments or functional areas. The steering committee writes the mission statement for the entire organization. Exhibit 4.4 shows the end result of this first step in the strategic planning process. The combined mission statements can be printed or silk-screened, framed, and displayed in every department. This enhances communication within the organization by increasing everyone's knowledge of the roles played by individual departments in the overall operation of the business. The framed mission statements should be graphically appealing, contain the property's logo, and match the general decor of the operation.

Collecting Data

After writing mission statements, the steering committee and planning groups collect data that provide a basis for analyzing operations. This data-gathering activity can be accomplished through external and internal scans.

To scan means to examine closely or to scrutinize. An external scan identifies outside factors affecting the profitability, productivity, and performance of a given area of operations. An internal scan identifies inside factors affecting the profitability, productivity, and performance of that same area of operations. The data collected through external and internal scans provide the basis for establishing priorities and determining strategic planning objectives.

External Scan. A planning group's external scan examines areas that are outside the group's department but still within the framework of property operations. The group typically focuses on defining its

Exhibit 4.4 Sample Mission Statements

Administration

The accuracy and efficiency with which we carry out accounting tasks and human resource responsibilities create fair and honest relationships with guests, employees, and creditors.

Sales

We sell and coordinate services and amenities provided by our resort's professional staff to fulfill commitments to our guests, produce profits, and generate repeat business.

Purchasing

We purchase, receive, and distribute products and equipment for our guests and co-workers, and we maintain friendly, clean, and safe production areas and storage environments.

Front Office

We serve as a communications / information center for the resort. Our professionalism and high standards provide comfort and ensure a memorable experience for our guests.

Housekeeping

We help keep the resort clean and provide friendly, professional service for our guests and fellow workers by training and supervising according to our standards.

Resort

The Guest comes first at the ABC Resort. We provide a luxurious resort experience, state-of-the-art convention facilities, and consistent, friendly, professional service.

Kitchen Operations

We consistently provide quality food items for our guests and employees in a clean, safe, sanitary, and professional environment while efficiently managing the owners' resources.

Restaurant Operations

Our prompt, courteous, and professional staff proudly welcomes each guest and graciously provides a variety of uniquely prepared dishes in an atmosphere of simple elegance.

Banquets

We fulfill our guests' needs and requests by providing quality meeting facilities and serving food and beverages in an expedient, professional, friendly, and attentive manner.

Maintenance

We promptly, cheerfully, and professionally complete work orders, repair equipment items, and maintain all the facilities in the resort for our guests and fellow employees.

Landscaping

We mow lawns, trim trees and shrubs, plant flowers, and keep outside areas clean and attractive for the resort's guests and for our fellow employees.

Beverage Operations

We provide beverages and entertainment for the resort's guests in a friendly and relaxed atmosphere, and we take pride in giving prompt, consistent, individualized service.

relationships with the other departments in the organization. Members begin by listing departments that relate to the operation of their own department. Departments on the list are ranked according to the degree to which they affect the profitability, productivity, and performance of the group's own department. The group then answers three questions about each department on its list:

1. What can we do to improve communications with this department?

2. What problems do we have with this department?

3. What can this department do to improve the service it provides for guests?

Answers to these questions provide the data necessary for establishing priorities and determining strategic planning objectives.

The external scan performed by the steering committee examines areas outside the framework of property operations that may affect the profitability, productivity, and performance of the entire organization during the upcoming year. Areas examined include:

- Markets
- Competition
- Local/national economy
- Legislation

Several members of the steering committee may feel that they are not as well-informed about these outside areas as are other committee members. To ensure participation of all steering committee members in this planning activity, it may be helpful to distribute (before the meeting) articles and sections from several trade publications that address relevant areas. For example, Laventhol & Horwath's *U.S. Lodging Industry Digest* and Pannell Kerr Forster's *Trends—USA* are useful sources of information relevant to the steering committee's external scan. Other useful sources of information include: articles in the American Hotel & Motel Association's *Lodging* magazine; articles in magazines and journals that focus on particular segments of the hospitality industry, such as *Hotel & Resort Industry*; and those magazines and journals that focus on specific areas of hotel operations, such as *Restaurant Business*, *Meetings and Conventions*, and others.

The steering committee also collects and organizes data relating to hotel operations about the wants, expectations, and needs of guests and owners (or the management company). Data may take the form of a composite analysis of responses from guest comment cards and copies of relevant communications from the owners (or the management company).

Internal Scan. The internal scan performed by a planning group examines areas within its own sphere of operations. Members of a planning group may consider such areas as:

- Facilities/location
- Daily department functions
- Product development
- Department communications
- Changing pool of job applicants
- Department growth/decline
- Equipment needs

The strategic planning steering committee performs its internal scan of operations by reviewing results from the manager/supervisor survey and employee survey. In relation to the manager/supervisor survey, each committee member receives (before the first steering committee meeting) the completed survey score sheet as well as a survey summary report. The summary report groups responses to survey statements into A, B, C, or D categories. As pointed out in the previous chapter, survey responses grouped into A or B categories indicate excellent or positive conditions within the property; statements grouped into C or D categories indicate areas that need management's immediate attention.

Each committee member also receives (before the first steering committee meeting) copies of the completed employee surveys of each department. The committee member highlights survey responses that indicate problems or give cause for concern. After reviewing the highlighted statements on a department-by-department basis, the committee writes three objectives for each department that, if accomplished, could resolve most of the problems indicated by that department's employee survey results.

When reviewing the results of the employee survey, it is important for steering committee members to realize that *feelings are facts*. If employees *feel* that they are not considered important to top management or to other departments, this is a *fact*—regardless of how top management or other departments actually regard the employees. If employees *feel* that they will be terminated if they ask for raises, this is a *fact*—regardless of current company policy. If employees feel that managers do not listen to their ideas, then this is a *fact*—regardless of whether managers listen to their ideas or not.

Determining Objectives

During this step in the strategic planning process the steering committee and planning groups analyze the data gathered from their external and internal scans. Conclusions are drawn from the analysis and objectives are determined. Each objective describes one problem and lists reasons why the situation is perceived as a problem.

When analyzing data it is important that steering committee members and members of planning groups encourage intuitive responses as well as systematic analysis. Intuition plays a vital role in all planning situations. Intuition can be defined as an immediate or direct understanding of a problem or situation. One member's intuitive "feeling" or "hunch" may prompt others to think differently about a particular problem. In the end, the group may arrive at a solution that would otherwise have been overlooked.

Members of a planning group analyze data gathered from external and internal scans by highlighting those items which seem to pose significant problems for their department. Whenever possible, highlighted items are combined as aspects of a single problem. Next, the group determines an objective for each highlighted problem. An objective describes a problem and lists reasons why the group perceives it to be a problem. For example, members of a banquets planning group determined the following objective:

> *Housekeeping needs a more flexible schedule for vacuuming public areas and banquet function areas.*
>
> - *Too much noise*
> - *Inconvenience to guests*
> - *Disrupts meetings*
> - *Poor appearance*

The information conveyed by an objective becomes helpful during the next planning activity when action plans are developed.

After objectives are written for all of the problems identified through external and internal scans, the planning group establishes priorities. The group accomplishes this by ranking the objectives in an order reflecting their importance to the profitability, productivity, and performance of its department. Exhibit 4.5 presents a partial list of objectives determined by a housekeeping planning group.

After planning groups have determined objectives and established priorities, their lists are sent to the strategic planning steering committee. The steering committee decides which objectives submitted by each planning group should be acted upon during the upcoming year.

Exhibit 4.5 Objectives from an External Scan

Date: 02/12/XX
Planning Group: Housekeeping
External Scan: All Departments

1. Front desk supervisors need to cross-train in housekeeping.

    - So they understand the mechanics of housekeeping.
    - So they know the rooms and what's in them.
    - So they know how long it takes to clean a room.
    - So they process out-of-order rooms correctly.

2. Sales/convention services needs to improve communications with housekeeping.

    - They don't notify housekeeping when they tour rooms.
    - They don't communicate guest problems with housekeeping or maintenance.
    - They don't notify housekeeping about special tours or complimentary rooms that require specific amenities.
    - They don't give advance notice of turn-down requests.

3. Banquets misuses furniture and fixtures.

    - They don't clean their carpets or blot stains.
    - They store broken equipment and tables behind the laundry.
    - They break lobby floor tiles by dragging six-foot tables across the lobby.

4. Room service needs to follow pick-up policies and procedures.

    - Pick-up sheets were designed by an employee problem-solving team, but are not being used.
    - They don't pick up trays, glasses, or dishes.
    - Can't get ahold of anyone but an order-taker.

5. Mini-bar attendants need to write job lists and follow policies and procedures.

    - They don't clean refrigerators properly.
    - They don't remove charge slips and tent cards.
    - They don't clean ice machines.
    - They don't blot and clean stains on carpets.

6. Rooms forecast needs to break out rooms by room type and location.

    - So we can schedule deep cleaning.
    - So we can clean rooms that are needed first.
    - So we can schedule room attendants efficiently.

The committee then steers approved objectives to the planning groups that have the authority to actually solve the problems.

For example, if the steering committee agreed that something should be done about the schedule for vacuuming public areas and banquet function areas, then the objective would not be returned to the banquets department for an action plan. Rather, the objective would be sent to the housekeeping planning group because the problem cannot be solved without action from the housekeeping department.

The steering committee also analyzes data gathered through its external scan and data gathered by individual committee members through their reviews of the manager/supervisor survey results. For each area of concern, the committee members agree upon a single objective.

The steering committee analyzes the employee survey results by reviewing the highlighted statements and the lists of objectives prepared by individual committee members. The committee reviews this material on a department-by-department basis and selects the three most significant areas of concern for each department. Next, members agree upon a single objective for each area of concern.

Before the final selection of objectives from its internal scan, the steering committee may wish to meet with department managers. Input from department managers may help the committee refine the objectives and clarify priorities.

Once the steering committee selects objectives from its internal scan, the objectives are sent to the appropriate planning groups. The planning groups then develop action plans for achieving the objectives.

Some objectives determined by the steering committee or by planning groups may cover problems that cannot be solved through the action of any single department. In these cases, the steering committee may divide into groups that take responsibility for developing action plans. Individual steering committee members are also assigned to develop action plans to achieve objectives selected from the committee's external scan.

Developing Action Plans

At this point in the strategic planning process, steering committee members and planning groups have been assigned objectives for the upcoming year. Their next task is to develop action plans by which to achieve their objectives. Effective action plans are developed by answering the following questions:

1. What is to be done?
2. How will it be done?
3. Who will do it?

4. Who will need to help?

5. How much will it cost?

6. When will each step be completed?

Answers to these questions provide all the information necessary to develop an action plan that lists what will be done, when it will be done, and who will be responsible for doing it. Exhibit 4.6 shows an action plan developed by a housekeeping strategic planning group. Action plans developed by steering committee members should follow the same format.

Once action plans have been developed, they are submitted to the steering committee for approval and the annual strategic plan for operations is assembled.

Assembling the Strategic Plan

At this step in the strategic planning process, the steering committee puts together the annual strategic plan for operations. This is accomplished by selecting action plans for implementation during the upcoming year. Important selection criteria include budget limitations and time frames.

The costs of implementing action plans must be evaluated in light of current and future budget constraints. While strategic planning for operations ideally should precede budget planning sessions, this does not guarantee that final budgets will be large enough to accommodate the costs of implementing all of the action plans which have been developed. Steering committee members must assess the financial feasibility of action plans and approve only those which they believe can be implemented within the limitations of current or future budgets.

The steering committee must also review the time frames projected for completion of action plans. Members of planning groups with little experience in strategic planning often try to do too much too quickly. Steering committee members may need to revise action plan time frames so that the problems are solved as completely as possible. Problems that are glossed over because of time constraints will only show up again in the next year's strategic planning sessions.

In addition, the steering committee must consider other factors that may affect action plan time frames. For example, the property may plan to introduce new equipment (such as a new telephone system or computer system) that will demand intensive training and may interfere with the time frames developed by some planning groups.

Once action plans are selected, revised, and approved by the steering committee, they are returned to the appropriate planning groups (or to individual steering committee members) for implementation. Department managers are responsible for implementing the action plans returned to their department's planning group.

Exhibit 4.6 Sample Action Plan

Planning Group	Housekeeping	
Strategic Planning Objective #5	Laundry needs to improve cleanliness and availability of rags.	

WHAT IS TO BE DONE	WHEN	BY WHOM	DATE COMPLETED
1. Laundry will wash, issue, and charge F&B and Housekeeping for rags and aprons.			
a. Develop procedures and meet with F&B Director.	03/15/88	Tony/Tom/ Burt	
b. Determine par levels.	03/15/88	Tony/Tom	
c. Store inventory in uniform room.	04/15/88	Tony/Tom	
d. Train F&B in new procedures.	04/30/88	Tony	
2. Develop system for washing rags and aprons in Laundry.	04/01/88	Tom	
3. Implement charge procedures.	04/30/88	Tony/Burt/ Pete	
4. Implement rag and apron program.	05/01/88	Tony	

Reviewing the Plan

The steering committee should review the strategic plan for operations and monitor results on a quarterly basis. Mistakes made in the first quarter should not be repeated in the second quarter. Some mistakes may necessitate revising the time frames of action plans. Other mistakes may indicate management deficiencies and/or training needs. All mistakes should be treated as learning experiences. The more experience that individuals obtain in the strategic planning process, the better they will become at strategic planning in the future.

Implementing the Strategic Planning Process

The success of strategic planning for operations depends a great deal on the administrative skills of the individual responsible for implementing the process. Depending upon the size of the hospitality organization, this individual could be the general manager, the human resources director, or the quality assurance manager.

Regardless of who spearheads the process, an implementation action plan must be developed to ensure an efficient and productive strategic planning process. The organizer of the strategic planning process develops an implementation action plan by specifying objectives that must be accomplished before strategic planning meetings can be conducted. Five fundamental objectives are:

1. Conduct surveys and summarize results.
2. Select strategic planning members.
3. Prepare strategic planning workbooks.
4. Schedule meetings.
5. Conduct meetings and process information.

The previous chapter discussed in great detail how to conduct and summarize the results of the manager/supervisor survey and the employee survey. The surveys should be conducted at least one month before the first steering committee meeting so that summarized results can be forwarded to each steering committee member before the meeting.

Previous sections of this chapter discussed criteria for selecting steering committee members as well as members of planning groups. The general manager and the organizer of the strategic planning process should be responsible for selecting steering committee members. Members of a planning group, on the other hand, should be selected by the general manager (or division director) and the ranking department manager.

Strategic planning workbooks should be prepared for steering committee members as well as for planning groups. These workbooks should contain:

● The objective of the strategic planning process

● How the strategic planning process achieves this objective

● An overview of strategic planning activities

● Detailed meeting agendas

The workbook prepared for steering committee members should also contain the mission statements prepared by planning groups. In addition, the workbook should contain materials needed for the external scan of markets, competition, national/local economy, and legislation.

Other materials that may be needed for the committee's external scan are:

- Relevant articles from industry trade publications
- Relevant communications from the owners (or management company)
- Composite analysis of guest comments

The workbook for steering committee members should also contain information needed for an internal scan of operations. This information includes the completed manager/supervisor survey score sheet as well as the survey summary report. The workbook should also include copies of the completed employee surveys of each department.

Scheduling meetings can be the most difficult aspect of administering the strategic planning process. The sequence of strategic planning meetings was shown earlier in this chapter in Exhibit 4.2. The nature of the strategic planning process requires that all planning groups meet before the first steering committee meeting. While the number and length of meetings may vary, it is usually possible to cover all of the strategic planning activities with three meetings (each four hours long) of planning groups and three meetings (each eight hours long) of the steering committee.

The organizer should allow enough lead time from the scheduled end of planning group meetings to the scheduled beginning of steering committee meetings so that any meetings missed by planning groups can be made up before the upcoming steering committee meeting. Also, time must be allotted within the schedule for processing information.

An implementation action plan should also indicate time frames for accomplishing objectives and identify the individuals responsible for carrying out specific tasks. Time frames will vary from property to property, and so will the positions held by individuals who are assigned various responsibilities. However, the previous descriptions of the basic implementation objectives should enable strategic planning organizers to specify time frames and assign responsibilities. Exhibit 4.7, at the end of this chapter, presents an action plan format which organizers can adapt to the special requirements of their individual organizations.

The next chapter explains in great detail how to conduct strategic planning meetings. The chapter provides the organizer of the strategic planning process with practical tools (such as sample meeting agendas, suggested meeting procedures, and sample flip chart sheets) with which to conduct productive meetings. In addition, the chapter alerts the organizer to the information which must be processed before, during, and after each meeting in order to ensure an efficient and successful strategic planning process at the hospitality property.

Exhibit 4.7 Implementation Action Plan

WHAT IS TO BE DONE	WHEN	BY WHOM	DATE COMPLETED
1. Conduct surveys and summarize results.			
Manager/Supervisor Survey			
a. Conduct surveys.			
b. Score survey results.			
c. Prepare summary report.			
Employee Survey			
a. Conduct surveys.			
b. Assemble survey responses by department.			
2. Select strategic planning members.			
a. Select steering committee members.			
b. Select planning group members.			
3. Prepare strategic planning workbooks.			
Planning Group Workbook			
a. Write the objective of the strategic planning process.			
b. Write an explanation of how the process achieves its objective.			
c. Write overview of strategic planning activities.			
d. Prepare detailed meeting agendas.			
Steering Committee Workbook			
a. Write the objective of strategic planning process.			
b. Write an explanation of how the process achieves its objective.			
c. Write overview of strategic planning activities.			
d. Prepare detailed meeting agendas.			
e. Insert materials for external scan.			
▸ Relevant trade articles			
▸ Composite analysis of guest comments			
▸ Relevant owner communications			

Exhibit 4.7 Continued

WHAT IS TO BE DONE	WHEN	BY WHOM	DATE COMPLETED
f. Insert materials for internal scan.			
▸ Manager/supervisor survey score sheet			
▸ Manager/supervisor survey summary report			
▸ Employee survey responses by department			
4. Schedule meetings.			
a. Planning groups meeting #1, 4 hours each			
b. Steering committee meeting #1, 8 hours			
c. Planning groups meeting #2, 4 hours each			
d. Steering committee meeting #2, 8 hours			
e. Planning groups meeting #3, 4 hours each			
f. Steering committee meeting #3, 8 hours			
g. Steering committee quarterly reviews, 4 hours each			
5. Conduct meetings and process information.			
Planning Groups Meeting #1			
a. Conduct the meetings.			
b. Process mission statements.			
c. Process data from external scans.			
d. Process data from internal scans.			
e. Distribute processed information before the next planning groups meeting.			
Steering Committee Meeting #1			
a. Conduct the meeting.			
b. Process mission statements.			
c. Process data from external scans.			
d. Process data from internal scans.			

Exhibit 4.7 Continued

WHAT IS TO BE DONE	WHEN	BY WHOM	DATE COMPLETED
e. Distribute processed information before the next steering committee meeting.			
Planning Groups Meeting #2 a. Conduct the meetings. b. Process objectives from external scan. c. Process objectives from internal scan. d. Distribute objectives to steering committee members before the next meeting.			
Steering Committee Meeting #2 a. Conduct the meeting. b. Process objectives selected by the committee. c. Distribute objectives to appropriate planning groups.			
Planning Groups Meeting #3 a. Conduct the meetings. b. Process action plans. c. Distribute action plans to steering committee members before the next meeting.			
Steering Committee Meeting #3 a. Conduct the meeting. b. Process approved action plans. c. Process annual strategic plan for operations. d. Distribute approved action plans to appropriate departments for implementation.			
Steering Committee Quarterly Review a. Conduct the meeting. b. Process review of strategic plan on a department-by-department basis. c. Distribute reviews to appropriate departments.			

5

How to Conduct Strategic Planning Meetings

Much of the success of strategic planning for operations rests on the talents of the organizer who conducts the meetings. The organizer must direct the strategic planning process without stifling the efforts of the participants. In order to accomplish this, the organizer must be able to communicate effectively not only with the high-ranking managers of the steering committee but also with the line employees who make up the strategic planning groups. The productivity of strategic planning meetings depends a great deal upon the organizer's ability to tactfully focus discussion on matters at hand.

A sizable amount of information must be processed and distributed to participants before, during, and after their meetings. Therefore, the organizer must have the support of administrative services and possess the necessary skill to coordinate the materials for each meeting.

This chapter provides practical tools by which to conduct productive strategic planning meetings. These tools include:

- Sample meeting agendas
- Suggested meeting procedures
- Sample flip chart sheets
- Information formats

The sample meeting agendas follow the sequence of strategic planning meetings shown in Exhibit 4.2 of the previous chapter. The suggested meeting procedures and sample flip chart sheets are designed to help an organizer lead participants in achieving meeting objectives listed on the sample agendas. The organizer can ensure a productive use of time during the meetings by preparing some flip chart sheets in advance.

The chapter also alerts the organizer to the information that must be processed before, during, and after each strategic planning meeting. Formats are presented to help the organizer record and process this information.

There are many ways by which to conduct successful strategic planning meetings. The tools presented in the following sections are meant to help organizers, not to hinder them. Organizers are encouraged to change the sample agendas, suggested meeting procedures, sample flip chart sheets, and information formats to meet the unique requirements of their properties.

Planning Groups: Meeting #1

Before the first planning group meeting, the organizer should distribute strategic planning workbooks to all of the participants. As indicated by the sample implementation action plan (shown in Exhibit 4.7 of the previous chapter), these workbooks should contain materials which:

- Define the objective of the strategic planning process.

- Explain how the strategic planning process achieves this objective.

- Provide an overview of strategic planning activities.

- Present detailed meeting agendas.

The workbooks introduce members to the strategic planning process and alert them to the tasks which lie ahead. Throughout the meetings, members refer to materials within their workbooks. Also, members add to their workbooks any materials which are distributed throughout the planning process.

The following sections provide step-by-step procedures by which the organizer can successfully conduct the first meeting of strategic planning groups.

Define Strategic Planning

Begin the meeting by asking members to open their strategic planning workbooks to the section which explains the objective of strategic planning for operations. Show flip chart PG 1.1. Explain that the strategic planning process achieves this objective by:

- Rallying everyone around a common vision of what the department stands for or strives to create

- Challenging members of the planning group to think beyond the demands of day-to-day department activities

- Increasing communication within their department and between their department and other departments (or functional areas)

- Identifying and solving problems that affect the quality of products and services delivered by their department and by the entire hospitality property

---

Strategic Planning Objective

To enhance the profitability of the hospitality business by increasing the productivity of:

- Managers
- Supervisors
- Employees

Flip Chart PG 1.1

Do not bog the meeting down with a lecture on the theoretical aspects of strategic planning. Members of planning groups are typically action-oriented. They want to do strategic planning, not talk it to death. Answer questions participants may have, but leave the more theoretical questions to be answered after the meeting.

Explain the Planning Process

Strategic Planning Activities

1. Write mission statements.
2. Collect data.
3. Determine objectives.
4. Develop action plans.
5. Assemble strategic plan.
6. Review the plan; monitor results.

Flip Chart PG 1.2

Turn the group's attention to flip chart PG 1.2 which identifies the sequence of strategic planning activities. Briefly define each planning activity. Definitions may be as brief as the following:

1. A mission statement answers basic questions about a department, such as: What do we do? How do we do it? For whom do we do it?

2. Collecting data provides a basis for analyzing operations.

3. Determining objectives means drawing conclusions from the data collected. An objective describes a problem and lists why the situation is seen as a problem.

4. An action plan identifies the steps that must be taken to achieve an objective. An action plan lists what will be done, when it will be done, and who will be responsible for doing it.

5. The steering committee puts together an annual strategic plan for operations by selecting objectives and action plans for implementation during the upcoming year. Some action plans may not be feasible because of budget limitations or other factors.

6. The steering committee reviews the strategic plan and monitors results on a quarterly basis.

Distribute a flowchart similar to the one shown in Exhibit 4.3 of the previous chapter. Use the flowchart to summarize the role of the steering committee and to show how the planning group fits into the total strategic planning process.

State the Purpose of the Meeting

```
                    Agenda for Meeting #1


        Date
        Department
        Starting Time _____/Ending Time _____

            Meeting Objectives                          Time

        1. Define strategic planning.
        2. Explain the planning process.
        3. State the purpose of the meeting.
        4. Write a mission statement.
        5. Perform external scan.
        6. Perform internal scan.
        7. Provide overview of next meeting.
```

Flip Chart PG 1.3

Turn the group's attention to flip chart PG 1.3 which presents the meeting's agenda. While reviewing the agenda, stress the time frame for accomplishing each meeting objective. After the review, put the flip chart sheet on the wall for all of the members to see. Point out that the group has accomplished the first two objectives, but there is still much work to be done.

State the purpose of the meeting as follows:

- To write a mission statement for the department
- To collect data so that objectives can be written at the next meeting

Point out the time frames for accomplishing these meeting objectives and move quickly to the task of writing a department mission statement.

Write a Mission Statement

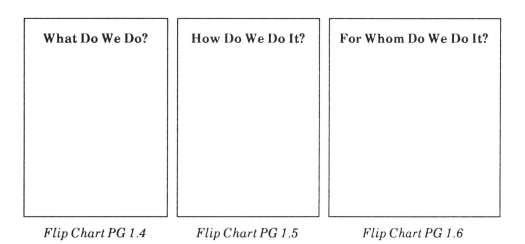

| **What Do We Do?** | **How Do We Do It?** | **For Whom Do We Do It?** |

Flip Chart PG 1.4   *Flip Chart PG 1.5*   *Flip Chart PG 1.6*

Explain that a department mission statement answers the following questions:

1. What do we do?
2. How do we do it?
3. For whom do we do it?

Point out that a well-written mission statement rallies everyone around a common vision of what the department stands for or strives to create. Stress that the mission statement which the group writes will help members of the steering committee to write a mission statement for the entire organization. Show flip chart PG 1.4 and ask the group to answer the question at the top of the sheet. Record their responses directly on the flip chart sheet. Follow the same procedure with flip charts PG 1.5 and PG 1.6. Put the completed flip chart sheets on the wall for all of the members to see. Exhibit 5.1 shows a partial list of responses from a banquets planning group.

Distribute sheets of paper and ask each member to write a mission statement for the department. Stress that mission statements must be 25 words. Encourage participants to use as many statements and phrases as they wish from flip charts PG 1.4, PG 1.5, and PG 1.6.

As members finish, ask them to write their mission statements on the flip chart. Put these sheets on the wall for everyone to see. This activity increases each member's involvement and shows that everyone's participation is important to the group's success.

After a brief discussion of these mission statements, use the flip chart and help the group to write a consensus mission statement. The consensus mission statement must be 25 words. This requirement forces members of the planning group to reach agreement on department priorities. Their interaction in keeping the consensus mission statement to exactly 25 words helps to set the tone for future strategic planning activities. The banquets planning group that produced the responses shown in Exhibit 5.1 agreed upon the following mission statement for its department:

> *We fulfill our guests' needs and requests by providing quality meeting facilities and serving food and beverages in an expedient, professional, friendly, and attentive manner.*

After the first draft of the consensus mission statement is written, put it on the wall for all of the members to see. Test the value of the statement by having the group answer the following questions:

● Does the mission statement foster common basic goals within the department?

● Can the mission statement serve as a basis for communication among everyone in the department?

● Can the mission statement serve as a basis for communication between their department and other departments?

● Is the mission statement unique to their particular department? (The mission statement should not apply to any other departments.)

● Can the mission statement be used to evaluate the department?

If the group answers "yes" to all of these questions, the consensus mission statement is complete. "No" answers to any of these questions should prompt appropriate revisions.

Exhibit 5.1 Mission Statement Responses: Banquets Department

What Do We Do?	**Sample Responses:**
	• Serve food and beverages.
	• Set up meeting rooms.
	• Break down meeting rooms.
	• Handle guest requests.
	• Train staff.
	• Clean rooms.
	• Work long hours.

Flip Chart PG 1.4

How Do We Do It?	**Sample Responses:**
	• In a friendly manner
	• Professionally
	• On time
	• Promptly
	• Courteously
	• With quality equipment

Flip Chart PG 1.5

For Whom Do We Do It?	**Sample Responses:**
	• Guests
	• Business people
	• Hotel staff
	• Ourselves
	• Owners
	• Hotel industry

Flip Chart PG 1.6

After the consensus mission statement has been written to the satisfaction of the members, remind them that members of the strategic planning steering committee will use their work (and the mission statements written by other planning groups) when they write a mission statement for the entire organization. Inform members of the group that copies of this mission statement and copies of the mission statements written by other planning groups will be distributed to them before the next meeting. Hand out copies of Exhibit 4.4 (shown in the previous chapter) as an example of the format that will be used to present the mission statements.

Turn the group's attention back to the meeting's agenda (shown on flip chart PG 1.3) and congratulate the members for accomplishing the fourth meeting objective. Stress that the data collected during the rest of the meeting will identify problems that affect the profitability, productivity, and performance of their department. Point out that the data collected by the group will be used at the next meeting to determine strategic planning objectives.

Perform External Scan

Explain that "to scan" means to examine closely or to scrutinize. Point out that an external scan examines other departments (or functional areas) within the property that may affect the profitability, productivity, and performance of their own department.

Begin by asking members to name the departments (or functional areas) within the property that affect the operation of their own department. Record their responses on the flip chart. Next, ask the members to rank the departments in terms of the degree to which they affect their own department. Exhibit 5.2 shows the list of departments ranked by a banquets planning group. After the departments (or functional areas) are ranked, the flip chart sheet should be put on the wall for all of the members to see.

Start with the highest ranked department on the list and ask members to answer the following three questions:

1. What can we do to improve communications with this department?
2. What problems do we have with this department?
3. What can this department do to improve the service it provides for guests?

Explain that the group should not spend a lot of time answering any single question. Point out that the goal of the external scan is to quickly collect data that will be analyzed at the next meeting. Stress that it is possible for the group to brainstorm 80% of the information

Exhibit 5.2 External Scan: Banquets Department

Date:	02/12/XX
Planning Group:	Banquets
External Scan:	Ranking Departments

Departments affecting the profitability, productivity, and performance of our department:

3.	Banquet kitchen
1.	Sales/convention services
7.	Maintenance
8.	Front desk/PBX
2.	Human resources
6.	Housekeeping/laundry
9.	Accounting/payroll
11.	Dining room/lounge
4.	Stewards
5.	Purchasing/receiving
10.	Security

that is needed in 20% of the time it would take to systematically collect all of the information. Instruct members not to dwell on the details of specific problems, but to state the problems quickly. Also, instruct members not to worry about which problems are more important than others. Point out that this kind of analysis will be performed at the next meeting.

As the group answers the questions for each department on its list, record responses on the flip chart. Exhibit 5.3 shows partial results of an external scan performed by a banquets planning group as it analyzed its relation to a convention services department.

After completing the external scan, inform the group that, before the next meeting, each member will receive typed copies of the data collected on the flip chart sheets. The first page of this material should list the departments ranked in order of importance to the profitability, productivity, and performance of the group's department. When participants receive this material, they should review it and place it in their strategic planning workbooks. This material will be used at the next meeting to determine strategic planning objectives.

Perform Internal Scan

Explain that an internal scan identifies factors inside their department that affect the profitability, productivity, and performance of the department.

Exhibit 5.3 External Scan of Convention Services: Banquets

Date: 02/12/XX
Planning Group: Banquets
External Scan: Convention Services

1. What can we do to improve communications with this department?

    - Cross train convention services staff in banquets.
    - Have daily meetings.
    - Banquets staff needs to be more open-minded.
    - Give convention services feedback on problems.
    - Track responses to feedback.

2. What problems do we have with this department?

    - Staff hard to locate.
    - Functions are booked in the East Room when some banquet rooms are empty.
    - Changes don't get to the right people on time and sometimes not at all.
    - Staff does not introduce banquet people to contact persons of groups.
    - Diagrams are not drawn to scale.
    - Too many last minute changes are made.
    - Daily reports come out too late.
    - Selling multiple choice menus creates problems for us.
    - Staff interferes too much during banquet functions.
    - Staff interferes with the structure of authority in our department.
    - Staff confuses people who work in banquets.
    - Staff lacks confidence in people who work in banquets.

3. What can this department do to improve the service it provides for guests?

    - Get accurate information from meeting planner sooner.
    - Wear beepers.
    - Make sure functions fit into the rooms that are booked for them.
    - Introduce banquets staff to meeting planners and function contacts.

```
┌─────────────────────────────────────┐
│            Internal Scan            │
│                                     │
│   ●  Facilities/location            │
│   ●  Daily department functions     │
│   ●  Product development            │
│   ●  Department communications      │
│   ●  Changing pool of job applicants│
│   ●  Departmental growth/decline    │
│   ●  Equipment needs                │
│                                     │
└─────────────────────────────────────┘
```

Flip Chart PG 1.7

Turn the group's attention to the categories listed on flip chart PG 1.7 and ask members to state problems (or opportunities) for their department in these areas during the upcoming year. Stimulate discussion by asking specific questions. Sample questions to ask are:

- *Facilities/Location*: What problems do you have with the facilities and location of your department?

- *Daily Department Functions*: What problems do you have with the way things are done in your department?

- *Product Development*: What products would you like your department to develop during the upcoming year?

- *Department Communications*: Are you satisfied with the type and format of information which your department currently receives? Is there any information that your department needs, but is not getting?

- *Changing Pool of Job Applicants*: What are the characteristics of people who apply for jobs in your department? How would these characteristics affect the operation of your department? How would these characteristics affect the experience of guests at our property?

- *Departmental Growth/Decline*: Do you see your department growing or declining during the upcoming year?

- *Equipment Needs*: What problems do you have with the equipment used by your department? What equipment would you include on a department "wish list"?

Responses for each category should be recorded on separate flip chart sheets. A partial list of responses given by a banquets planning group for the category of product development is shown in Exhibit 5.4.

Once data has been collected through this internal scan, turn the group's attention back to the meeting's agenda shown on flip chart PG

Exhibit 5.4 Internal Scan of Product Development

Date:	02/12/XX
Planning Group:	Banquets
Internal Scan:	Product Development

- Theme coffee breaks for functions
- Theme receptions and cocktail parties
- Upgrade physical meeting sets
- Different uniforms for special functions
- French service
- Flambé service

1.3. The group should be congratulated for accomplishing the meeting objectives.

Provide Overview of Next Meeting

Agenda for Meeting #2

Date
Department
Starting Time _____/Ending Time _____

Meeting Objectives   Time

1. Review accomplishments.
2. State the purpose of the meeting.
3. Write objectives from external scan.
4. Write objectives from internal scan.
5. Rank objectives.
6. Provide overview of next meeting.

Flip Chart PG 1.8

Turn the group's attention to flip chart PG 1.8 which presents the agenda for the next meeting. Inform the members that, at their next meeting, they will analyze the data gathered from their external and internal scans. Explain that this analysis is a two-step process:

Step 1   Members highlight items which seem to pose significant problems for their department.

Step 2   The group combines highlighted items and writes objectives.

Explain that an objective describes a problem and lists why it is seen as a problem. Stress that the information conveyed by an objective becomes helpful when action plans are developed later in the planning process.

After announcing the place and time of the next meeting, thank members for their valuable contributions to the strategic planning process.

Steering Committee: Meeting #1

Before the first meeting, the organizer should assemble and distribute strategic planning workbooks to all steering committee members. These workbooks provide an orientation to the strategic planning process and alert committee members to tasks which must be completed before their first meeting. The workbook should contain instructions for these tasks and any materials which are needed to complete them. The organizer should personally deliver these workbooks to committee members and, at that time, review the agenda for the first meeting, explain the tasks which must be completed before the meeting, and answer any questions.

Tasks which must be accomplished by each steering committee member before the first meeting are:

1. Review the mission statements prepared by department planning groups.

2. Review materials for the committee's external scan. These materials may include articles and information from trade publications, a composite analysis of guest comments, and relevant communications from the owners (or the management company).

3. Review results of the manager/supervisor survey.

4. Review results of the employee survey and write three objectives for each department.

The following sections provide step-by-step procedures by which the organizer can successfully conduct the first steering committee meeting.

Define Strategic Planning

Begin the meeting by asking committee members to open their strategic planning workbooks to the section that explains the objective of strategic planning for operations. Show flip chart SC 1.1. Explain that the strategic planning process achieves this objective by:

- Aligning all levels within the organization around a common vision of what the hospitality business stands for or strives to create

- Engaging managers, supervisors, and employees in a planning process that challenges them to think beyond the demands of day-to-day activities

- Increasing communication within and among the diverse departments and functional areas that make up the organization.

- Identifying and solving problems that affect the quality of products and services delivered by the organization.

Strategic Planning Objective

To enhance the profitability of the hospitality business by increasing the productivity of:

- Managers
- Supervisors
- Employees

Flip Chart SC 1.1

Some members of the steering committee may be inclined to debate other benefits of strategic planning for operations. The organizer should answer questions participants may have, but the more theoretical questions should be answered after the meeting. If necessary, tactfully point out that the committee has a great deal to accomplish and quickly move to an explanation of the strategic planning process.

Explain the Planning Process

Turn the committee's attention to flip chart SC 1.2 which identifies the sequence of strategic planning activities. Do not bog the meeting down with a lecture on the theoretical aspects of strategic planning. Briefly define each planning activity. Definitions may be as brief as the following:

1. A mission statement answers basic questions about operations, such as: What do we do? How do we do it? For whom do we do it?

2. Collecting data provides a basis for analyzing operations.

3. Determining objectives means drawing conclusions from the data collected. An objective describes a problem and lists why the situation is perceived as a problem.

4. An action plan identifies the steps that must be taken to achieve an objective. An action plan lists what will be done, when it will be done, and who will be responsible for doing it.

5. The steering committee puts together the overall strategic plan for operations by selecting objectives and action plans for implementation during the upcoming year. Some action plans may not be feasible because of budget limitations or other factors.

6. The steering committee reviews the strategic plan and monitors results on a quarterly basis.

Strategic Planning Activities

1. Write mission statements.
2. Collect data.
3. Determine objectives.
4. Develop action plans.
5. Assemble strategic plan.
6. Review the plan; monitor results.

Flip Chart SC 1.2

Distribute a flowchart similar to the one shown in Exhibit 4.3 of the previous chapter. Use the flowchart to summarize the role of department planning groups and to show how the steering committee fits into the total strategic planning process.

State the Purpose of the Meeting

Turn the committee's attention to flip chart SC 1.3 which presents the meeting's agenda. While reviewing the meeting's agenda, stress the time frame for accomplishing each meeting objective. After the review, put the flip chart sheet on the wall for all of the members to see.

State the purpose of the meeting as follows:

● To review department mission statements and write a mission statement for the entire organization

● To collect data so objectives can be determined

```
Agenda for Meeting #1


Date
Steering Committee
Starting Time _____/Ending Time _____

     Meeting Objectives                              Time
  1. Define strategic planning.
  2. Explain the planning process.
  3. State the purpose of the meeting.
  4. Review department mission statements.
  5. Write a mission statement.
  6. Perform external scan.
  7. Perform internal scan.
  8. Provide overview of next meeting.
```

Flip Chart SC 1.3

Remind members of the time frames for accomplishing these meeting objectives and move quickly to a review of department mission statements.

Review Department Mission Statements

Refer committee members to the series of department mission statements that appear in their strategic planning workbooks. Committee members should have reviewed these mission statements before the meeting.

Inform the committee that these mission statements will be combined with the mission statement that the committee writes for the entire organization. Hand out copies of Exhibit 4.4 (shown in the previous chapter) as an example of the format that will be used to combine the mission statements.

Write a Mission Statement

Show flip chart SC 1.4. Ask committee members to answer the question at the top of the flip chart. Record their responses directly on the flip chart sheet. Follow this same procedure with flip charts SC 1.5 and SC 1.6.

After the flip chart sheets have been put on the wall for all of the members to see, distribute sheets of paper and ask each member to write a mission statement for the entire organization. Encourage committee members to use as many statements and phrases as they wish from flip charts SC 1.4, SC 1.5, and SC 1.6. Stress that mission statements must be 25 words. As members finish, collect their mission statements, write them on the flip chart, and put the flip chart sheets on the wall for everyone to see.

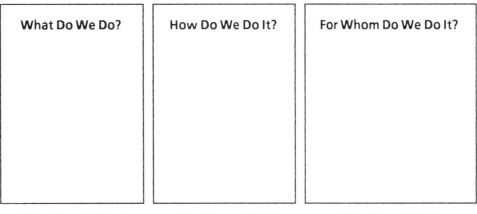

What Do We Do?	**How Do We Do It?**	**For Whom Do We Do It?**

Flip Chart SC 1.4   *Flip Chart SC 1.5*   *Flip Chart SC 1.6*

After a brief discussion of these mission statements, use the flip chart and help the group to write a consensus mission statement. The consensus mission statement must be 25 words. This requirement forces members of the steering committee to begin reaching agreement on priorities for the property. It also allows members to experience the kind of work that planning groups put into the writing of their department mission statements. The interaction of members during this activity sets the tone for the committee's future strategic planning activities.

After the first draft of the consensus mission statement is written, put it on the wall for all of the members to see. Test the value of the statement by having committee members answer the following questions:

- Does the mission statement foster common basic goals within the organization?

- Can the mission statement serve as a basis for communication for everyone within the organization?

- Does the mission statement assert the organization's unique philosophy of doing business? (The mission statement should not apply to other hospitality properties.)

- Can the mission statement be used to evaluate the organization?

If the committee answers "yes" to all of these questions, the consensus mission statement is complete. "No" answers to any of these questions should prompt appropriate revisions. The final version of the mission statement should be put on the wall for all of the members to see.

Remind committee members that, before their next meeting, they will receive a typed copy of the combined mission statements (similar in format to Exhibit 4.4 distributed earlier in the meeting). Inform the committee that copies will also be distributed to department planning groups.

Refer committee members to the meeting's agenda shown on flip chart SC 1.3 and point out that the committee has accomplished more than half of the meeting's objectives.

Perform External Scan

External Scan

- Markets
- Competition
- Local/national economy
- Legislation
- Owners
- Guests

Flip Chart SC 1.7

Explain that "to scan" means to examine closely or to scrutinize. Explain that the external scan examines areas outside the framework of property operations that may affect the profitability, productivity, and performance of the entire organization during the upcoming year. Refer members to materials related to the external scan in their strategic planning workbooks. Committee members should have reviewed these materials before the meeting.

Turn the committee's attention to flip chart SC 1.7 which lists the areas of the committee's external scan. Ask committee members to draw upon their reading of articles from industry and trade publications and identify factors which may affect property operations during the upcoming year in the areas of: markets, competition, local/national economy, and legislation. During this activity, encourage intuitive responses. Stress that an intuitive "feeling" or "hunch" from one member may prompt others to think differently about a particular area. Point out that, in the end, the committee may perceive a problem (or an opportunity) that would otherwise have gone unnoticed.

Use the flip chart to record committee responses for each area of the external scan. Exhibit 5.5 shows sample committee responses given during an external scan of markets and industry trends.

Exhibit 5.5 Sample Steering Committee External Scan

Date: 02/20/XX
Steering Committee: Meeting #1
External Scan: Markets

During the upcoming year, we can expect the following:

Markets
- Lower occupancy percentages
- Expansion of the resort segment of the lodging industry
- Domestic and leisure travel increasing faster than corporate travel
- A decrease in convention business over the next two years

Industry Trends
- Difficulty in raising average daily rates
- An increase in small meetings and close-to-home travel
- Prospering conference facilities
- New markets such as senior citizens, baby boomers, business trip extenders, and spouses accompanying business travelers

---

Stimulate discussion about owners and guests by asking specific questions and recording responses on the flip chart. Sample questions to ask are:

Owners

1. What do the owners want, expect, or need from managers of the property?

2. What problems are caused by managers not meeting these wants, expectations, or needs?

3. What steps can be taken to resolve these problems and minimize their effect on property operations?

4. What does management want, expect, or need from the owners of the property?

5. What problems are caused by the owners not meeting these wants, expectations, or needs?

6. What steps can be taken to resolve these problems and minimize their effect on property operations?

Guests

1. What do guests want, expect, or need from management?

2. What problems are caused by management not meeting these wants, expectations, or needs?

3. What steps can be taken to resolve these problems and minimize their effect on property operations?

4. What does management want, expect, or need from the guests who stay at the property?

5. What problems are caused by guests not meeting these wants, expectations, or needs?

6. What steps can be taken to resolve these problems and minimize their effect on property operations?

After all responses have been recorded on the flip chart, move quickly to the next item on the agenda and assist committee members in performing an internal scan.

Perform Internal Scan

Explain that an internal scan examines areas inside property operations that may affect the profitability, productivity, and performance of the entire organization during the upcoming year. Alert committee members to the two parts of the internal scan: the first part addresses results of the manager/ supervisor survey; the second part addresses results of the employee survey.

Begin the first part of the internal scan by stimulating discussion about top management's perception of department managers and supervisors. Ask specific questions and record responses on the flip chart. Sample questions to ask are:

Department Managers

1. What do department managers want, expect, or need from top management?

2. What problems are caused by top management not meeting these wants, expectations, or needs?

3. What steps can be taken to resolve these problems and minimize their effect on property operations?

4. What does top management want, expect, or need from department managers?

5. What problems are caused by department managers not meeting these wants, expectations, or needs?

6. What steps can be taken to resolve these problems and minimize their effect on property operations?

Supervisors

1. What do supervisors want, expect, or need from department managers?

2. What problems are caused by department managers not meeting these wants, expectations, or needs?

3. What steps can be taken to resolve these problems and minimize their effect on property operations?

4. What do department managers want, expect, or need from supervisors?

5. What problems are caused by supervisors not meeting these wants, expectations, or needs?

6. What steps can be taken to resolve these problems and minimize their effect on property operations?

After all responses are recorded on the flip chart, refer committee members to the manager/supervisor survey materials in their strategic planning workbooks. These materials include:

- Survey score sheet
- Survey summary report

Refer committee members to the statements sorted into the C and D categories on the survey summary report. Point out that these statements indicate problems that need management's immediate attention.

Assign each member to write a total of ten objectives from the data collected by the committee's external scan and by the committee's review of results from the manager/supervisor survey. Explain that, at the next meeting, the committee will review these objectives, rank them in order of importance, and assign them to appropriate committee members to develop action plans.

Begin the second part of the committee's internal scan by stimulating discussion about top management's perception of employees. Ask specific questions and record responses on the flip chart. Sample questions to ask are:

Employees

1. What do employees want, expect, or need from management?

2. What problems are caused by management not meeting these wants, expectations, or needs?

3. What steps can be taken to resolve the problems and minimize their effect on property operations?

4. What does management want, expect, or need from employees?

5. What problems are caused by employees not meeting these wants, expectations, or needs?

6. What steps can be taken to resolve the problems and minimize their effect on property operations?

Refer members to the employee survey materials in their strategic planning workbooks. These materials include:

- Survey results, by department

- Three objectives for each department (written by committee members before the meeting)

Use the flip chart to record the objectives proposed by committee members. Record the group's work on flip chart sheets so that the written objectives conform to the format shown in Exhibit 5.6. Each objective should:

1. Describe a problem.

2. Identify why the situation is seen as a problem.

Encourage committee members not to be defensive about objectives that concern their areas of operations.

At the end of this activity, collect the flip chart sheets and inform committee members that, before the next meeting, they will receive typed copies of the objectives determined during this second part of the internal scan.

Provide Overview of Next Meeting

Turn the committee's attention to flip chart SC 1.8 which provides an overview of the next meeting. Explain that, at the next meeting, committee members will select objectives for the upcoming year.

Inform committee members that, before the next meeting, they will receive typed copies of the following materials:

- Combined mission statements (similar in format to Exhibit 4.4 distributed earlier in the meeting)

- Data collected from the committee's external scan of markets, competition, local/national economy, legislation, owners, and guests

Exhibit 5.6 Sample Objectives: Banquets Planning Group

Date: 03/03/XX
Planning Group: Banquets
Objectives: Convention Services

Objective #1   Convention services staff need to carry beepers.
- Hard to locate staff.

Objective #2   Convention services needs to improve the timeliness and accuracy of communication with banquets.
- Changes don't get to the right people on time and sometimes not at all.
- Diagrams are not drawn to scale.
- Too many last minute changes are made.
- Daily reports come out too late.
- Selling multiple choice menus creates problems for us.

Objective #3   Convention services should introduce contacts to banquets managers.
- So banquets knows who should sign the check.
- So banquets knows who to see about guest needs.
- So guests don't call the front desk or other outlets for information they should get directly from banquets.

Objective #4   Convention services should not book functions into the East Room when other banquet rooms are empty.
- East Room is too far from the banquets kitchen.
- Banquets can service other banquet rooms at less cost.
- Banquets can provide higher food quality at banquet rooms nearer to the banquets kitchen.

Objective #5   Convention services should stay out of the function after banquets takes over.
- Staff interferes too much during banquet functions.
- Staff interferes with the structure of authority in our department.
- Staff confuses people who work in banquets.
- Lack of confidence rubs off on everyone.

- Objectives written by the committee in response to results of the employee survey
- Objectives written by each strategic planning group

Explain that, at the next meeting, the committee will review the combined mission statements and decide how they will be displayed throughout the property.

```
┌─────────────────────────────────────────────────────────────┐
│                                                               │
│                   Agenda for Meeting #2                       │
│                                                               │
│                                                               │
│   Date                                                        │
│   Steering Committee                                          │
│   Starting Time _____/Ending Time _____     │
│                                                               │
│        Meeting Objectives                            Time     │
│   1. State the purpose of the meeting.                        │
│   2. Review combined mission statements.                      │
│   3. Select objectives from external scan.                    │
│   4. Select objectives from internal scan.                    │
│   5. Select objectives from planning groups.                  │
│   6. Discuss how to write an action plan.                     │
│   7. Provide overview of next meeting.                        │
│                                                               │
└─────────────────────────────────────────────────────────────┘
```

Flip Chart SC 1.8

Remind members to come to the next meeting with a total of ten objectives written from data collected by the committee's external scan and by the committee's review of results from the manager/supervisor survey. Point out that, at the next meeting, the committee will review these objectives, rank them in order of importance, and assign them to appropriate committee members to use for developing action plans. If, before the next meeting, the steering committee wishes to meet with department managers to refine these objectives or to clarify priorities, the organizer should make appropriate arrangements.

Point out that, during the next meeting, the committee will discuss how to write effective action plans. Distribute copies of Exhibit 4.6 from the previous chapter which shows an action plan developed by a housekeeping planning group. Inform the committee that all action plans will follow the format shown in Exhibit 4.6.

Inform committee members that, after receiving typed copies of the objectives written in response to results of the employee survey, they should:

1. Highlight three objectives for each department for which action plans should be developed.

2. Rank the highlighted objectives for each department by assigning them point values of three, two, or one.

Explain that, at the next meeting, the committee will select objectives by totaling the point values assigned to objectives for each department. The three objectives with the highest point totals will be assigned to department planning groups to use for developing action plans.

Explain that, at the next meeting, committee members will also select objectives written by strategic planning groups. Remind members that, before the next meeting, they will receive copies of these objectives. Instruct committee members to review the objectives of each planning group and assign point values to those objectives for which action plans should be developed. Explain that, for each set of objectives submitted by planning groups, committee members can assign one five-point value, one four-point value, one three-point value, one two-point value, and as many one-point values as are needed. Stress that committee members do not have to assign a point value to each objective, but only to those objectives for which they feel action plans should be developed.

Point out that, at the next meeting, the committee will review the objectives submitted by each planning group. Objectives will be selected by totaling the total point values assigned by members and agreeing upon a cut-off point total. Objectives with point totals at or below this figure will not be acted upon during the upcoming year. Objectives with point totals above this figure will be steered to appropriate planning groups (or will be assigned to individual committee members) for action plans to be developed. Explain that, if necessary, the cut-off point total will be decided by a vote.

After announcing the place and time of the next meeting, thank members for their valuable contributions to the strategic planning process.

Planning Groups: Meeting #2

Before the second meeting, the organizer should distribute results from the first meeting to each member of the group. These materials include the following:

- The combined mission statements
- Data collected by the planning group's external scan
- Data collected by the planning group's internal scan

Distributing these materials before the second meeting allows participants time to review their past accomplishments and to revise, refine, or add to the data collected.

The following sections provide step-by-step procedures by which the organizer can successfully conduct the second meeting of planning groups.

Review Accomplishments

Begin the meeting by turning the group's attention to flip chart PG 2.1 which defines the objective of strategic planning. After quickly

---

Strategic Planning Objective	Strategic Planning Activities
To enhance the profitability of the hospitality business by increasing the productivity of: • Managers • Supervisors • Employees	1. Write mission statements. 2. Collect data. 3. Determine objectives. 4. Develop action plans. 5. Assemble strategic plan. 6. Review the plan; monitor results.

Flip Chart PG 2.1   *Flip Chart PG 2.2*

reviewing this definition, draw the group's attention to flip chart PG 2.2 which lists strategic planning activities. Point out that the group completed the first two activities during the first meeting. Identify the group's accomplishments by turning attention to flip chart PG 2.3 which shows the agenda for the first meeting.

Agenda for Meeting #1

Date
Department
Starting Time _____/Ending Time _____

    Meeting Objectives   Time

1. Define strategic planning.
2. Explain the planning process.
3. State the purpose of the meeting.
4. Write a mission statement.
5. Perform external scan.
6. Perform internal scan.
7. Provide overview of next meeting.

Flip Chart PG 2.3

End this brief review by referring members of the group to the combined mission statements which were recently added to each member's strategic planning workbook. Point out the good work that all of the planning groups and the steering committee have done.

Turn the group's attention to flip chart PG 2.4 which shows the current meeting's agenda. While reviewing the agenda, stress the time frame for accomplishing each meeting objective. After the review, put

---

the flip chart sheet on the wall for all of the members to see. Point out that the group has just completed the first meeting objective, and that the meeting is off to a fast start.

Agenda for Meeting #2

Date
Department
Starting Time _____/Ending Time _____

    <u>Meeting Objectives</u>   <u>Time</u>

1. Review accomplishments.
2. State the purpose of the meeting.
3. Write objectives from external scan.
4. Write objectives from internal scan.
5. Rank objectives.
6. Provide overview of next meeting.

Flip Chart PG 2.4

State the Purpose of the Meeting

An Objective

1. Describes a problem.
2. Lists why a situation is a problem.

Flip Chart PG 2.5

State that the purpose of the meeting is to write objectives from data gathered through the group's external and internal scans. Turn the group's attention to flip chart PG 2.5 which explains the two functions performed by an objective.

Illustrate the process of writing objectives by presenting examples of work performed by other planning groups. Refer members to their copies of Exhibit 5.3, which were distributed at the first meeting. This exhibit shows the results of the external scan performed by a banquets planning group. Next, distribute copies of Exhibit 5.6, which lists objectives written by the same banquets planning group. Stress how the format in which the objectives are written reflects the two functions performed by an objective: each statement describes a problem; each list explains why the situation is seen as a problem. Stress that the same format will be used when the group writes its own objectives.

Point out that some of the problems identified by the banquets planning group were combined under a single objective. Explain that Objective #2 in Exhibit 5.6 covers many of the problems originally listed in the external scan shown in Exhibit 5.3. Point out that some of the problems listed in the external scan appear as reasons suporting the perception that a more general communication problem exists.

Explain the procedure that the group will use to write objectives. A suggested two-step procedure is as follows:

Step 1   Members highlight items which seem to pose significant problems for their department.

Step 2   The group combines highlighted items and writes objectives.

Point out that, after objectives are written, members of the planning group will rank them according to their importance to the profitability, productivity, and performance of their own department.

Write Objectives from External Scan

Refer members to the material in their strategic planning workbooks containing the results of the group's external scan. The first page of this material should list departments in the order of their importance to the profitability, productivity, and performance of the group's own department.

Inform participants that they will write objectives for the highest priority department first. Ask members to highlight items which pose significant problems for their own department. After the members have highlighted the items, use the flip chart and help the group combine highlighted items and write objectives. Each objective should:

1. Describe a problem.
2. Identify why the situation is seen as a problem.

Record the group's work on flip chart sheets so that the written objectives conform to the format shown in Exhibit 5.6. As flip chart sheets are completed, put them on the wall for all of the members to see.

The same procedure should be used to write objectives for all of the departments scanned by the group at its first meeting.

Write Objectives from Internal Scan

Refer members to the material in their strategic planning workbooks containing the results of the group's internal scan. This material should cover the following areas:

- Facilities/location
- Daily department functions
- Product development
- Department communications
- Changing pool of job applicants
- Departmental growth/decline
- Equipment needs

Ask members to highlight items which pose significant problems (or opportunities) for their department. After the members have highlighted the items, use the flip chart and help the group combine highlighted items and write objectives. Each objective should:

1. Describe a problem.

2. Identify why the situation is seen as a problem.

Record the group's work on flip chart sheets so that the written objectives conform to the format shown in Exhibit 5.6. As flip chart sheets are completed, put them on the wall for all of the members to see.

Rank Objectives

After objectives have been determined for all of the areas covered by both the external and internal scans, have the members set priorities by ranking the objectives according to their importance to the profitability, productivity, and performance of their department. Record their responses on the flip chart sheets.

After this activity is completed, inform the group that the objectives will be typed and forwarded to the steering committee. Point out that the steering committee decides which objectives submitted by each planning group should be acted upon during the upcoming year. The committee then steers approved objectives to the planning groups that have the authority to actually solve the problems.

Provide Overview of Next Meeting

Turn the group's attention to the current meeting's agenda on flip chart PG 2.4 and congratulate the members for accomplishing the meeting's objectives. Provide an overview of the next meeting by turning the group's attention to flip chart PG 2.6.

Inform members of the group that, before the next meeting, they will receive copies of the objectives for which they will write action plans. Point out that, at the next meeting, the planning group will write action plans for some of the objectives which they have just written. Explain that the group will also write action plans for objectives which have been written by other departments and by the steering committee.

Agenda for Meeting #3

Date
Department
Starting Time _____/Ending Time _____

<u>Meeting Objectives</u>   <u>Time</u>

1. State the purpose of the meeting.
2. Review objectives.
3. Discuss how to write an action plan.
4. Write action plans.
5. Discuss implementation process.

Flip Chart PG 2.6

Briefly explain that an action plan identifies the steps that must be taken in order to achieve an objective. Inform the group that an action plan lists three things:

1. What will be done

2. When it will be done

3. Who will be responsible for doing it

Explain that effective action plans are developed by answering the following questions:

1. What is to be done?

2. How will it be done?

3. Who will do it?

4. Who will need to help?

5. How much will it cost?

6. When will each step be completed?

Point out that answers to these questions provide all of the information necessary to develop an action plan. Distribute copies of Exhibit 4.6 from the previous chapter which shows an action plan developed by a housekeeping planning group. Inform the group that all action plans will follow the format shown in Exhibit 4.6.

After announcing the place and time of the next meeting, thank members for their valuable contributions to the strategic planning process.

Steering Committee: Meeting #2

Before the second steering committee meeting, the organizer should distribute to all committee members typed copies of the following materials:

- Combined mission statements (similar in format to Exhibit 4.4 distributed during the first meeting)

- Data collected from the committee's external scan of markets, competition, local/national economy, legislation, guests, and owners

- Objectives written by the committee in response to results of the employee survey

- Objectives written by each strategic planning group

The following sections provide step-by-step procedures by which the organizer can successfully conduct the second steering committee meeting.

State the Purpose of the Meeting

```
┌─────────────────────────────────────────────────────────────┐
│                   Agenda for Meeting #2                      │
│                                                              │
│                                                              │
│   Date                                                       │
│   Steering Committee                                         │
│   Starting Time _____/Ending Time _____      │
│                                                              │
│       Meeting Objectives                          Time       │
│                                                              │
│   1. State the purpose of the meeting.                       │
│   2. Review combined mission statements.                     │
│   3. Select objectives from external scan.                   │
│   4. Select objectives from internal scan.                   │
│   5. Select objectives from planning groups.                 │
│   6. Discuss how to write an action plan.                    │
│   7. Provide overview of next meeting.                       │
│                                                              │
└─────────────────────────────────────────────────────────────┘
```

Flip Chart SC 2.1

State that the purpose of the meeting is to select objectives for which action plans are to be developed. Turn the committee's attention to flip chart SC 2.1 which presents the meeting's agenda. While reviewing the meeting's agenda, stress the time frame for accomplishing each meeting objective. After the review, put the flip chart sheet on the wall for all of the members to see.

Review Combined Mission Statements

Refer committee members to the combined mission statements which were distributed before the meeting. After a brief review, have the committee decide how the combined mission statements will be displayed throughout the property.

Suggest that the combined mission statements can be printed or silk-screened, framed, and displayed throughout every department within the organization. Stress how this enhances communication within the organization by increasing everyone's knowledge of the roles played by individual departments in the overall operation of the business. Suggest that the framed mission statements should be graphically appealing, contain the property's logo, and match the general decor of the operation.

Select Objectives from External Scan

Ask committee members to open their strategic planning workbooks to the ten objectives which they have written from data collected through the external scan and from the results of the manager/ supervisor survey. Explain that the committee will review these objectives, rank them in order of importance, and assign them to appropriate committee members to develop action plans.

Suggest that committee members may have written similar objectives. Explain that, during the review, these objectives will be combined. A suggested procedure for reviewing and combining objectives is as follows:

1. Ask the committee member on your immediate right to state one objective.

2. Ask if other committee members have written a similar objective.

3. Use the flip chart to write a single objective which covers aspects of the problem brought out by each committee member.

Ask the next committee member on your right to state an objective, and combine that objective with similar objectives written by other committee members. Continue around the room until all objectives have been recorded on the flip chart. As flip chart sheets are filled, put them on the wall for all of the members to see.

After all of the objectives are written, ask the committee to rank them in order of importance by assigning point values. A suggested procedure for assigning point values is as follows:

1. Ask each member to assign a point value to each objective.

2. If there are 30 objectives, each committee member assigns 30 points to what he or she believes is the highest priority objective, 29 points to the next highest priority objective, and so on down to one point for the lowest priority objective. Alert committee members that they can assign each number only once.

3. Total the point values assigned to each objective.

After the objectives have been ranked in terms of their point totals, assign objectives to appropriate committee members who will develop action plans.

Select Objectives from Internal Scan

Ask committee members to open their strategic planning workbooks to the objectives which they have written in response to results of the employee survey. Before the meeting, committee members should have:

1. Highlighted three objectives for each department for which they will develop action plans

2. Ranked the highlighted objectives for each department by assigning them point values of three, two, or one

Use the flip chart to total the point values assigned to objectives for each department. Have the committee assign the three objectives with the highest point totals to the appropriate department planning group which will develop action plans.

Record the committee's decisions, and, after the meeting, type the objectives and route them to the appropriate planning groups.

Select Objectives from Planning Groups

Ask committee members to open their strategic planning workbooks to the objectives written by department planning groups. Before the meeting, committee members should have assigned point values to those objectives for which action plans should be developed. For each set of objectives submitted by planning groups, committee members should have assigned one five-point value, one four-point value, one three-point value, one two-point value, and as many one-point values as were needed.

For each set of planning group objectives, use the flip chart to total the point values assigned by committee members. After point totals have been computed, have the committee decide on the cut-off point total for all sets of planning group objectives. Objectives with point totals at or below this figure will not be acted upon during the upcoming year. Objectives with point totals above this figure are steered to appropriate planning groups for action plans to be developed.

Suggest that, since committee members did not have to assign a point value to every objective, the committee may wish to reconsider objectives which fall below the cut-off point but which received point values from at least half of the committee members.

After objectives have been selected, have the committee steer objectives to the planning groups that have the authority to actually solve the problems. Record the committee's decisions, and, after the meeting, type the objectives and route them to the appropriate planning groups.

Discuss How to Write an Action Plan

An Action Plan States:	Effective Action Plans Answer:
1. What will be done. 2. When it will be done. 3. Who will be responsible for doing it.	1. What is to be done? 2. How will it be done? 3. Who will do it? 4. Who will need to help? 5. How much will it cost? 6. When will each step be completed?

Flip Chart SC 2.2   *Flip Chart SC 2.3*

Explain that an action plan identifies the steps that must be taken in order to achieve an objective. Turn the committee's attention to flip chart SC 2.2 and review the definition of an action plan.

Next, refer members to their copies of Exhibit 4.6 which were distributed at the previous meeting. The exhibit shows an action plan developed by a housekeeping strategic planning group. Stress that action plans must conform to the format shown in Exhibit 4.6.

Turn the committee's attention to flip chart SC 2.3 which lists questions that must be answered in order to write an effective action plan. Point out that the answers will provide all the information necessary to write an action plan. Put the flip chart sheet on the wall for all of the members to see.

Answer any questions committee members may have about writing action plans and move quickly to provide an overview of the next meeting.

Provide Overview of Next Meeting

Agenda for Meeting #3

Date
Steering Committee
Starting Time _____/Ending Time _____

Meeting Objectives   Time

1. State the purpose of the meeting.
2. Present action plans.
3. Assemble strategic plan.
4. Set dates for quarterly reviews.

Flip Chart SC 2.4

Provide an overview of the next meeting by turning the committee's attention to flip chart SC 2.4. Explain that, at the next meeting, committee members will select action plans developed by strategic planning groups and assemble the overall strategic plan for operations.

Inform committee members that, before the next meeting, they will receive typed copies of the action plans written by each strategic planning group. Point out that, before submitting these action plans, planning groups will already have obtained approval from their department managers (or division directors). Advise committee members to review this material and come to the meeting prepared to select which action plans should be implemented during the upcoming year.

Explain that, once action plans are selected, an overall strategic plan for operations will be assembled by arranging the action plans of each department according to their projected implementation dates. Point out that this format will ensure an efficient quarterly review of the plan and allow the steering committee to monitor results.

After announcing the place and time of the next meeting, thank members for their valuable contributions to the strategic planning process.

Planning Groups: Meeting #3

Before the third meeting, distribute the appropriate list of objectives to the members of each planning group. This list contains objectives selected by the steering committee which have been routed to planning groups which will develop action plans.

The following sections provide step-by-step procedures by which the organizer can successfully conduct the third planning group meeting.

State the Purpose of the Meeting

Agenda for Meeting #2

Date
Department
Starting Time _____/Ending Time _____

    <u>Meeting Objectives</u>   <u>Time</u>

1. Review accomplishments.
2. State the purpose of the meeting.
3. Write objectives from external scan.
4. Write objectives from internal scan.
5. Rank objectives.
6. Provide overview of next meeting.

Flip Chart PG 3.1

Agenda for Meeting #3

Date
Department
Starting Time _____/Ending Time _____

    <u>Meeting Objectives</u>   <u>Time</u>

1. State the purpose of the meeting.
2. Review objectives.
3. Discuss how to write an action plan.
4. Write action plans.
5. Discuss implementation process.

Flip Chart PG 3.2

State that the purpose of the meeting is to develop action plans for objectives which have been selected by the steering committee. Turn the group's attention to flip chart PG 3.1 and briefly review what the group accomplished at the previous meeting. Next, show flip chart PG 3.2 which presents the agenda for the current meeting. While reviewing the meeting's agenda, stress the time frame for accomplishing each meeting objective. After the review, put the flip chart sheet on the wall for all of the members to see.

Review Objectives

Ask the members to open their strategic planning workbooks to the list of objectives which was distributed before the meeting. Explain that the list contains objectives which were written by the group, the steering committee, and other planning groups. Stress that all of the objectives on the list have been selected by the steering committee and have been routed to the planning group which will develop action plans.

Briefly review the list of objectives and move quickly to a discussion of how to write an action plan.

Discuss How to Write an Action Plan

Explain that an action plan identifies the steps that must be taken in order to achieve an objective. Turn the group's attention to flip chart PG 3.3 and review the definition of an action plan.

Next, refer members to their copies of Exhibit 4.6 which were distributed to them at the previous meeting. The exhibit shows an action plan developed by a housekeeping strategic planning group. Explain that the action plans which the group will write during the meeting will conform to the format of the sample action plan.

An Action Plan States:	Effective Action Plans Answer:
1. What will be done. 2. When it will be done. 3. Who will be responsible for doing it.	1. What is to be done? 2. How will it be done? 3. Who will do it? 4. Who will need to help? 5. How much will it cost? 6. When will each step be completed?
Flip Chart PG 3.3	*Flip Chart PG 3.4*

Turn the group's attention to flip chart PG 3.4 which lists questions that must be answered in order to write an effective action plan.

Explain that the group will answer these questions for each objective on its list. Point out that the answers will provide all the information necessary to write an action plan. Put the flip chart sheet on the wall for all of the members to see.

Write Action Plans

Action Plan Format			

Date
Planning Group
Strategic Planning Objective # _____

WHAT IS TO BE DONE	WHEN	BY WHOM	DATE COMPLETED
1.			
2.			
3.			
4.			

Flip Chart PG 3.5

Focus the group's attention on one objective at a time and elicit answers to each question listed on flip chart PG 3.4. After the answers have been recorded on flip chart sheets, assist the group in filling out an action plan for the objective. Use the flip chart sheets which were prepared as action plan formats before the meeting. These flip chart sheets should be similar in format to that shown on flip chart PG 3.5.

The organizer should follow the same procedure until action plans have been developed for all of the objectives on the group's list.

After all action plans have been written, instruct members of the planning group to meet with their department manager (or division director) to obtain approval for their action plans.

Discuss Implementation Process

After the action plans have been approved by the group's department manager (or division director), explain that they will be typed and forwarded to the steering committee for presentation. Point out that, due to budgetary constraints or other factors, the committee may not approve all of the action plans submitted by the planning group. Explain that the steering committee will also assemble an overall strategic plan for operations. Explain that this plan is assembled by arranging the action plans of each department according to their projected implementation dates.

Point out that the department manager of the planning group will receive the approved action plans. Stress that action plans are to be implemented according to the timetables indicated. Stress that the department's progress in implementing the action plans will be monitored by the steering committee on a quarterly basis.

Before dismissing the group, congratulate the members for successfully participating in the strategic planning process. However, point out that while the members have planned their work well, actual success is measured by how well they work their plan.

Steering Committee: Meeting #3

Before the steering committee meeting, distribute typed copies of the action plans written by each strategic planning group. Steering committee members should review this material before the meeting.

The following sections provide step-by-step procedures by which the organizer can successfully conduct the third steering committee meeting.

State the Purpose of the Meeting

Agenda for Meeting #3

<u>Meeting Objectives</u>   <u>Time</u>

1. State the purpose of the meeting.
2. Select action plans.
3. Assemble strategic plan.
4. Set dates for quarterly reviews.

Flip Chart SC 3.1

State that the purpose of the meeting is to select action plans to be implemented by strategic planning groups during the upcoming year. Show flip chart SC 3.1 which contains the agenda for the current meeting. After reviewing the agenda, explain that, once action plans are selected, an overall strategic plan for operations is assembled by arranging the action plans of each department according to their projected implementation dates. Point out that this format ensures an efficient quarterly review of the plan and allows the steering committee to monitor results.

Select Action Plans

Refer committee members to the action plans which were distributed before the meeting. Explain the criteria that will be used to select action plans for implementation during the upcoming year.

Although these criteria will vary among hospitality properties, they should include department budget limitations and projected time frames of the action plans. Whatever selection criteria are used, the organizer should list them on a flip chart sheet and put the sheet on the wall for all of the members to see.

Record the responses of the committee as it selects action plans on a department-by-department basis. Once action plans are approved, they should be returned to the appropriate department managers for implementation.

Assemble Strategic Plan

Explain that, after the meeting, action plans which have been selected for implementation will be sorted on a department-by-department basis according to their projected implementation dates. Point out that this document will constitute the overall strategic plan for operations.

Inform participants that copies of the strategic plan will be distributed to committee members and department managers. Stress that department managers will be responsible for implementing the action plans returned to their departments.

Set Dates for Quarterly Reviews

Explain that department managers are responsible for updating action plans and forwarding copies to the steering committee on a quarterly basis. Point out that, at quarterly review meetings, the steering committee monitors results on a department-by-department basis and, if necessary, revises some of the action plans.

Close the meeting by restating the objectives of strategic planning for operations. Stress that the committee and the planning groups have planned their work and now must work their plan. Announce the place and time of the first quarterly review and thank members for their valuable contributions to the strategic planning process.

Part III
Problem-Solving Teams

6

An Overview of the Problem-Solving Process

The purpose of the problem-solving process is to enable individuals to work together as a team in solving work-related problems. Problem-solving teams are groups of managers, supervisors, or employees that meet on a voluntary basis for one hour each week to identify and solve problems. A team may be composed of five to seven individuals from the same department or from related departments or functional areas within the property. Individuals are paid for the time they spend attending team meetings, and they should be rewarded for successfully solving problems that affect the productivity and overall performance of the hospitality operation.

Problem-solving teams are formed at the management level first. When teams of department managers successfully solve problems and receive the necessary support from their managers, teams can be formed at the supervisory level. When teams of supervisors successfully solve problems and receive the necessary support from their managers, employee problem-solving teams can be formed.

Upper management support is absolutely crucial to the success of the problem-solving process. This support must be more than mere lip service; it must be a real commitment to the problem-solving process as a way of doing business. This commitment must be made crystal clear to all division directors, department managers, and supervisors before any employee teams are formed.

Top management commitment to the problem-solving process takes a variety of forms. Some of the more essential forms of commitment are:

- Creating the position of a quality assurance manager
- Holding department managers and supervisors accountable for supporting the efforts of problem-solving teams

- Providing the resources for training individuals to function as productive members of problem-solving teams
- Providing administrative services, such as typing or word processing services, for team leaders and the quality assurance manager
- Designating a room for team meetings
- Implementing a reward system for teams that successfully solve problems

Top management commitment means a substantial investment of time, expertise, and funds in the problem-solving process. It may take from six months to a year for a significant return on this investment to be reflected in the financial statements of the business. However, more immediate returns will appear as increased communication within the property, higher employee morale, more teamwork within and among departments, and more positive employee attitudes. These immediate benefits eventually become long-term returns in the form of lower employee turnover, higher guest satisfaction, and substantial increases in repeat business. As problem-solving teams become self-sufficient, revenue should increase and expenses should decrease, resulting in greater profits for the business.

This chapter provides an overview of a problem-solving process which has proven to be successful in a variety of hospitality operations. However, it is beyond the scope of this book to examine the many problem-solving procedures and techniques that can be used effectively in a quality assurance system. Top management executives may wish to contract the services of professional consultants who can design a unique problem-solving system to meet the special needs of their hospitality operations.

The overview that follows introduces the contents of subsequent chapters in this part of the book. First, the four stages of the problem-solving process are described. Chapter 7 examines the specific procedures followed by problem-solving teams as they complete each stage of the process. In addition, Chapter 7 describes the progress of a problem-solving team, the Saloonkeepers, as it completes each stage of the process.

Next, the present chapter addresses the kind of training that individuals must receive in order to function productively as members of problem-solving teams. Chapter 8 provides quality assurance managers with practical training materials which have been used successfully in a variety of hospitality operations. Chapter 9 examines additional training topics as well as the specific problem-solving procedures in which team leaders should receive training.

The final sections of the present chapter describe some of the duties and responsibilities of a quality assurance manager, and examine recognition and reward systems that have been adopted by hospitality organizations with quality assurance programs.

The Stages of the Problem-Solving Process

There are four stages to the problem-solving process presented in this book. They are:

1. Identifying a problem to solve
2. Developing a solution to the problem
3. Completing a cost/benefit analysis
4. Proposing the solution to management

The following sections briefly describe the steps involved in each of these stages.

Identifying a Problem to Solve

Exhibit 6.1 shows the sequence of steps that enable teams to identify problems to solve. It is crucial to the success of the problem-solving process that teams be permitted to select their own problems. These problems may not always be those which management would select. However, it is only natural for co-workers to want to solve the problems that bother them the most.

Teams begin this stage of the process by brainstorming a list of problems. Brainstorming is a technique that is used by teams throughout the problem-solving process to generate ideas quickly and efficiently. This technique normally allows a team to collect 80% of the information that it needs in 20% of the time it would take to systematically collect all of the information. Within 30 minutes, an average team may brainstorm 50 or more problems. Exhibit 7.2 (shown in Chapter 7) lists useful brainstorming guidelines that team leaders may use as they direct the efforts of a team in identifying problems to solve.

The second step in identifying a problem to solve is to group the problems into categories. Next, the team selects the most important category of problems. From the most important category, the team selects a particular problem to solve.

The final step in problem identification is for the leader to complete appropriate portions of the team's track record. Exhibit 6.2 presents a sample form which can be used as the track record for problem-solving teams. The form identifies all of the stages in the problem-solving process and provides space for indicating the date each stage is completed. By reviewing the track records of teams, the quality assurance manager can evaluate the performance of each team and

Exhibit 6.1 Sample Procedures for Identifying Problems to Solve

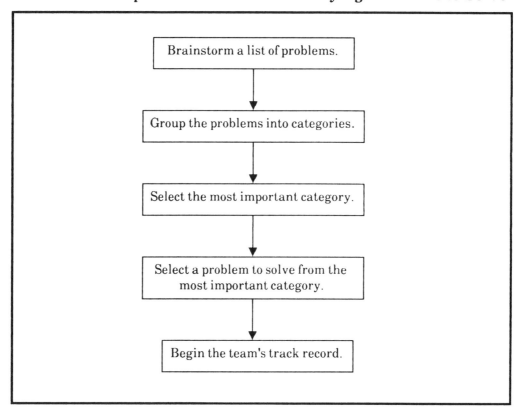

measure the overall success of the problem-solving process. Chapter 9 discusses additional ways quality assurance managers can monitor the progress of teams and evaluate the success of the process at their hospitality organizations.

Developing a Solution to the Problem

After identifying a problem to solve, the team's next task is to develop a solution. Exhibit 6.3 diagrams procedures which enable problem-solving teams to efficiently develop effective solutions. Detailed explanations of these procedures are provided in Chapter 7.

Without a set of well-defined procedures, problem-solving teams can waste a great deal of time in fruitless discussion and haphazard data collection. Disorganized efforts usually produce ineffective solutions. Ineffective solutions disappoint management, frustrate team members, lower team morale, and may eventually cause a team to disband.

By following the procedures outlined in Exhibit 6.3, a good team will be able to develop an effective solution in about two one-hour meetings. The first meeting is taken up with exploring everybody's angle, examining causes and effects, stating specific desired results,

Exhibit 6.2 Sample Team Track Record

Team:
Problem Categories: A.
　　　　　　　　　　B.
　　　　　　　　　　C.
　　　　　　　　　　D.
　　　　　　　　　　E.

Category		Dates			
Problems/ Solutions	Problem Identified	Solution Developed	Cost/Benefit Analysis Completed	Management Proposal Approved	Solution Evaluated (months) 1 2 3 6
Problem					
Solution					
Problem					
Solution					
Problem					
Solution					

Exhibit 6.3 Sample Procedures for Developing Solutions

brainstorming possible solutions, listing the good news and the bad news, and obtaining feedback.

When listing the good news and the bad news, problem-solving teams examine the positive and the negative aspects of each solution suggested by team members. The good news is what members of the team like about a solution, what they believe people in positions that are affected by the problem will like about the solution, and what they believe guests will like about the solution. The bad news is what people will not like about the solution. Looking at both the good news and the bad news guides the team in selecting the best solution to a problem.

While examining causes and effects, teams brainstorm how the problem affects the hospitality operation. The team leader structures this activity according to categories that will be useful when completing a cost/benefit analysis. Generally, the team leader directs the activity by proposing types of effects for the team to brainstorm such as: wasted time, wasted money, and guest dissatisfaction.

At the second meeting, the team continues to obtain necessary feedback and then assembles an action plan. Generally, the effects brainstormed by a team indicate areas in which further information must be gathered. One of the ways teams gather additional information is by obtaining feedback from people in positions at the property that are affected by the problem. Individuals who are affected by the problem may be able to provide important information that team members have overlooked. Exhibit 6.4 presents a sample form which teams can use to obtain important feedback.

The last step in developing a solution is for the problem-solving team to assemble an action plan. Exhibit 6.5 outlines procedures which enable a problem-solving team to assemble an effective action plan. Detailed explanations of these procedures are provided in Chapter 7.

An action plan lists what will be done, when it will be done, and who will be responsible for doing it. Exhibit 6.6 presents a sample action plan format. Before putting the plan into action, the team leader reviews the plan with the department manager and obtains approval. The department manager may suggest additional information that the team should analyze, or may offer advice on how to proceed with certain aspects of the plan.

Approval should not be difficult to obtain. The department manager should be extremely well-informed about the progress of the problem-solving team because he or she has received minutes of each team meeting as well as oral reports from the team leader and the quality assurance manager. Reviewing and approving action plans provides a manager with a perfect opportunity to share his or her expertise with the team leader and play the role of a coach in developing the team.

Completing a Cost/Benefit Analysis

After completing each step of the action plan, the team prepares a written proposal to management by completing a cost/benefit analysis on the solution to the problem under investigation. The cost/benefit analysis translates the work of the team into the language that management understands best—dollars and cents. Exhibit 6.7 presents a sample cost/benefit analysis form. Exhibit 6.8 presents a sample cost of effect form which serves as supporting documentation for items listed in section B of the cost/benefit analysis form. Chapter 7 provides a detailed explanation of how problem-solving teams complete a cost/benefit analysis.

After a team completes its cost/benefit analysis, the leader marks the progress on the team's track record, and invites to the next team

Exhibit 6.4 Sample Feedback Form

Feedback Form

To: _____ Date: _____

From: _____

We are currently analyzing a problem. The problem is: _____

_____

To do a complete job of solving this problem we need your opinions on how the problem can be solved. Please take the time to list any opinions and ideas you have and return the form to:

_____ (Team Leader)

by : _____ (Date)

Comments:

Thank you!

meeting the highest ranking manager whose area of responsibility is affected by the problem. At the meeting the manager reviews the cost/ benefit analysis and the supporting cost of effect forms. Mistakes are treated as learning experiences. The manager may suggest revisions and offer additional advice that will help the team prepare for its management proposal.

Proposing the Solution to Management

When problem-solving teams present their proposals to management, they should follow the authority structure within their

Exhibit 6.5 Steps in Assembling an Action Plan

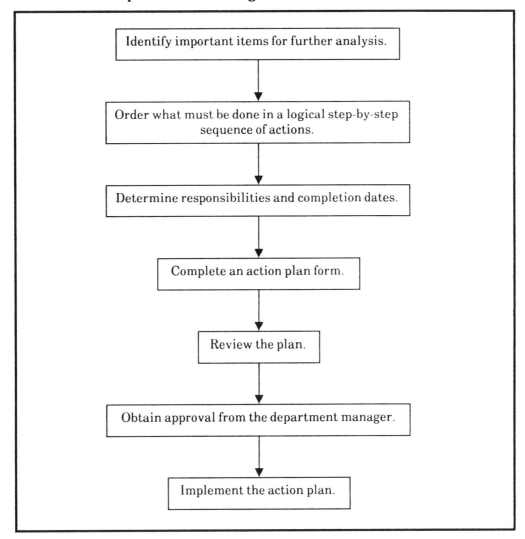

organizations. In order to have their proposal approved, team members must invite all the managers affected by the problem and the management representative who has the authority to approve the proposal.

For example, a housekeeping problem-solving team proposing a solution that affects housekeeping, the front desk, and the restaurant, would invite six managers to its presentation: the executive housekeeper, the front office manager, and the restaurant manager would be invited because the problem affects their areas of responsibility. The rooms director would be invited because he or she has authority over the executive housekeeper and the front office manager; the food and beverage director would be invited because he or

Exhibit 6.6 Sample Action Plan Format

	WHAT IS TO BE DONE	WHEN	BY WHOM	DATE COMPLETED

Problem-Solving Team:

Problem:

Solution:

1.
   a.
   b.
   c.

2.
   a.
   b.
   c

3.
   a.
   b.
   c

4.
   a.
   b.
   c

5.
   a.
   b.
   c

she has authority over the restaurant manager. And, in this particular case, the general manager would be invited to attend because he or she has authority over the rooms director and the food and beverage director.

After a team's proposal is approved, the leader marks this progress on the team's track record. Copies of the track record are given to the team's department manager and the quality assurance manager. When the department manager receives the track record, it becomes his or her responsibility to monitor the follow-up to the solution and to complete the evaluation portion of the team's track record. As each evaluation indicates that the solution has indeed solved the problem, members of the team are rewarded for their work according to procedures adopted by the property.

Exhibit 6.7 Sample Cost/Benefit Analysis Form

Cost/Benefit Analysis

Facility: Team:
Proposed to: Date:

A. Problem/Solution

B. Annual Cost of Effects Caused by the Problem
    (see attached Cost of Effect forms for cost calculations)

Effect	Cost
#1	
#2	
#3	
#4	
#5	
#6	
#7	
#8	
#9	
Total Annual Cost	

C. Non-Costed Effects

D. Follow-up Responsibility

    Assigned to: Date

    Evaluation Dates: 1.
                       2.
                       3.
                       4.

E. Anticipated Annual Savings

    Approved By: Date

Training Problem-Solving Teams

Everyone who volunteers to become a member of a problem-solving team must receive appropriate training. Ideally, the individuals who will eventually function together as a team should receive training as a group. The quality assurance manager is responsible for planning and conducting the training sessions.

Exhibit 6.8 Sample Cost of Effect Form

Cost of Effect

Facility: Team:
Proposed to: Date:

A. Problem/Solution

B. Effect

C. Annual Cost of Effect

    1. What is the cost of the effect each time it might occur?

    2. What percent of the time does the effect occur?

    3. What is the actual cost of the effect each time that it occurs? (Multiply the answer in step 1 by the answer in step 2.)

    4. How many times will the effect occur each year?

    5. What is the annual cost of the effect? (Multiply the answer in step 3 by the answer in step 4.)

Quality assurance managers should tailor training programs to meet the specific needs of the participants. For instance, the training provided for hourly employees may differ from that provided for supervisors and managers. However, everyone who participates in the problem-solving process must be required to attend training sessions which cover the following topics:

- Introduction to the problem-solving process
- Interpersonal communication
- Group dynamics
- Problem-solving techniques
- Cost/benefit analysis
- Presentations to management

The number and length of training sessions will vary in relation to the problem-solving process used and the needs of the participants. The quality assurance manager is also responsible for conducting training sessions for team leaders. Chapter 9 provides details about these special training sessions. Quality assurance managers are encouraged to revise and supplement the materials presented in Chapters 8 and 9 in order to effectively train teams in the details and mechanics of the problem-solving processes which their organizations plan to use.

The Role of the Quality Assurance Manager

Like everyone else connected with the problem-solving process, the individual selected to serve as the quality assurance manager must receive specific training. The general manager should assume some of these training responsibilities. For example, the general manager should ensure that the individual selected to serve as the quality assurance manager is given the opportunity to acquire a good working knowledge of the various departments and functional areas within the hospitality organization. In addition, the general manager should act as a mentor and instruct the quality assurance manager in how to communicate effectively with division directors, department managers, supervisors, and employees. Throughout the early implementation stages of the process, the general manager must provide the quality assurance manager with the guidance, advice, and support that will ensure a successful quality assurance system.

Exhibit 6.9 presents a partial job list for a quality assurance manager. The responsibilities of the position span the implementation, maintenance, and evaluation of the problem-solving process. Specific duties range from promoting the problem-solving process and training leaders and team members, to tracking team performance and administering the reward system adopted by the hospitality organization.

Recognition and Reward Systems

Before implementing the problem-solving process, top management executives and the quality assurance manager should determine the

Exhibit 6.9 Partial Job List for a Quality Assurance Manager

JOB LIST

Position: Quality Assurance Manager   Date Prepared: xx/xx/xx
Tasks: Manager must be able to:

1. Build and maintain organizational support for the activities of problem-solving teams.

2. Implement recognition and reward systems for participants in the problem-solving process.

3. Prepare a budget for the quality assurance system.

4. Communicate the progress of problem-solving teams to management and to everyone employed by the organization.

5. Recruit new team members.

6. Develop training materials.

7. Conduct training sessions for team leaders in the following areas:
   a. Introduction to the problem-solving process
   b. Interpersonal communication
   c. Group dynamics
   d. Problem-solving techniques
   e. Cost/benefit analysis
   f. Presentations to management

8. Assist leaders in training team members in the following areas:
   a. Introduction to the problem-solving process
   b. Interpersonal communication
   c. Group dynamics
   d. Problem-solving techniques
   e. Cost/benefit analysis
   f. Presentations to management

9. Ensure that team members follow an established code of conduct.

10. Ensure that teams follow the stages of the problem-solving process.

11. Offer teams suggestions regarding collecting and analyzing data and about methods for implementing and tracking solutions.

12. Assist team leaders in completing cost/benefit analysis forms.

13. Assist teams in preparing management presentations.

14. Review meeting agendas with team leaders before meetings.

15. Offer advice and guidance to team leaders after meetings.

16. Evaluate the performance of team leaders.

17. Evaluate the performance of problem-solving teams with team leaders.

18. Track the progress of problem-solving teams by reviewing minutes of meetings and team track records.

19. Measure the progress of the quality assurance system by analyzing the results of the manager/supervisor survey and the employee survey.

20. Communicate the goals and progress of the problem-solving process by producing a monthly or quarterly quality assurance newsletter.

21. Supervise the distribution of rewards to successful problem-solving teams.

means by which individuals and teams will be recognized and rewarded for their efforts. Recognition and reward systems can include:

- Badges
- Pins
- Certificates of achievement
- T-shirts
- Coffee mugs
- Free dinners
- Lunch with the general manager

However, they should all have one primary message, which is simply, "Thank You!" One of the most effective forums for recognizing contributions and distributing significant awards is an annual quality assurance banquet at the property.

A quarterly quality assurance newsletter can promote the problem-solving process while extending recognition to successful teams and supportive departments, managers, and supervisors. The newsletter can be used to inform non-participants about fundamental features of the problem-solving process, and can also alert members of teams to innovative problem-solving techniques.

Bulletin boards can be an effective means of communicating the activities of problem-solving teams. The quality assurance manager can use a general bulletin board to post a list of all active teams and their members, photographs of all new team members, the record number of problems brainstormed in 30-minute period, photographs of teams proposing solutions to management, the solution that has produced the record amount of anticipated annual savings, and other items of general interest.

Each problem-solving team can also maintain a bulletin board in its work area or department. Teams can post meeting times, problems which they have identified, the problem they are currently attempting to solve, and photographs of individuals from other departments who are assisting the team in its problem-solving efforts. Again, care should be taken to update the bulletin board postings on a regular basis.

Distributing cash is not necessarily the best type of reward system. It may be more effective to devise a system in which team members purchase their own rewards and are reimbursed by the hospitality operation. The reward system at the Sheraton Scottsdale Resort in Phoenix, Arizona, distributes "property money" to team members as they achieve success in the problem-solving process.

Exhibit 6.10 shows examples of property money. The name and logo of the resort, the property's quality assurance logo, the denomination,

Exhibit 6.10 Samples of Property Money

and serial numbers are printed on each bill. Serial numbers are necessary in order to track who receives and who spends the money. Team members use their own money to purchase the rewards they wish, bring their receipts to the accounting department, and redeem their property money at a ratio of 16 property dollars for one real dollar.

The amount of property money that a team receives is based on the team's cost/benefit analysis. The value of the team's work is computed in terms of "hard dollar" savings and "soft dollar" savings. Hard dollar savings are actual cash savings that the team's solution produces for the hospitality operation. For example, a team's solution to a problem may save the operation money in relation to supplies or materials that are presently wasted. The value of these wasted supplies or materials is considered to be a hard dollar saving. For each hard dollar saved by their solutions, teams receive three dollars of property money.

Soft dollar savings do not represent actual cash savings that the team's solution produces for the hospitality operation. For example, a team's solution to a problem may save the operation money because it reduces the amount of time wasted by employees. Since the employees will be paid for hours worked regardless of time wasted or time saved, there is no direct cash savings for the property. However, eliminating wasted time does benefit the property in terms of increasing employee productivity. Therefore, for each soft dollar saved by their solutions, teams receive one dollar of property money.

The cost of the team's solution is subtracted from the property money earned through hard and soft dollar savings to arrive at the amount of property money actually distributed to the team. At the Sheraton Scottsdale Resort property money is distributed in a series of payments to a team. The payment schedule is as follows:

- 25% when the team's solution is approved
- 25% after 30 days if the solution works 50% of the time
- 25% after 60 days if the solution works 75% of the time
- 25% after 90 days if the solution works 100% of the time

In order to receive full payment, the team must follow up on its solution for 90 days. With holding full payment until the solution proves to be successful teaches teams that the process does not end with developing solutions; the process ends when solutions have been successfully implemented.

7

Problem-Solving Teams in Action

This chapter examines the specific procedures that problem-solving teams use at each stage of the problem-solving process presented in Chapter 6. The present chapter follows the progress of an actual problem-solving team as it:

- Identifies a problem to solve
- Develops a solution to the problem
- Completes a cost/benefit analysis
- Proposes the solution to management

The procedures presented in this chapter have proven to be successful in a variety of hospitality operations. However, it is beyond the scope of this book to examine the many problem-solving techniques that can be used effectively in a quality assurance system. Top management executives may wish to contract the services of professional consultants who can design a unique problem-solving system to meet the special needs of their hospitality operations.

Identifying a Problem to Solve

The first task of a newly formed problem-solving team is to identify problems and to select the first problem to solve. It is crucial to a team's success that the members be permitted to select their own problems to solve. These problems may not always be those that management would select. However, it is only natural for co-workers to want to solve the problems that bother them the most. If management selects the problems for teams to solve, individuals may become disenchanted with the entire process because they feel management lacks confidence in their abilities.

Exhibit 6.1 (shown in Chapter 6) diagrams procedures which enable a newly formed problem-solving team to identify its first problem to solve. These procedures have been used with success in a variety of hospitality operations. However, there are many ways by which problem-solving teams can identify problems. Quality assurance managers are encouraged to adapt the procedures presented in the following sections to the unique needs of their hospitality organizations.

Brainstorm a List of Problems

Brainstorming is a technique that teams use throughout the problem-solving process to generate ideas quickly and efficiently. This technique normally allows a team to collect 80% of the information that it needs in 20% of the time it would take to systematically collect all of the information.

Brainstorming is also fun. Like the players in a game, team members involved in brainstorming pursue well-defined objectives by following an established set of rules. When a team brainstorms problems, its objectives are:

- To ensure the participation of everyone on the team

- To identify as many problems as possible in the team's department

- To identify problems between the team's department and other departments in the property

Since brainstorming encourages everyone to participate in a free flow of ideas, the activity helps to create an identity for the group and shape individuals into members of a team.

Exhibit 7.1 lists useful guidelines with which team leaders can direct the process of brainstorming problems. The team leader directs the brainstorming activity by setting a time limit (usually 30 minutes) and systematically going around the table, eliciting one problem from each team member. As problems are suggested, the leader records them on a flip chart. After each member has suggested one problem, the team leader goes around the table again. On any given round, a member may draw a blank and have nothing to contribute. In this case, the team does not wait for the person to come up with an idea. The member simply "passes" until the next round. This procedure is repeated until all of the members pass, or until the time limit is reached.

During this activity, no discussion takes place. Members of the team are *not* permitted to criticize any of the problems suggested. Also, the names of individuals (working on the team or at the property) are not connected to any of the problems. The objective is to identify problems, not personalities. In relation to the team, this provides

Exhibit 7.1 Sample Guidelines for Brainstorming Problems

Rules for Brainstorming

1. Once brainstorming starts, everyone on the team is free to identify problems.

2. No one on the team can comment on anything that someone else says.

3. No one on the team can ridicule anything that another team member says.

4. As the team identifies problems, the team leader lists them on a flip chart.

5. The team leader must make sure that everyone on the team has the opportunity to speak.

6. Brainstorming ends 30 minutes after it begins.

7. Problems identified are listed in the meeting minutes in the same order in which they were written on the flip chart.

8. No names are associated with any of the problems.

9. Who said what does not go out of the room.

---

anonymity for individuals and helps to build a group identity. All should consider the list of problems to be the result of teamwork, not the result of individuals.

All problems, no matter how outlandish, are recorded as part of the meeting minutes. To avoid bias, the ideas are recorded in the same sequence in which they were suggested. Within 30 minutes, an average team may brainstorm 50 or more problems. Exhibit 7.2 shows a list of problems brainstormed by the "Saloonkeepers," a problem-solving team made up of employees who work at the main lounge of a resort. The problems are numbered only as a means to quickly identify them; the numbering system does not indicate an order of importance.

Group the Problems into Categories

The second step in identifying a problem to solve is to group the problems into categories. Team members suggest the categories by which to group the problems. The team leader ensures that everyone on the team has the opportunity to propose categories. The categories chosen by the Saloonkeepers were:

- Equipment
- Maintenance
- Management

Exhibit 7.2   Problems Brainstormed by the Saloonkeepers

Problems Identified

1. Need bigger beer coolers.
2. Need to repair existing beer coolers.
3. Need more ashtrays.
4. Need more glasses.
5. Need to raise happy hour prices.
6. Need drink specials on a nightly basis.
7. Need better lighting at server station.
8. Need new soda guns.
9. Need for an electric dishwasher at the bar.
10. Need better communication with managers.
11. Need to repair ice machine.
12. Need more storage.
13. Need a designated bar server for the dining room.
14. Need to sell more wine in the dining room.
15. Need to address the bar towel shortage.
16. Need a better selection of imported beer.
17. Need to address the garbage problem in the bar area.
18. Need to repair the wood floor in the bar.
19. Need to rewrite job descriptions.
20. Need to train servers behind the bar for emergencies.
21. Need better behavior from employees on Employee Night.
22. We should have Employee Night on Sundays also.
23. Banquets keeps stealing our glasses.
24. Banquets should use its own liquor.
25. Need to be able to serve coffee at the pool.
26. Sales people need to communicate special activities to us.
27. Need Sunday entertainment.
28. Need to get rid of the stand-up bar.
29. Need new cocktail trays.
30. Front desk needs more cash to make change.
31. Need shorter breaks for the band.
32. Need new songs for the band.
33. Need different server stations at the bar.
34. Need access to liquor room key.
35. Need bigger dance floor.
36. The fire on the terrace is not always lit.
37. Need smaller chairs at the tables.

Exhibit 7.2 Continued

Problems Identified - Continued

38. Need better bar stools.
39. Need better air conditioning in the bar.
40. Need better communication with the dining room.
41 Need new bar mats.
42. Need better happy hour hors d'oeuvres.
43. Need buspersons to do a better job keeping the hors d'oeuvres stocked.
44. Need to serve wine through dispensing guns.
45. Need new drain plugs for the sinks.
46. Need to re-do par stock in the bar.
47. Need better candles on the terrace.
48. Need better shot glasses.
49. Need another cash register at the bar.
50. Employees need a tour of the hotel's facilities.
51. Need a better variety of light beer.
52. Room service needs to have its own glassware.
53. Guest checks signed off as complimentary should have an automatic 15% gratuity.
54. Need cash caddies for the bar servers.

- Training
- Other Departments

The team leader directs the team's work by systematically going down the list of problems. The team decides which problems belong in each category. If disputes arise, a problem may be listed under more than one category. During the activity, the team leader records responses on the flip chart. Rather than writing out each problem under the category's title, the team leader simply records the number designating the problem on the problem identification list. Exhibit 7.3 shows a sample flip chart categorizing the problems identified in Exhibit 7.2.

Select the Most Important Category

The third step in identifying a problem to solve requires that the team select the most important category. This can be done quickly by having members of the team assign point values to the categories. Each team member assigns three points to the category which he or she

Exhibit 7.3 Flip Chart Format for Categorizing Problems

3/2/1/3/1 10 Equipment	1/3/2/1 7 Maintenance	3/2/2 7 Management	2/2/1 5 Training	3/3/1 7 Other Deparments
1	2	5	13	21
3	7	6	19	22
4 (3/2/2 = 7)	11	10	20	23
8	17	12	43	24
9 (3/3/2/3 = 11	18	14	46	25
15	39	16	50	30
29 (3/1/1/1 = 6)		26		36
33 (2/2/3/1 = 8)		27		40
35		28		42
37		31		52
38		32		
41		34		
44		51		
45		53		
47				
48 (1/2/1 = 4)				
49				
54				

considers the most important; two points to the second-most important category; and one point to the third-most important category. The team leader records the point values directly on the flip chart sheet which lists the categorized problems. The points are totaled and the category with the most points is the one from which the team selects a problem to solve. The numerical values across the top of the categories listed in Exhibit 7.3 indicate the point values assigned by members of the Saloonkeepers. The point totals indicate that the team chose equipment as the most important category.

Select a Problem to Solve from the Most Important Category

The fourth step requires that team members select, from the most important category, a problem that they are committed to solving. To accomplish this, members of the team assign point values. Each team member assigns three points to the problem which he or she considers the most important; two points to the second-most important problem; and one point to the third-most important problem. The team leader records the point values directly on the flip chart sheet which lists the categorized problems. The points are totaled, and the problem with the most points becomes the problem that the team will solve. The numerical values alongside the problem numbers listed under the category of equipment in Exhibit 7.3 indicate the point values assigned by members of the Saloonkeepers. Problem #9 received the most points. Therefore, the team chose "Need for an electric dishwasher at the bar" as its first problem to solve.

Begin the Team's Track Record

At the final step in problem identification, the leader completes appropriate portions of the team's track record. Exhibit 7.4 presents a sample form which problem-solving teams can use as their track record. The form identifies all of the stages in the problem-solving process and provides space for indicating the date upon which each stage is completed. The form alerts the team to the work which lies ahead, and, over the course of time, the form reminds the team of its accomplishments.

The completed portions of Exhibit 7.4 reflect the work completed by the Saloonkeepers. After the team has completed all of the tasks involved in solving problem #9, the team leader records the solution in the first column of the form. Then, the team reviews the track record, and proceeds by:

- Selecting a category of problems

- Selecting a problem within that category

- Completing all of the tasks involved in solving the new problem

The next section follows the Saloonkeepers as the team develops a solution to problem #9.

Developing a Solution to the Problem

After identifying a problem to solve, the team's next task is to develop a solution. Exhibit 6.3 (shown in Chapter 6) lists procedures which enable problem-solving teams to efficiently develop effective solutions. These procedures have been used with success in a variety of hospitality operations. Without a set of well-defined procedures, problem-solving teams can waste a great deal of time in fruitless discussion and haphazard data collection. Disorganized efforts usually produce ineffective solutions. Ineffective solutions disappoint management, frustrate team members, lower team morale, and may eventually cause a team to disband.

By following the procedures presented in this section, a good team will be able to develop an effective solution in about two one-hour meetings. At the first meeting, the team explores everybody's angle, examines causes and effects, states specific desired results, brainstorms possible solutions, lists the good news and the bad news, and obtains

Exhibit 7.4 Sample Team Track Record

Team: Saloonkeepers
Problem Categories: A. Equipment
                       B. Maintenance
                       C. Management
                       D. Other Departments
                       E. Training

Category	Dates				
Problems/ Solutions	Problem Identified	Solution Developed	Cost/Benefit Analysis Completed	Management Proposal Approved	Solution Evaluated (months) 1 2 3 6
Problem A4 Need more glasses.					
Solution					
Problem A9 Need for an electric dishwasher at the bar. Solution					
Problem A29 Need new cocktail trays.					
Solution					

feedback. At the second meeting, the team continues to obtain necessary feedback and then assembles an action plan. The quality assurance manager should direct the first efforts of a newly formed problem-solving team in developing a solution. Thereafter, the team leader, with guidance from the quality assurance manager, should be able to direct the process.

There are many other procedures by which problem-solving teams can efficiently generate effective solutions to problems. Quality assurance managers are encouraged to adapt the procedures presented in the following sections to the unique needs of their hospitality organizations.

Explore Everybody's Angle

A problem is like a complex geometric shape with many angles and sides. The angles create the sides of a problem and the sides give the problem its shape. The angles of a problem are the viewpoints of the managers, supervisors, and employees whose work is affected by the problem. The sides of a problem are the immediate effects that the problem has on people working at the property. Since there are many sides to any one problem, a team must explore all the angles before it can develop an effective solution.

The first step in developing a solution is to get an overview of the problem by looking at it from the angles of the people whose work the problem affects. A team accomplishes this by brainstorming positions within the property that the problem affects. The team leader records their responses on a flip chart. Next, the team brainstorms how these positions are immediately affected by the problem. Exhibit 7.5 shows the positions and immediate effects brainstormed by the Saloonkeepers.

Since all of the people affected by a problem generally are not represented on the problem-solving team, members may have to conduct interviews after the meeting in order to obtain more detailed information. The team leader notes who must be interviewed, and, near the end of the meeting, brings this to the team's attention.

After the team has explored the angles and identified the sides, the problem takes on a more definite shape. At this point, team members are able to clarify the problem and state it in a form that will be easily understood by everyone involved.

When problems are first identified, they are usually not well defined. Often, they are simply made up of key words and catch phrases generated in the heat of brainstorming. Vaguely-worded problems cause confusion and block communication. At this point in the problem-solving process, it is essential that team members clarify the problem so that almost anyone in the property will be able to understand it.

For example, a housekeeping team that brainstormed a problem as "lost and found," could clarify it as, "Lack of follow-through on lost and

Exhibit 7.5 Brainstorming Immediate Effects of the Problem

Problem: Inadequate supply of clean glasses at the bar.

Bartender Immediate Effects:

- Tries to keep up with the glasses.
- Wipes each glass to get the spots off.
- Orders new brushes.
- Mixes drinks as fast as he can.
- Talks to customers when there is time.

Bar Server Immediate Effects:

- Waits for drinks.
- Works around stacked-up glasses on busy nights.
- Tries to satisfy complaining guests.

Busperson Immediate Effects:

- Carries glasses to and from kitchen and bar when not busy busing tables.
- May get grief from dining room servers.

Dishmachine Operator Immediate Effects:

- Puts bar glasses through machine before restaurant dishes.
- Tries to get someone to take cleaned glasses to the bar.
- Gets grief from everyone.

Hostess Immediate Effects:

- Wastes time on weekends looking for people to carry glasses to and from bar.
- Tries to satisfy complaining guests.

Bar Manager F&B Director Immediate Effects:

- Helps wash glasses if not too busy.
- Carries glasses to and from the kitchen when busperson is not available.
- Tries to schedule extra help when the bar will be busy.

found procedures." Similarly, a kitchen team that brainstormed a problem as "spillage and spoilage," could clarify it as, "Inadequate procedures for controlling spillage and spoilage in the kitchen."

The original wording of the problem identified by the Saloonkeepers was "Need for an electric dishwasher at the bar." This wording does not convey a problem; it communicates a solution to a problem that is never actually stated. After exploring the angles and sides to the problem, the team restated the problem as "Inadequate supply of clean glasses at the bar." After the problem is properly defined, the wording of the problem on the team's track record is revised accordingly.

Properly defining the problem increases everyone's understanding, and makes it easier for the team to examine causes and effects in the next step of developing a solution.

Examine Causes and Effects

Exploring everyone's angle shapes the problem from the viewpoints of the people involved. The next step in developing a solution focuses on the causes of the problem and how the problem affects the hospitality operation.

A problem-solving team brainstorms causes by identifying why the problem exists. The team leader directs the brainstorming activity and records responses on the flip chart. The number of causes a team identifies will, of course, depend on the type of problem involved. Exhibit 7.6 shows the causes brainstormed by the Saloonkeepers.

After identifying causes, the team brainstorms how the problem affects the hospitality operation. It is important to structure this activity according to categories that will be useful in the later cost/benefit analysis. Generally, the team leader directs the activity by proposing types of effects for the team to brainstorm. Important categories by which to structure the brainstorming activity include:

- Wasted time
- Wasted money
- Guest dissatisfaction

The leader encourages the team to be as specific as possible when determining effects within each category. For example, effects listed under "wasted time" should indicate whose time is wasted and whether the time is wasted on a daily, weekly, or monthly basis. Effects listed under "wasted money" may include broken equipment, wasted supplies, or wasted products. The team leader must also encourage the team to be specific when stating how or why the problem produces "guest dissatisfaction." Exhibit 7.6 lists the effects brainstormed by the Saloonkeepers.

Exhibit 7.6 Brainstorming Causes and Effects

Problem: Inadequate supply of clean glasses at bar.

Causes

1. There is too much business in the bar to wash the glases by hand.
2. When the bar and the restaurant are both busy, the dishmachine operator can't clean the glasses fast enough to supply the bar.
3. When the restaurant and bar are both busy, no one is available to take glasses from the bar to the kitchen and back.
4. Nobody thought about this problem when the bar was built.

Effects: Wasted Time

Bartender	Takes more time daily to wash glasses by hand than it would to wash them in an electric dishwasher.
Bar Server	Wastes time daily waiting for drinks because there are no glasses available.
Busperson	Wastes time taking glassses from the bar to the kitchen and bringing them back.
Dishmachine Operator	Wastes time every week trying to find someone to take glasses back to the bar.
	Wastes time sorting restaurant and bar glasses on weekends.
	Wastes time rewashing restaurant glasses that are sent back from the bar on weekdays.
Hostess	The hostess wastes time on weekends looking for people to take glasses to and from the bar and kitchen.
Bar Manager	Wastes time washing glasses.
F&B Manager	Wastes time with overly-complicated scheduling.

Effects: Wasted Money

Breakage	Lots of glasses get broken when they are stacked waiting to get washed.
Products	Free drinks are given to guests who have to wait too long to get their orders.
Supplies	Chemicals and brushes for the manual glass washers are expensive.

Effects: Guest Dissatisfaction

1. Drinks are mixed in the wrong glasses.
2. Lipstick stains appear on glasses that have been washed at the bar.
3. Takes too long to deliver the drinks.
4. Bartenders are too busy washing glasses to talk with our guests sitting at the bar

Generally, the effects the team brainstorms indicate areas in which further information must be gathered. During the brainstorming activity, the team leader notes the areas in which data must be collected, and, near the end of the meeting, brings this to the team's attention.

The information brainstormed in examining causes and effects provides a good picture of the problem's magnitude. It also serves as an excellent starting point for stating specific desired results.

State Specific Desired Results

The next step in developing a solution is to state specific desired results that a solution to the problem must produce. The specific desired results suggest what it will ideally be like when the problem is completely solved.

The team leader directs this activity by referring the team to the same categories which were used in listing the effects of the problem on the hospitality operation. If the problem were completely solved, these negative effects should disappear. Exhibit 7.7 shows the specific desired results that the Saloonkeepers produced.

The specific desired results serve as criteria for judging the value of the solutions that are brainstormed in the next activity.

Brainstorm Possible Solutions

Team members often have solutions in mind as they identify problems at the very first stage of the problem-solving process. After looking at the problem from different angles, examining the causes and effects, and stating specific desired results, the initial solutions can be more thoroughly developed.

Before directing the brainstorming activity, the team leader reviews the work that the team has accomplished. As the team brainstorms possible solutions, the leader records the responses on the flip chart. Solutions are numbered on the flip chart in the order in which they are suggested. The Saloonkeepers brainstormed the following solutions to the problem of an inadequate supply of clean glasses at the bar:

1. Buy a new electric dishwasher.

2. Buy a used electric dishwasher.

3. Add an extra bartender to the staff.

4. Buy more glasses.

5. Create a full-time position to help the bartender.

6. Hire an extra busperson.

Exhibit 7.7 Specific Desired Results

If the problem of an inadequate supply of clean glasses at the bar were completely solved, then:

Bartender	Will be able to make drinks faster so servers won't have to wait.
	Will mix drinks in the proper glasses.
	Won't have infected cuticles.
	Will have time to talk to our guests.
Bar Servers	Won't have as many complaints.
	Will receive more tips.
	Will have better working conditions.
	Will be able to provide more prompt, professional service to our guests.
Busperson	Won't have to carry glasses to and from the bar and kitchen.
Dishmachine Operator	Won't have to wash bar glasses. Won't be hassled by everyone.
Hostess	Won't have to carry glasses back and forth or look for other people to do it.
Bar Manager	Won't have to wash glasses.
F&B Director	Won't have to schedule extra workers.
Breakage	Breakage of bar glasses will decrease.
Products	Revenue will increase because the number of free drinks to guests who had to wait too long to get their orders will decrease.
Supplies	Will cost less.
Guest Satisfaction	Will increase because there will be fewer complaints.

List the Good News and the Bad News

During this step in the problem-solving process the team examines the positive and the negative aspects of each solution brainstormed in the previous activity. Looking at both the good news and the bad news of each solution prepares the team for selecting the best solution to a problem.

The good news is what members of the team like about a solution, what they believe people in positions that are affected by the problem will like about it, and what they believe guests will like about it. The bad news is what people will dislike about the solution.

The leader directs the activity by asking team members to state first the good news and then the bad news about each solution on the list. Responses are recorded on the flip chart. Exhibit 7.8 shows what members of the Saloonkeepers considered to be the good news and the bad news of each solution they brainstormed earlier.

Obtain Feedback

Before selecting a solution to investigate, the team gets the opinions of the people in the positions that the problem affects. Obtaining feedback communicates to others within the property exactly what the team is trying to accomplish. Persons affected by the problem may be able to provide important information that team members have overlooked. Also, feedback may enable a team to improve the solution that it has already identified.

The team leader directs this activity by reviewing the positions that the team identified as it explored everybody's angle. If possible, team members add more positions to the list. After the meeting, the team leader sends a feedback form to the persons in those positions. Exhibit 6.4 (shown in Chapter 6) presents a sample feedback form that team members can adapt to obtain information that may help them select the best possible solution.

The leader of the Saloonkeepers used a form similar to the one shown in Exhibit 6.4, collected the completed feedback forms and, at the next meeting, summarized the results on a flip chart. The feedback is shown in Exhibit 7.9. Obtaining feedback is the final step before the team assembles an action plan by which to solve the problem as completely as possible.

Assemble an Action Plan

The last step in developing a solution requires that the problem-solving team assemble an action plan. An action plan lists what must be done in order to further analyze important aspects of the problem and of the team's solution. An action plan lists what will be done, when it will be done, and who will be responsible for doing it.

The team members determine what will be done by reviewing their work in developing a solution and identifying important items for further analysis. The leader then directs a brainstorming activity in

Exhibit 7.8 The Good News and the Bad News

Solution #1:   Buy a new electric dishwasher.

Good News: Would solve all aspects of the problem and satisfy specific desired results.

Bad News: Bar setup would have to be modified.
Management doesn't want to spend the money.

Solution #2:   Buy a used electric dishwasher.

Good News: Same as Solution #1.
Would cost less than a new electric dishwasher.

Bad News: Bar setup would have to be modified.
Management doesn't want to spend the money.
Might not work as well or last as long as a new machine.

Solution #3:   Add an extra bartender to the staff.

Good News: Could carry glasses to and from the kitchen.

Bad News: Not enough room behind the bar.
Would cost too much.
Would not solve the problem completely.

Solution #4:   Buy more glasses.

Good News: Would have more glasses available to mix drinks.
Could have all glasses washed before the bar opens.
Would mix the right drinks in the right glasses.

Bad News: Would cost a lot more money.
No place to store the glasses.
More glasses would get broken.
Management doesn't want to spend the money.

Solution #5: Create a full-time position to help the bartender.

Good News: Wouldn't have to look for someone to carry glasses.

Bad News: No room behind the bar.
Would still be hauling glasses in front of guests.
Glasses would still get tied up in the kitchen.
Might have to split tips with the person.
Management doesn't want to spend the money.

Solution #6: Hire an extra busperson.

Good News: Same as #5.

Bad News: Same as #5

Exhibit 7.9 Feedback Obtained by the Saloonkeepers

Feedback Summary

- Sounds like a good idea.

- It's about time.

- Can't afford it.

- Need to improve the system instead of buying equipment.

- Good idea; it saves money.

- Good idea; the sooner the better.

- What would be done with the equipment that's in there now?

- What systems do other hotels and bars use?

- Great idea.

- Need to check plumbing and electrical setup in the bar before looking at dishwashers.

---

which team members generate a list of everything that must be done to thoroughly analyze each item of importance. Next, the leader helps the team to order what must be done into a logical, step-by-step sequence of actions. Individual team members then accept responsibility for completing the actions by specified dates. After all of this information is recorded on an action plan form, the team reviews the plan to ensure that all important aspects of the problem and its solution are addressed. Before putting the plan into action, the team leader reviews the plan with the department manager and obtains his or her approval.

Exhibit 6.5 (shown in Chapter 6) diagrams the steps that a problem-solving team takes in assembling an action plan. The following sections examine each of these steps in detail by describing how the Saloonkeepers assembled its action plan.

Identify Important Items for Further Analysis. A problem-solving team identifies important items for further analysis by reviewing all of the previous meetings' work which the leader recorded on flip chart sheets. The team leader organizes the activity by hanging all of the flip chart sheets on the wall for the members to see. These flip chart sheets include those completed during the following activities:

Exploring everybody's angle (see Exhibit 7.5)

Examining causes and effects (see Exhibit 7.6)

Stating specific desired results (see Exhibit 7.7)

Brainstorming possible solutions (see Exhibit 7.8)

Listing the good news and the bad news (see Exhibit 7.8)

Obtaining feedback (see Exhibit 7.9)

The leader directs the activity by focusing the team's attention on one set of flip chart sheets at a time, and asks each member of the team to underline what he or she considers the most important item listed.

Exhibit 7.5 presents the results of the Saloonkeepers's exploration of everyone's angle. The team underlined the following items from its work in brainstorming the immediate effects of an inadequate supply of clean glasses at the bar:

Bartender	*Talks to customers when there is time.*
Bar Server	*Works around stacked-up glasses on busy nights.*
Hostess	*Wastes time on weekends looking for people to carry glasses to and from bar.*

In reviewing the causes of the problem (shown in Exhibit 7.6), the team underlined the following:

1. There is too much business in the bar to wash the glasses by hand.

Exhibit 7.6 also presents the results of the team's examination of the problem's effects on the hospitality operation. The team underlined the following effects:

Bartender	*Takes more time daily to wash glasses by hand than it would to wash them in an electric dishwasher.*
Breakage	*Lots of glasses get broken when they are stacked waiting to get washed.*
Products	*Free drinks are given to guests who have to wait too long to get their orders.*
Guests	*Drinks are mixed in the wrong glasses.*

Exhibit 7.7 lists the specific desired results that the team believes a solution to the problem should accomplish. In reviewing these results, the team underlined the following items:

Bar Servers	*Won't have as many complaints. Will receive more tips. Will be able to provide more prompt, professional service to our guests.*

Breakage	*Breakage of bar glasses will decrease.*
Products	*Revenue will increase because the number of free drinks to guests who had to wait too long to get their orders will decrease.*
Guest Satisfaction	*Will increase because there will be fewer complaints.*

When reviewing the possible solutions to the problem (see Exhibit 7.8), the team underlined the following:

Solution #1: Buy a new electric dishwasher.

Solution #2: Buy a used electric dishwasher.

Exhibit 7.8 also presents the team's work in examining the good news and the bad news of each possible solution. When reviewing these positive and negative aspects of each solution, the team underlined the following:

Solution #1: Buy a new electric dishwasher.

> *Good News: Would solve all aspects of the problem and satisfy specific desired results.*

> *Bad News: Bar setup would have to be modified.*

Solution #2: Buy a used electric dishwasher.

> *Bad News: Might not work as well or last as long as a new machine.*

In reviewing the feedback obtained from those working in positions which the problem affects (see Exhibit 7.9), the team underlined the following comments:

Good idea; it saves money.

Good idea; the sooner the better.

What systems do other hotels and bars use?

Need to check plumbing and electrical setup in the bar before looking at dishwashers.

After important items have been underlined, the team leader further narrows the number of items that must be thoroughly investigated by asking team members to assign point values to the three most important items. Each team member assigns three points to the item which he or she considers the most important; two points to the second-most important item; and one point to the third-most important item. The team leader records the point values directly on the flip chart sheets, totals the points each item receives, and lists the items on the flip chart in the order indicated by the point totals. Exhibit 7.10 shows the results of this activity for the Saloonkeepers.

Order What Must Be Done in a Logical Step-by-Step Sequence of Actions. In the next step of assembling an action plan, the team brainstorms actions that must be taken to thoroughly analyze the items of importance. It may not be possible, or necessary, to take action in relation to each item. The leader directs the activity by first focusing the team's attention on the most important item on the flip chart and asking team members to state what must be done to thoroughly analyze it. The team leader records the team's responses on the flip chart. The Saloonkeepers brainstormed the following action steps:

Item: Buy a new electric dishwasher.

Action: Find out how much new (and used) dishwashers cost.

    1. Contact vendors.

    2. Make appointments for vendors to meet with the team to discuss costs and answer questions.

Item: Bar setup would have to be modified.

Action: Determine what modifications are necessary in the bar.

    1. Contact maintenance.

    2. Get before and after scale drawings of the bar.

    3. Calculate cost of modifications.

    4. Determine who will perform the work.

Item: What systems do other hotels and bars use?

Action: Check systems that other bars use.

    1. Visit XYZ hotel.

    2. Visit ABC hotel.

    3. Visit XXX bar and grill.

    4. Visit CCC dance hall.

Item: There is too much business in the bar to wash glasses by hand.

Action: Calculate the number of glasses used in the bar.

    1. Check daily revenue sheets.

Exhibit 7.10 Items for Further Analysis

Points Received	Item
9 Points	Buy a new electric dishwasher.
7 Points	Bar setup would have to be modified.
5 Points	What systems do other hotels and bars use?
3 Points	Bar servers won't have as many complaints.
	Buy a used electric dishwasher.
	Would solve all aspects of the problem and satisfy specific desired results.
	There is too much business in the bar to wash glasses by hand.
2 Points	Drinks are mixed in the wrong glasses.
	Lots of glasses get broken when they're stacked waiting to get washed.
1 Point	Bar servers will receive more tips.
	Breakage of bar glasses will decrease.
	Good idea; it saves money.
	The bartender takes more time to wash glasses by hand than it would to wash them in an electric dishwasher.
	Revenue will increase because the number of free drinks to guests who had to wait too long to get their orders will decrease.

      2. Get guest checks from accounting.

      3. Estimate totals by month and year.

Action: Time the bartender at washing a rack of glasses for each type of glass used.

Item: Lots of glasses get broken when they're stacked waiting to get washed.

Action: Track breakage of bar glasses for the past year.

      1. Get inventory levels from F&B director.

2. Get from accounting invoices for all bar glass purchases during the last 12 months.

3. Calculate the total number of glasses broken during one year.

Item: Revenue will increase because the number of free drinks to guests who had to wait too long to get their orders will decrease.

Action: Calculate the cost of free drinks to guests for the past year.

Determine Responsibilities and Set Completion Dates. The next step in assembling an action plan is to divide the work among the members of the team and establish the dates on which each action should be completed. Whatever system is used to divide the work, it is the team leader's responsibility to ensure that work is distributed fairly among the team members. Once the work is as evenly divided as possible, individual team members commit to completion dates. The team leader records who is responsible for completing each action and the dates by which the actions are expected to be completed.

Complete an Action Plan Form. By this point in the problem-solving process, the team will have collected the necessary information with which to complete an action plan form that lists what will be done, when it will be done, and who will be responsible for doing it. Exhibit 7.11 shows the format the Saloonkeepers used to record their action plan. Individual properties are encouraged to adapt this format to their own requirements. Note that the actions are listed in order of their expected completion dates. This format makes it easy for team members, the team leader, the department manager, and the quality assurance manager to track the team's progress.

Review the Plan. After the team leader has completed the action plan form, the entire team reviews the plan to ensure that it includes all the steps necessary to thoroughly analyze items of importance. The team leader follows up on team member comments by adding to the plan or making appropriate revisions before presenting it to the team's department manager for approval.

Obtain Approval From Department Manager. The department manager may suggest additional information that the team should analyze, or may offer advice on how to proceed with certain aspects of the plan.

Approval should not be difficult to obtain. The department manager should already be extremely well-informed about the team's progress because he or she has received a copy of the minutes of each team

Exhibit 7.11 The Saloonkeepers Action Plan

Problem-Solving Team: Saloonkeepers

Problem: Inadequate supply of clean glasses at the bar.

Solution: Buy a new electric dishwasher.

WHAT IS TO BE DONE	WHEN	BY WHOM	DATE COMPLETED
1. Check systems that other bars use.			
a. Visit XYZ hotel.	11/1	Sally	
b. Visit ABC hotel.	11/1	Sue	
c. Visit XXX bar and grill.	11/1	Brenda	
d. Visit CCC dance hall.	11/1	Vince	
2. Calculate the number of glasses used in the bar.			
a. Check daily revenue sheets.	11/1	Laura	
b. Get guest checks from accounting.	11/1	Tim	
c. Estimate totals by month and year.	11/8	Laura & Tim	
3. Time the bartender at washing a rack of glasses for each type of glass used.	11/8	Sue	
4. Track breakage of bar glasses for the past year.			
a. Get inventory levels from F&B Director.	11/1	Jorge	
b. Get from accounting invoices for all bar glass purchases during the last 12 months.	11/1	Brenda	
c. Calculate the total number of glasses broken during one year.	11/8	Jorge & Brenda	
5. Calculate the cost of free drinks to guests for the past year.	11/8	Sally	
6. Find out how much new (and used) dishwashers cost.			
a. Contact vendors.	11/1	Vince	

Exhibit 7.11 Continued

	WHAT IS TO BE DONE	WHEN	BY WHOM	DATE COMPLETED
b.	Make appointments for vendors to meet with the team to discuss costs and answer questions.	11/15	Vince	
7.	Determine what modifications are necessary in the bar.			
a.	Contact maintenance.	11/1	Tim	
b.	Get before and after scale drawings of the bar.	11/15	Tim	
c.	Calculate cost of modifications.	11/22	Tim	
d.	Determine who will perform the work.	11/22	Tim	

meeting, as well as oral reports from the team leader. Reviewing and approving action plans provides a manager with a perfect opportunity to share his or her expertise with the team leader and to play the role of a coach in developing the team.

Implement the Action Plan. After obtaining the department manager's approval, the leader reviews the final action plan with the team members and explains any modifications that were made. The leader organizes the implementation of the plan by distributing copies of the action plan and stressing that, while team members have planned their work well, actual success is measured by how well they work their plan. As steps of the action plan are completed, the leader marks the progress on the team's track record.

Completing a Cost/Benefit Analysis

After completing each step of the action plan developed in the previous stage of the problem-solving process, the team prepares a written proposal to management by completing a cost/benefit analysis of the solution to the problem under investigation. The cost/benefit analysis translates the work of the team into the language that management understands best—dollars and cents.

Exhibit 7.12 presents a sample cost/benefit analysis form. The Saloonkeepers used this form in preparing for their proposal to management for the purchase of a new electric dishwasher. Quality assurance managers are encouraged to adapt this form to the unique requirements of their properties. The following sections describe in detail how each portion of the sample cost/benefit form is completed.

Exhibit 7.12 Sample Cost/Benefit Analysis Form

Cost/Benefit Analysis

| Facility: | Mandrew Resort | Team: | Saloonkeepers |
| Proposed to: | Food and Beverage Director | Date: | 12/06/XX |

A. Problem/Solution

Problem: Inadequate supply of clean glasses at the bar.

Solution: **Buy a new electric dishwasher for the bar.**

B. Annual Cost of Effects Caused by the Problem
(see attached Cost of Effect forms for cost calculations)

Effect	Cost
#1	$1,938.59
#2	817.97
#3	620.87
#4	78.84
#5	413.91
#6	236.52
#7	615.60
#8	2,080.00
#9	3,561.60
Total Annual Cost	**$10,363.90**

C. Non-Costed Effects

Guest dissatisfaction with slow service; possible loss of business; low employee morale; bartenders get infected cuticles; lack of control.

D. Follow-up Responsibility

Assigned to:	Bar Manager	Date 12/20/XX
Evaluation Dates:	1. 01/20/XX	
	2. 02/20/XX	
	3. 03/20/XX	
	4. 06/20/XX	

E. Anticipated Annual Savings

Total Annual Cost of Effects	$10,363.90
Less: Cost of new dishwasher	(2,400.00)
Less: Cost of installation	(150.00)
Less: One year supply of chemicals	(27.38)
Anticipated Annual Savings	**$7,786.52**

Approved By: Food and Beverage Director   Date: 12/20/XX

Section A: Problem/Solution

Before filling out section A, the team lists the following information at the top of the cost/benefit analysis form:

● Name of facility

● Name of the problem-solving team

● The date on which the form is completed

● The highest ranking management representative to whom the proposal will be made

The team then records the definition of the problem and the proposed solution in the space provided in Section A.

Section B: Annual Cost of Effects Caused by the Problem

This section lists the number of effects that the problem causes and totals their annual cost to the hospitality operation. The calculations used in determining the cost of each effect appear on the cost of effect forms which the team attaches to its cost/benefit analysis. The team completes a separate cost of effect form for each effect that costs the hospitality operation money. Exhibits 7.13 through 7.21 appear at the end of this chapter. They show the cost of effect forms the Saloonkeepers used to support the figures that appear on their cost/benefit analysis. Quality assurance managers are encouraged to develop their own cost of effect forms in order to meet the requirements of their hospitality organizations.

In order to calculate the cost of an effect, the problem-solving team must collect the pertinent information. Most of this information will already have been collected by members who have completed the steps of the action plan. However, teams usually must collect additional information to complete the cost of effect forms.

In order to compute labor time, the team uses an average hourly figure of $4.50. All of the teams at the property use this figure. Deciding on an average hourly figure maintains the confidentiality of actual salaries and hourly wages.

The leader helps the members of the team to fill out the cost of effect forms. Next, the team members invite the highest-ranking manager who is involved in the problem to their next meeting to review the cost of effect forms. Mistakes are treated as learning experiences. The manager may suggest revisions and offer additional advice that will help the team prepare its management proposal.

Section C: Non-Costed Effects

This section of the cost/benefit analysis lists effects of the problem that cost money, but the amount of money cannot be calculated with any degree of certainty. Many of the items recorded in this section are from the list of immediate effects which the team brainstormed while exploring everybody's angle.

Section D: Follow-up Responsibility

This section identifies the person who will be responsible for monitoring the success of the solution to the problem for one year. The success of the solution to a problem should be evaluated 30 days, 60 days, 90 days, and 6 months after the solution is implemented. This ensures that the problem is completely solved.

Section E: Anticipated Annual Savings

In this section the team members calculate the anticipated annual savings that will result from implementing their solution. Most of the figures necessary for the calculations will already have been collected by members who have completed the steps of the action plan. Once the cost/benefit analysis form is completed, the leader marks the progress on the team's track record.

Presenting a Proposal to Management

When problem-solving teams present their proposals to management, they follow the authority structure within their organizations. In order to have their proposal approved, team members must invite all managers affected by the problem, as well as the management representative who has the authority to approve the proposal.

The members of the Saloonkeepers invited the bar manager because this person is responsible for the department within which the problem exists. The members also invited the chef because this person supervises the dishmachine operator whose work is affected by the problem. The team invited the restaurant manager because the problem affects the busperson's work. The food and beverage director was invited because this person supervises the other managers invited, and, therefore, this person has the authority to approve the solution.

Before the Saloonkeepers presented its proposal to management, each member prepared a complete packet of information to present. At the meeting, the packets were distributed to each manager. These packets included the following:

- A meeting agenda
- Background information on the problem
- A summary of the team's research
- The completed cost/benefit analysis form

- Brochures from dishmachine vendors
- Scale drawings of necessary modifications to the bar

After a team's proposal is approved, the leader marks the progress on the team's track record. Copies of the track record are given to the team's department manager and the quality assurance manager. When the department manager receives the track record, it becomes his or her responsibility to monitor the solution's follow-up and complete the evaluation portion of the team's track record. As each evaluation indicates that the solution has indeed solved the problem, members of the team are rewarded for their work according to the procedures adopted by the property.

Exhibit 7.13 Cost of Effect #1

Cost of Effect

Facility: Mandrew Resort   Team: Saloonkeepers
Proposed to: Food and Beverage Director   Date: 12/06/XX

A. Problem/Solution

   Problem: Inadequate supply of clean glasses at the bar.

   Solution: Buy a new electric dishwasher for the bar.

B. Effect

   **1. The bartender takes more time to wash glasses by hand than it would
       to wash them in an electric dishwasher.**

C. Annual Cost of Effect

   1. What is the cost of the effect each time it might occur?
       Labor cost base is $4.50 per hour.
       $4.50 per hour

   2. What percent of the time does the effect occur?

       16,300 glasses are used by the bar each month.

       The bartender washes 80% of the glasses used at the bar.
       The dishmachine operator cleans the other 20%.

       16,300 x 80% = 13,040

       The bartender washes 13,040 glasses at the bar each month.

       $$\frac{13{,}040 \text{ glasses}}{31 \text{ days}} = 420.65$$

       The bartender washes 420.65 glasses each evening shift.

       The bartender can wash one glass in 10 seconds. 10 seconds equals .0028
       hours (10 seconds divided by 60 seconds divided by 60 minutes).

       420.65 x .0028 = 1.18

       The bartender spends 1.18 hours washing glasses each evening shift.

       The evening shift is 6 hours long.

       $$\frac{1.18 \text{ hours}}{6.0 \text{ hours}} = .1967$$

       The bartender spends 19.67% of each evening shift washing bar glasses.

       19.67%

Exhibit 7.13 Continued

3. What is the actual cost of the effect each time that it occurs? (Multiply the answer in step 1 by the answer in step 2.)

   Step 1 $ 4.50
   Step 2   x 19.67%
           $ .8852

4. How many times will the effect occur each year?

   The bartender will wash bar glasses whenever the bar is open.

   There are 365 6-hour shifts at the bar each year.

   365 days x 6 hours = 2,190 hours the bar is open.

   2,190

5. What is the annual cost of the effect? (Multiply the answer in step 3 by the answer in step 4.)

   Step 3 $ .8852
   Step 4   x 2,190
          $1,938.59

Exhibit 7.14 Cost of Effect #2

Cost of Effect

Facility: Mandrew Resort   Team: Saloonkeepers
Proposed to: Food and Beverage Director   Date: 12/06/XX

A. Problem/Solution

Problem: Inadequate supply of clean glasses at the bar.

Solution: Buy a new electric dishwasher for the bar.

B. Effect

   2. **The bar server wastes time daily waiting for drinks to serve because no clean glasses are available.**

C. Annual Cost of Effect

   1. What is the cost of the effect each time it might occur?

       Labor cost base is $4.50 per hour.

       $4.50 per hour

   2. What percent of the time does the effect occur?

       The bar servers report that they spend a total of 30 minutes every night waiting for drinks to serve because no clean glasses are available.

       30 minutes = .5 hours

       The bar is open for business 6 hours a night.

       $\frac{.5 \text{ hours}}{6 \text{ hours}}$ = .083

       8.3% of the time

   3. What is the actual cost of the effect each time that it occurs? (Multiply the answer in step 1 by the answer in step 2.)

       Step 1 $ 4.50
       Step 2   x   8.3%
                  $.3735 per hour

   4. How many times will the effect occur each year?

       Bar servers will wait for drinks to serve whenever the bar is open.

       There are 365 6-hour shifts at the bar each year.

       365 days x 6 hours = 2,190 hours the bar is open.

       2,190

   5. What is the annual cost of the effect? (Multiply the answer in step 3 by the answer in step 4.)

       Step 3 $. 3735
       Step 4   x 2,190
                   $817.97

Exhibit 7.15 Cost of Effect #3

Cost of Effect

Facility: Mandrew Resort   Team: Saloonkeepers
Proposed to: Food and Beverage Director Date: 12/06/XX

A. Problem/Solution
Problem: Inadequate supply of clean glasses at the bar.

Solution: Buy a new electric dishwasher for the bar.

B. Effect
3. Time wasted by the dishmachine operator.

C. Annual Cost of Effect
1. What is the cost of the effect each time it might occur?

Labor cost base is $4.50 per hour.

$4.50 per hour

2. What percent of the time does the effect occur?

The dishmachine operator spends 3 minutes per rack of bar glasses and washes 7.5 racks per night.

3 x 7.5 = 22.5 minutes per night washing bar glasses

$\frac{22.5 \text{ minutes}}{60 \text{ minutes}}$ = .375 hours per night washing bar glasses

The bar is open for 6 hours each night.
$\frac{.375 \text{ hours}}{6 \text{ hours}}$ = .063

6.3% of the time

3. What is the actual cost of the effect each time that it occurs? (Multiply the answer in step 1 by the answer in step 2.)

Step 1 $ 4.50
Step 2   x 6.3%
              $.2835

4. How many times will the effect occur each year?

The dishmachine operator will wash bar glasses whenever the bar is open.

There are 365 6-hour shifts at the bar each year.

365 days x 6 hours = 2,190 hours the bar is open.

2,190

5. What is the annual cost of the effect? (Multiply the answer in step 3 by the answer in step 4.)

Step 3 $.2835
Step 4   x 2,190
              $620.87

Exhibit 7.16 Cost of Effect #4

Cost of Effect

Facility: Mandrew Resort   Team: Saloonkeepers
Proposed to: Food and Beverage Director   Date: 12/06/XX

A. Problem/Solution
Problem: Inadequate supply of clean glasses at the bar.
Solution: Buy a new electric dishwasher for the bar.

B. Effect
   4.   The hostess wastes time on weekends looking for people to take glasses to and from the bar and kitchen.

C. Annual Cost of Effect
   1. What is the cost of the effect each time it might occur?
   Labor cost base is $4.50 per hour.
   $4.50 per hour

   2. What percent of the time does the effect occur?
   The hostess reports that she wastes 3 minutes each night looking for someone to take glasses to or from the bar.

   $$\frac{3 \text{ minutes}}{60 \text{ minutes}} = .05 \text{ hours wasted each night}$$

   The bar is open for 6 hours each night.

   $$\frac{.05 \text{ hours}}{6 \text{ hours}} = .008$$

   .8% of the time

   3. What is the actual cost of the effect each time that it occurs? (Multiply the answer in step 1 by the answer in step 2.)

   Step 1 $ 4.50
   Step 2   x .8 %
             $ .036

   4. How many times will the effect occur each year?
   The hostess will look for someone to carry the bar glasses whenever the bar is open.
   There are 365 6-hour shifts at the bar each year.
   365 days x 6 hours = 2,190 hours the bar is open.
   2,190

   5. What is the annual cost of the effect? (Multiply the answer in step 3 by the answer in step 4.)

   Step 3 $ .036
   Step 4 x 2,190
           $78.84

Exhibit 7.17 Cost of Effect #5

Cost of Effect

Facility: Mandrew Resort   Team: Saloonkeepers
Proposed to: Food and Beverage Director   Date: 12/06/XX

A. Problem/Solution
    Problem: Inadequate supply of clean glasses at the bar.
    Solution: Buy a new electric dishwasher for the bar.

B. Effect
    5. The busperson wastes time taking glasses from the bar to the kitchen and bringing them back.

C. Annual Cost of Effect
    1. What is the cost of the effect each time it might occur?
        Labor cost base is $4.50 per hour.
        $4.50 per hour

    2. What percent of the time does the effect occur?
        The busperson reports that it takes him 2 minutes to carry 2 racks of glasses to the bar and 2 minutes to return them to the kitchen.
        The busperson wastes 2 minutes for each rack of glasses.
        The dishmachine operator washes 7.5 racks per night.
        2 minutes x 7.5 racks = 15 minutes
        The busperson wastes .25 hours each night.
        The bar is open for 6 hours each night.

        $$\frac{.25 \text{ hours}}{6 \text{ hours}} = .042$$

        4.2% of the time

    3. What is the actual cost of the effect each time that it occurs? (Multiply the answer in step 1 by the answer in step 2.)
        Step 1 $ 4.50
        Step 2   x   4.2%
                 $ .189

    4. How many times will the effect occur each year?
        The busperson will carry the bar glasses whenever the bar is open.
        There are 365 6-hour shifts at the bar each year.
        365 days x 6 hours = 2,190 hours the bar is open.
        2,190

    5. What is the annual cost of the effect? (Multiply the answer in step 3 by the answer in step 4.)
        Step 3 $. 189
        Step 4   x 2,190
                 $413.91

Exhibit 7.18 Cost of Effect #6

Cost of Effect

Facility: Mandrew Resort   Team: Saloonkeepers
Proposed to: Food and Beverage Director   Date: 12/06/XX

A. Problem/Solution

  Problem: Inadequate supply of clean glasses at the bar.

  Solution: Buy a new electric dishwasher for the bar.

B. Effect

  6.   The bar manager and F&B director waste time washing glasses at the bar and rescheduling help.

C. Annual Cost of Effect

  1. What is the cost of the effect each time it might occur?

    Labor cost base is $4.50 per hour.

    $4.50 per hour

  2. What percent of the time does the effect occur?

    The bar manager and the F&B director report that, together, they spend about 1 hour per week washing bar glasses and rescheduling staff.

    The bar is open for 6 hours 7 nights a week.

    6 x 7 = 42 hours the bar is open per week.

    $$\frac{1 \text{ hour}}{42 \text{ hours}} = .024$$

    2.4% of the time

  3. What is the actual cost of the effect each time that it occurs? (Multiply the answer in step 1 by the answer in step 2.)

    Step 1 $ 4.50
    Step 2   x   2.4%
           $ .108

  4. How many times will the effect occur each year?

    The bar manager and the F&B director will waste time washing bar glasses and rescheduling staff whenever the bar is open.

    There are 365 6-hour shifts at the bar each year.

    365 days x 6 hours = 2,190 hours the bar is open.

    2,190

  5. What is the annual cost of the effect? (Multiply the answer in step 3 by the answer in step 4.)

    Step 3 $. 108
    Step 4   x 2,190
          $236.52

Exhibit 7.19 Cost of Effect #7

Cost of Effect

Facility: Mandrew Resort   Team: Saloonkeepers
Proposed to: Food and Beverage Director   Date: 12/06/XX

A. Problem/Solution

   Problem: Inadequate supply of clean glasses at the bar.

   Solution: Buy a new electric dishwasher for the bar.

B. Effect

   7. Lots of glasses get broken when they are stacked waiting to get washed.

C. Annual Cost of Effect

   1. What is the cost of the effect each time it might occur?

      Past invoices indicate that the average cost per bar glass is $1.35.

      $1.35 per glass

   2. What percent of the time does the effect occur?

      The bar manager estimates that 50% of the total breakage cost for the bar glasses is due to stacking the bar glasses for cleaning.

      50% of the time

   3. What is the actual cost of the effect each time that it occurs? (Multiply the answer in step 1 by the answer in step 2.)

      Step 1 $ 1.35
      Step 2   x   50 %
                 $ .675

   4. How many times will the effect occur each year?

      Comparing bar glass purchases to past inventory par levels indicates that, on the average, 76 bar glasses are broken each month.

      76 x 12 = 912 bar glasses are broken each year.

      912

   5. What is the annual cost of the effect? (Multiply the answer in step 3 by the answer in step 4.)

      Step 3 $ .675
      Step 4 x 912
              $615.60

Exhibit 7.20 Cost of Effect #8

Cost of Effect

Facility: Mandrew Resort   Team: Saloonkeepers
Proposed to: Food and Beverage Director   Date: 12/06/XX

A. Problem/Solution

   Problem: Inadequate supply of clean glasses at the bar.

   Solution: Buy a new electric dishwasher for the bar.

B. Effect

   8. Free drinks to guests who had to wait too long to get their orders.

C. Annual Cost of Effect

   1. What is the cost of the effect each time it might occur?

   2. What percent of the time does the effect occur?

   3. What is the actual cost of the effect each time that it occurs? (Multiply the answer in step 1 by the answer in step 2.)

   4. How many times will the effect occur each year?

   5. What is the annual cost of the effect? (Multiply the answer in step 3 by the answer in step 4.)

   Accounting reports that non-sales related free drinks amounted to $2,080 during the past year.

   $2,080

Exhibit 7.21 Cost of Effect #9

Cost of Effect

Facility: Mandrew Resort   Team: Saloonkeepers
Proposed to: Food and Beverage Director   Date: 12/06/XX

A. Problem/Solution

    Problem: Inadequate supply of clean glasses at the bar.

    Solution: Buy a new electric dishwasher for the bar.

B. Effect

    9. Chemicals and brushes for the manual glass washers are expensive.

C. Annual Cost of Effect

    1. What is the cost of the effect each time it might occur?

    2. What percent of the time does the effect occur?

    3. What is the actual cost of the effect each time that it occurs? (Multiply the answer in step 1 by the answer in step 2.)

    4. How many times will the effect occur each year?

    5. What is the annual cost of the effect? (Multiply the answer in step 3 by the answer in step 4.)

    Accounting reports that $254.40 is spent each month for chemicals and $42.40 is spent each month for brushes to clean glasses at the bar.

    $254.40 x 12 months = $3,052.80 per year for chemicals.

    $42.40 x 12 months = $508.80 per year for brushes.

    $3,052.80
    + 508.80
    $ 3,561.60

8
Training Problem-Solving Teams

The previous chapter demonstrated what problem-solving teams are capable of doing. This chapter examines the training that members of problem-solving teams must have in order for them to function productively. Everyone who volunteers to become a member of a problem-solving team must receive appropriate training.

The quality assurance manager is responsible for planning and conducting the training sessions. Ideally, the individuals who will eventually function together as a team will receive training as a group. Group training sessions help build team solidarity. However, it is sometimes necessary to train a group that will not stay together as a team. After the training sessions, these individuals may be assigned to different problem-solving teams that are already functioning but need additional members.

Quality assurance managers should tailor training programs to meet the specific needs of the participants. For instance, the training provided for hourly employees may differ from that provided for supervisors and managers. However, everyone who participates in the problem-solving process must be required to attend training sessions which cover the following topics:

- Introduction to the problem-solving process
- Interpersonal communication
- Group dynamics
- Problem-solving techniques
- Cost/benefit analysis
- Management proposals

This chapter provides practical training materials that quality assurance managers can use to conduct effective sessions covering the first three topics. A team receives training in problem-solving techniques, in completing a cost/benefit analysis form, and in presenting management proposals when they actually use the process to solve their first problem. Chapter 9 examines these training topics as well as the type of training that team leaders need in areas involving specific problem-solving procedures.

The number and length of training sessions will vary in relation to the problem-solving process used and the needs of the participants. Quality assurance managers are strongly encouraged to revise and supplement the materials presented in this chapter in order to effectively train teams in the details and mechanics of the problem-solving processes which their organizations plan to use.

Introducing the Problem-Solving Process

The first training session should provide an introduction to the problem-solving process. The quality assurance manager can structure an effective introductory session by:

1. Stating the purpose of the problem-solving process

2. Describing how teams solve problems

3. Identifying how managers, supervisors, and employees benefit from participating in the problem-solving process

4. Reviewing a code of conduct by which the members of problem-solving teams are expected to abide

The following sections provide useful information that will help quality assurance managers conduct an effective introductory training session.

State the Purpose of the Problem-Solving Process

The quality assurance manager should begin the introductory session by stating the purpose of the problem-solving process. Write a statement of purpose on a flip chart. The statement can be as brief as the following example:

The purpose of the problem-solving process is to enable individuals to work together as a team in solving work-related problems.

Hang the flip chart sheet on the wall for all of the members to see, and refer to it as often as possible when answering questions from the participants.

Participants generally come to an introductory session with many important questions that they want answered right away. Take the time to address some of the questions participants may have. Allow each participant to ask questions. Answer each question as thoroughly as possible without getting bogged down in the complexities of the problem-solving process. If some questions cannot be thoroughly answered at this point, indicate when they will be addressed.

Describe How Teams Solve Problems

The next part of the introductory session should provide an overview of the process that the team will use to solve problems. This overview should not attempt to cover the step-by-step details of the process. Team members will learn these details as they solve their first problem.

Stress that the procedures used by problem-solving teams are designed to ensure that problems are solved as completely as possible. Explain that teams are not after "quick fixes" or partial solutions to the problems which they address.

List the following stages in the problem-solving process on the flip chart:

1. Identify a problem to solve.

2. Develop a solution to the problem.

3. Complete a cost/benefit analysis.

4. Present a proposal to management.

Briefly describe the steps involved in each stage of the process. It may be helpful to distribute copies of Exhibits 6.1 and 6.3 (shown in Chapter 6) when describing how teams identify a problem to solve and how teams develop a solution to the problem. However, be careful not to overwhelm the participants. Stress that you are only providing an overview of the process. Tell the participants that they will learn more about how these tasks are accomplished when they begin to work as a team to solve their first problem.

At this point in the training, there is no need to present a detailed explanation of how to complete a cost/benefit analysis. Simply inform the participants that a cost/benefit analysis translates their solution to a problem into the language that management understands best— dollars and cents. Point out that this analysis proves very useful when the team presents its solution for management approval. Inform participants that they will receive appropriate training in cost/benefit analysis procedures when they work as a team to solve their first problem.

Explain "What's in It for Me?"

At this time in the introductory session, the quality assurance manager should explain how managers, supervisors, and employees

Exhibit 8.1 How a Department Benefits from Problem-Solving Teams

---

Department Benefits

- Managers and supervisors spend less time "putting out fires" and can devote more time to planning, organizing, and coordinating activities within the department.

- Managers, supervisors, and employees experience greater job satisfaction.

- Morale within the department increases.

- Less turnover occurs within the department.

- Managers and supervisors experience less stress on the job.

- Better communication takes place within the department.

- Better communication takes place between the department and other departments in the property as other managers, supervisors, and employees are called upon to support the efforts of the department's problem-solving team.

- The productivity of the department increases as the staff applies problem-solving skills on the job.

- Supervisors and employees gain a "dollar and cents" appreciation of the department's economic goals.

- Supervisors and employees become more aware of the difficulties involved in solving problems affecting their departments.

---

may benefit from participating in the problem-solving process. Exhibit 8.1 lists some of these benefits. Quality assurance managers are encouraged to add to this list of benefits and prepare appropriate flip chart sheets to use during the introductory session. In addition, they should explain the reward system that is used at their properties.

This is also a convenient time to answer additional questions that participants may have. Once again, allow each participant to ask questions. Answer each question as thoroughly as possible without getting bogged down in the complexities of the problem-solving process. If some questions cannot be thoroughly answered at this time, indicate when they will be addressed.

Explain the Code of Conduct

Before the end of the introductory session, the quality assurance manager should review the code of conduct by which team members are expected to abide. Exhibit 8.2 presents a sample code of conduct which lists some duties and responsibilities of problem-solving team members.

Exhibit 8.2 Sample Code of Conduct

Code of Conduct for Members of Problem-Solving Teams

1. Participate in problem-solving training sessions.

2. Attend all scheduled meetings. Members must arrive on time and not leave early. Absences, tardiness, etc., will be recorded in the minutes of the meetings.

3. Ensure that meeting minutes are sent to your department manager and to the quality assurance manager.

4. Use the problem-solving process by following the procedures outlined during training sessions.

5. Choose to solve problems that relate to your area of responsibility.

6. Do not choose problems that are off-limits for problem-solving teams. Members cannot choose problems in the following areas: pay, benefits, scheduling, and personnel policies and procedures.

7. Participate actively in all team activities and encourage others to do the same.

8. Complete assignments on time. Members must collect feedback and contact resources according to the dates designated by the team's action plan.

9. Keep to the agenda set for each team meeting.

10. Evaluate the productivity of team meetings.

11. Complete a cost/benefit analysis form for each solution your team develops.

12. Review your completed cost/benefit analysis form with your department manager before scheduling a meeting to propose a solution to management.

13. Prepare a written proposal of the solution you wish to present to management.

14. Participate in your team's presentation of solutions to management.

15. Follow up and ensure that the solution which your team implements completely solves the problem.

The code of conduct also indicates the types of problems that are off-limits to problem-solving teams. Quality assurance managers should prepare a code of conduct that meets the needs of their hospitality organizations. Distribute copies to the participants and answer any questions they may have.

Training in Interpersonal Communications

The quality assurance manager cannot hope to cover the full length and breadth of the communications field in a single training session.

Communications is one of the most complex areas of human behavior. Hundreds of books have been written on the subject and entire departments of large universities are devoted to its study. The training session on interpersonal communication should focus on a limited set of specific objectives. This section presents training activities which are designed to achieve the following objectives:

- To make members of the team aware of the need to develop effective communication skills

- To present a model of interpersonal communication that members can understand and apply in their everyday lives

- To present practical tips that will help members to become better communicators

There are many ways to make members aware of a need to develop effective communication skills. The activity presented in this chapter heightens awareness by simply suggesting that the number of communications which take place in a hospitality organization is astronomical. Quality assurance managers are encouraged to develop their own techniques for making members aware of a need to become better communicators.

Likewise, there are many models of the interpersonal communication process. However, most of these models are extremely complex and they may easily overwhelm the training session participants. The model presented in this chapter tries to simplify the process of interpersonal communication while still doing justice to the complexities that the process involves. However, quality assurance managers are encouraged to revise the model presented in this chapter in order to satisfy their own specific training objectives.

One of the best ways of explaining a model of interpersonal communication is with a story. The story should be entertaining, full of humor, and should relate to the work environment of the people attending the training session. The stories that work best are those that describe cases in which two people fail to communicate successfully. The model is used to pinpoint what went wrong and what the two people could have done to ensure more successful communication.

The story presented in this chapter was used in a training session involving members of a housekeeping problem-solving team. Different stories could be used to train a front office team, a maintenance team, and so on. The stories that work best are those that you make up yourself. Quality assurance managers are encouraged to create their own sets of stories that can be used to explain the communication models they choose to use.

Establish the Need to Develop Effective Communication Skills

Establish the need to develop effective communication skills by posing the following question to the team members:

How many messages will it take to communicate the mission of our hospitality operation to each of our guests during a single year?

Use the flip chart to list the data necessary to answer the question. If your property is a hotel or motel, simply change the appropriate figures and perform the following calculations accordingly:

Property:	150 rooms
Communicators:	1 owner
	1 general manager
	8 department managers
	16 supervisors
	80 hourly employees
Guests:	39,420 (based on a 72% annual occupancy rate, single occupancy only)

1. The owner communicates the mission of the hospitality operation to the general manager.
   Total communications: _1_

2. The general manager communicates the owner's message to the eight department managers. (1 general manager x 8 department managers = 8 messages)
   Total communications: _9_

3. Each department manager communicates the general manager's message to all of the supervisors. (8 department managers x 16 supervisors = 128 messages)
   Total communications: _137_

4. Each supervisor communicates the department managers' messages to all of the hourly employees. (16 supervisors x 80 employees = 1,280 messages)
   Total communications: _1,417_

5. Each employee communicates the supervisors' messages to all of the guests during the year. (80 employees x 39,420 guests = 3,153,600 messages)
   Total communications: _3,155,017_

Suggest that, if it takes over three million communications to convey the mission of the property to each guest during a single year, the total number of communications in the operation during the year must be astronomical.

Stress that this example only focuses on the number of communications and does not consider whether or not the owner's message was successfully communicated to the guests. Ask members of the team to suggest what could happen to prevent the owner's message from being successfully communicated to the guests. List their responses on the flip chart. Expect responses such as:

● The owner's message could change as it passes through the levels of the organization.

● The owner's message could be unclear.

● Some of the communicators may not understand the owner's message.

After listing the responses, hang the flip chart on the wall for all of the members to see. As you explain the model for interpersonal communication, refer to these responses (as often as possible) and explain what could be done to ensure the successful communication of the owner's message to the guests.

Explain the Model of Interpersonal Communications

Stress that successful communication takes place when a message is received, understood, and acted upon by both the speaker and the listener. Exhibit 8.3 diagrams a model of interpersonal communications. Distribute copies of this model to the members of the team. Point out that the model identifies 20 steps that are necessary to ensure successful interpersonal communications. Use a story to explain the steps presented in the model. The following sections demonstrate how a story can be used to explain the interpersonal communications model shown in Exhibit 8.3.

Step 1

1. Speaker begins by: Thinking about the message he or she is about to send

Matthew is a new houseman at the property. He knows that Dorothy, the executive housekeeper, is short of help today. He pops into Dorothy's office and offers to lend a hand. Dorothy sits thinking about the message she is about to send to Matthew.

Step 2

2. The speaker sorts and selects from: Knowledge, past experience, feelings, attitudes, emotions

Exhibit 8.3 A Model of Interpersonal Communications

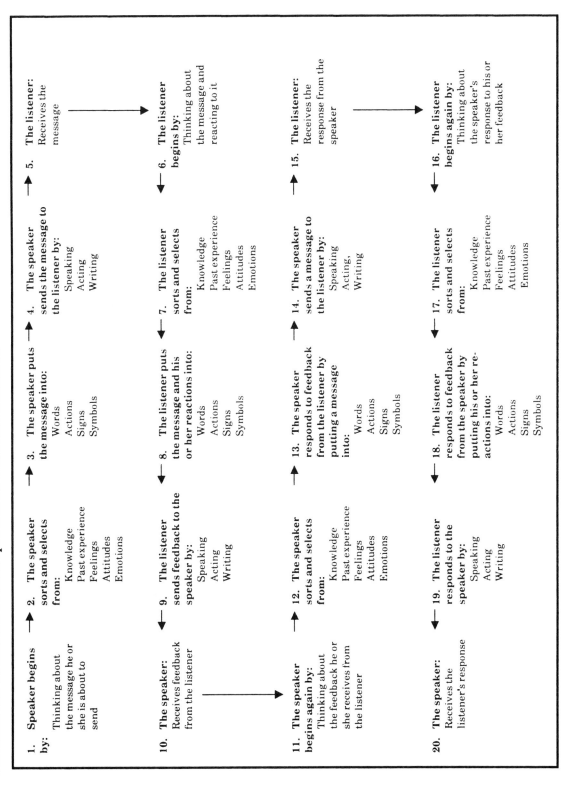

1. **Speaker begins by:**
   Thinking about the message he or she is about to send

2. **The speaker sorts and selects from:**
   Knowledge
   Past experience
   Feelings
   Attitudes
   Emotions

3. **The speaker puts the message into:**
   Words
   Actions
   Signs
   Symbols

4. **The speaker sends the message to the listener by:**
   Speaking
   Acting
   Writing

5. **The listener:**
   Receives the message

6. **The listener begins by:**
   Thinking about the message and reacting to it

7. **The listener sorts and selects from:**
   Knowledge
   Past experience
   Feelings
   Attitudes
   Emotions

8. **The listener puts the message and his or her reactions into:**
   Words
   Actions
   Signs
   Symbols

9. **The listener sends feedback to the speaker by:**
   Speaking
   Acting
   Writing

10. **The speaker:**
    Receives feedback from the listener

11. **The speaker begins again by:**
    Thinking about the feedback he or she receives from the listener

12. **The speaker sorts and selects from:**
    Knowledge
    Past experience
    Feelings
    Attitudes
    Emotions

13. **The speaker responds to feedback from the listener by putting a message into:**
    Words
    Actions
    Signs
    Symbols

14. **The speaker sends a message to the listener by:**
    Speaking,
    Acting,
    Writing

15. **The listener:**
    Receives the response from the speaker

16. **The listener begins again by:**
    Thinking about the speaker's response to his or her feedback

17. **The listener sorts and selects from:**
    Knowledge
    Past experience
    Feelings
    Attitudes
    Emotions

18. **The listener responds to feedback from the speaker by putting his or her re-actions into:**
    Words
    Actions
    Signs
    Symbols

19. **The listener responds to the speaker by:**
    Speaking
    Acting
    Writing

20. **The speaker:**
    Receives the listener's response

Dorothy sorts through her knowledge, past experience, feelings, attitudes, and emotions. It isn't often that someone volunteers to help clean rooms. She's surprised. She's also busy and could use the help.

Step 3

3. The speaker puts the message into: Words, actions, signs, symbols

Dorothy arranges a message in her mind.

Step 4

4. The speaker sends the message to the listener by: Speaking, acting, writing

She puts her message into words and actions. She smiles, breathes a sigh of relief, and says, "We can sure use another pair of hands today. Clean room 604. And thanks."

Step 5

5. The listener: Receives the message

Matthew nods.

Step 6

6. The listener begins by: Thinking about the message and reacting to it

He also starts thinking about what it means to clean a room.

Step 7

7. The listener sorts and selects from: Knowledge, past experience, feelings, attitudes, emotions

Matthew doesn't know very much about cleaning rooms but he begins to sort through his knowledge, past experience, feelings, attitudes, and emotions: "What's there to know about cleaning a room? Dirt is dirt. I appreciate dirt. I had a tomato farm with all different kinds of dirt. Andrew would pick a tomato, bring it to me, and I could tell him where he picked it, just by smelling the dirt still on it. But cleaning rooms? I know when my rooms are clean. That's when I can get from the front door to the fridge and over to the sofa. Clean is clean. Easy job, can do."

Step 8

8. The listener puts the message and his or her reactions into:	Words, actions, signs, symbols

Matthew arranges a message in his mind.

Step 9

9. The listener sends feedback to the speaker by:	Speaking, acting, writing

Matthew puts his message into words and actions. "Sure thing, Dorothy. I'll get on it right away."

Step 10

10. The speaker:	Receives feedback from the listener

Dorothy smiles.

Step 11

11. The speaker begins again by:	Thinking about the feedback he or she receives from the listener

Dorothy doesn't have time to think about the feedback she has just received from Matthew. In fact, she doesn't have time for any thinking today; she's too busy working. Matthew said he'd "get on it right away," and that's really all that Dorothy wanted to hear. She continues working without thinking, while Matthew goes to clean room 604. Let's follow Matthew and see what he meant by helping out housekeeping.

Matthew decides that the bed sheets don't look dirty, so he throws the crumpled bedspread back over the bed. He doesn't straighten the spread because he knows "the guy staying in here is just going to mess it up again anyway." He uses one of the hand towels to wipe off the vanity, and puts the towel back on the rack with the dirty side folded in. He looks into the bathroom; but, since he doesn't do bathrooms, he just closes the door.

The amenities are scattered all over the vanity, but Matthew leaves them that way. He thinks, "Every time I stay in a hotel, I have to dig through the shower cap, hand cream, soap, cream rinse, and all the rest of the junk to get to the shampoo, so I'll save this guy the trouble."

Matthew watches T.V. for a bit and decides that there's no point in vacuuming the carpet. "It gets vacuumed almost every day anyway," he thinks. He doesn't see any dust so he can't see any point in dusting. Since there's only a little trash in the waste basket, he leaves it because

"Someone will empty it when it's full." Matthew looks around the room once more, decides that his job is finished, and walks back to housekeeping to tell Dorothy.

"Hi, Dorothy! Room 604 is clean. See you later. Anytime you need any more help, just let me know."

"Wait a minute," says Dorothy. "I have to inspect the room before you're finished."

They go to room 604. When Dorothy opens the door, she finally receives feedback from Matthew about her message. When she sees the "clean" room, she begins to think about her message and the listener and says, "I thought you said this room was clean!"

Step 12

12. The speaker sorts and
    selects from:

    Knowledge, past experience, feelings, attitudes, emotions

Dorothy compares her knowledge of clean to Matthew's knowledge of clean, her past experience to his. She concludes, "This is the worst job of cleaning that I've seen in 20 years of housekeeping!"

Her feelings, attitudes, and emotions about cleaning become quickly apparent to Matthew.

Step 13

13. The speaker responds to
    feedback from the listener
    by putting a message into:

    Words, actions, signs, symbols

Dorothy arranges a message in her mind.

Step 14

14. The speaker sends a message
    to the listener by:

    Speaking, acting, writing

Dorothy drags Matthew from room 604 to room 601 and shows him what she means by a "clean room." They go back to room 604. Dorothy is clearly irritated. Shaking her finger at Matthew she says, "Now clean this room the way I mean clean!"

Step 15

15. The listener:

    Receives the response from the speaker

Matthew stands wide-eyed.

Step 16
16. The listener begins again by:

Thinking about the speaker's response to his or her feedback

He begins thinking about the differences between room 601 and 604. He also begins thinking about how upset Dorothy is.

Step 17
17. The listener sorts and selects from:

Knowledge, past experience, feelings, attitudes, emotions

Matthew compares his knowledge, past experience, feelings, attitudes, and emotions about cleaning to what he senses to be Dorothy's knowledge, past experience, feelings, attitudes, and emotions about cleaning.

Step 18
18. The listener responds to feedback from the speaker by putting his or her reactions into:

Words, actions, signs, symbols

Matthew arranges a message in his mind.

Step 19
19. The listener responds to the speaker by:

Speaking, acting, writing

Matthew reluctantly concludes that he should clean the room the way Dorothy wants it done. He shuffles his feet, shrugs his shoulders, and says, "OK, Dorothy, I get the message." He decides that, in the future, he needs to know what he's getting into before he volunteers to help someone.

Step 20
20. The speaker:

Receives the listener's response

Dorothy nods and storms off to her office. On the way she begins to cool down and feels bad about how she treated Matthew. "He was only trying to help," she reminds herself. Dorothy wonders what she could have been thinking when she let Matthew clean the room without any direction or explanation. She decides that "When he's done we need to talk."

After finishing the job, Matthew returns to Dorothy's office. They talk together for some time about how to avoid misunderstandings in the future. They decide that the best way to communicate more effectively is to ensure that the message is received, understood, and acted upon by both the speaker and the listener.

Improving Interpersonal Communication Skills

Remind the members that successful communication takes place when a message is received, understood, and acted upon by both the speaker and the listener. Suggest that better communication results when people develop effective speaking and listening skills.

Ask the members to state what tips they would give to Dorothy and Matthew to help them become better speakers and listeners. Record their responses on the flip chart. Hang the flip chart sheets on the wall for all of the members to see. Whenever possible, refer to these tips while discussing ways by which to develop effective speaking and listening skills.

Speaking. Ask the members to state which of the following is their favorite type of communication activity: speaking, listening, acting, or writing. Expect most members to respond that speaking is their favorite.

Distribute copies of Exhibit 8.4 which lists tips for more effective speaking. Carefully review each of these tips with the members of the team and, if possible, refer to the tips they suggested earlier.

Ask the members to identify the most important tip listed in Exhibit 8.4. Expect them to identify the most important tip as: "Always ask questions to see how much your listener understands." Suggest that, in some situations, people speak just so that they can hear themselves talk. Point out that, in these cases, speakers are not concerned with communicating to others, but only to themselves. Stress that in order to communicate successfully with others, a speaker must actively seek feedback from the listeners. Point out that one of the best ways to get feedback is to ask the listener questions to see whether or not the listener understands the message.

Listening. Ask the members which of the following is probably the most important type of communication activity: speaking, listening, acting, or writing. Expect them to respond that listening is the most important activity. Stress that the best listener is often the most effective communicator.

Distribute copies of Exhibit 8.5 which lists tips for more effective listening. Carefully review each of these tips with the members of the team and, if possible, refer to the tips they suggested earlier. The following sections present important points to stress while discussing how to develop effective listening skills.

Exhibit 8.4 Developing Effective Speaking Skills

Tips for More Effective Speaking

- Know exactly what you want to say before you say it.
- Say what must be said in as few words as possible.
- Put your message into words that your listeners will understand.
- Keep your messages simple.
- Pause frequently to allow listeners to ask questions.
- Avoid exaggerations and unfounded generalizations.
- Focus on the best way to state your main idea.
- Whenever possible, look at the person(s) to whom you are speaking.
- Be sensitive to your listeners' nonverbal behavior.
- Always ask questions to see how much your listeners have understood.

Exhibit 8.5 Developing Effective Listening Skills

Tips for More Effective Listening

- Look directly at the speaker.
- Show interest and enthusiasm while listening.
- Don't let your mind wander.
- Identify the speaker's main idea.
- Suspend judgment until the speaker is finished.
- Avoid forming arguments against the speaker's ideas until you fully understand them.
- Do not let your emotions affect what you hear.
- Be sensitive to the speaker's nonverbal behavior.
- Concentrate on what the speaker is saying.
- Try not to anticipate what the speaker is about to say.
- Always ask questions.

Suggest that listening seems easy because listening speed is twice as fast as the speed with which most people can speak. Suggest that members can prove this to themselves by adjusting the playing speed of a tape recorder. Stress that good listening is hard work. Point out that it requires discipline and concentration for listeners to keep their minds from wandering while a speaker is talking, and to prevent their own ideas from distorting the message that a speaker is trying to communicate. Suggest that lazy listeners hear only what they want to hear.

Stress that sometimes it is difficult to identify a speaker's main idea. Point out that, in some cases, the speaker may not even have a main idea to express. For example, a person may simply be "thinking out loud." Stress that, when a listener cannot identify a speaker's main idea, he or she should wait until the speaker stops talking and then ask him or her to summarize the main idea.

Answer any questions that members may have about the tips in Exhibits 8.4 and 8.5. Ask the members to use these tips throughout the rest of the training program, especially during the next part of the training that covers group dynamics. Stress that the more they apply these communication techniques now, the more successful their problem-solving team will be in the future. Stress again that successful communication takes place when a message is received, understood, and acted upon by both the speaker and the listener.

Training in Group Dynamics

The best way to begin a training session on group dynamics is with an exercise that engages the members in a group problem-solving activity. One of the more interesting and informative exercises to use is the NASA survival test. This exercise was developed by the National Aeronautics and Space Administration (NASA) and can be used to demonstrate that groups outperform individuals in decision-making situations.

Exhibit 8.6 contains the worksheet used for this exercise. Pass out copies of the worksheet to each team member. Direct them to read the instructions and complete the exercise without discussing the material or their answers with the other members. When they have finished, collect the worksheets and distribute another blank copy of the exercise to each member. Explain that, this time, they are to complete the exercise as a team. Instruct the team that differences of opinion should be settled by a group vote.

Once the team begins the exercise, refrain from interfering with their work. However, occasionally remind them to settle differences of opinion by voting. As the team completes the exercise, score their individual worksheets according to the following instructions:

Exhibit 8.6 Survival Exercise Worksheet

Instructions:

You are a member of a space crew originally scheduled to rendezvous with a mother ship on the lighted surface of the moon. Due to mechanical difficulties, however, your ship was forced to land at a spot some 200 miles from the rendezvous point. During landing, much of the equipment aboard was damaged, and, since survival depends on reaching the mother ship, the most critical items available must be chosen for the 200-mile trip.

Listed below are the 15 items left intact and undamaged after landing. Your task is to order them in terms of their importance to your crew in allowing them to reach the rendezvous point.

Place the number 1 by the most important item, the number 2 by the second most important, and so on, through number 15.

You have 15 minutes to complete this phase of the exercise.

_____ Box of matches
_____ Food concentrate
_____ Fifty feet of nylon rope
_____ Parachute silk
_____ Portable heating unit
_____ Two .45 caliber pistols
_____ One case of dehydrated milk
_____ Two 100-pound tanks of oxygen
_____ Stellar map (of the moon's constellations)
_____ Life raft
_____ Magnetic compass
_____ Five gallons of water
_____ Signal flares
_____ First aid kit containing injection needles
_____ Solar-powered FM receiver-transmitter

1. Compute the *net difference* between each individual's answer and the correct answer. For example, if an individual's answer is 9, and the correct answer is 12, the net difference is 3. The individual's score for that particular item is 3 points. Similarly, if the individual's answer is 12, and the correct answer is 9, the net difference is 3. In this case, the individual's score for that particular item would also be 3 points.

2. Total the points to determine each individual's overall score.

3. Total all of the scores computed in step 2, and divide by the number of individuals to arrive at an average individual score.

After 15 minutes have passed, stop the exercise and record the group's answers on the flip chart. Review the correct answers and explanations (as shown in Exhibit 8.7), and compute the team's score as follows:

1. Compute the net difference between each answer and the correct answer. (This is the same procedure used to score the individual worksheets.)

2. Total the points to determine the team's overall score.

Both individual and group scores for the exercise can be evaluated as follows:

00-20	Excellent
21-30	Good
31-40	Average
41-50	Fair
51 +	Poor

The results of the activity should show that the group scored better than the average individual. In rare cases, the results of the exercise may indicate that the group scored worse than the average individual on the team. If this happens, point out that the members need to learn more about how to work together. Stress that the training which they are about to receive will provide them with important information and useful techniques to help them become productive members of a successful problem-solving team.

Explain How a Group Develops

Explain that as groups mature, they typically pass through several stages of development. List the following stages on the flip chart:

1. Membership

2. Individual influence

3. Shared feelings

4. Respect for individual differences

5. Productive teamwork

Suggest that these stages can be identified in terms of the kinds of questions that members often ask themselves about their relationship to the group.

Exhibit 8.7 Survival Exercise: Answers and Explanations

15	Box of matches *No oxygen*
4	Food concentrate *Can live for some time without food*
6	Fifty feet of nylon rope *For travel over rough terrain*
8	Parachute silk *For carrying objects*
13	Portable heating unit *Lighted side of the moon is hot*
11	Two .45 calibre pistols *Some use for propulsion*
12	One case of dehydrated milk *Needs water to work*
1	Two 100-pound tanks of oxygen *No air on the moon*
3	Stellar map (of the moon's constellations) *Needed for navigation*
9	Life raft *Some value for shelter or carrying objects*
14	Magnetic compass *Moon's magnetic field is different from the earth's*
2	Five gallons of water *You can't live long without water*
10	Signal flares *No oxygen*
7	First aid kit containing injection needles *First aid kit may be needed, but needles are useless*
5	Solar-powered FM receiver-transmitter *Communication*

Stage 1: Membership. Point out that individuals on new problem-solving teams generally pass through this membership stage during the first few training sessions. Suggest that, before attending the first training session, individual members of the team probably had a number of concerns. For example, they may have asked themselves such questions such as:

- What will it mean to be a member of this team?
- How will I benefit from being a member of this team?
- Will it be alright for me to arrive early for the meetings? Can I leave late?
- What will the other members expect from me?
- How will I go about speaking at the meetings?
- Will I find that being a member of this team is stimulating? boring? exciting? threatening? rewarding?

Stress that these are typical questions that people have whenever they join any kind of group. Point out that some of these questions were answered at the first training session. Ask the members to share any other questions which they had before the first meeting. If possible, answer these questions before explaining the next stage of group development.

Stage 2: Individual Influence. Explain that after individuals understand what it means to be a member of a group, they begin to think about what kind of influence they can exert on the group. Suggest that, during the NASA survival exercise, individual members of the team probably had a number of concerns. For example, they may have asked themselves such questions as:

- Who is the leader of this group?
- How do decisions get made in this group?
- In what ways are the members trying to influence each other?
- Should I let the members of this group influence my decisions?
- What opportunities are there for me to influence other members of the group?
- Do some members in this group care more about influence and power than they do about solving the problem?

Stress that these are typical concerns that individuals have when they engage in their first activities with a new group. Point out that some of these concerns are addressed by the problem-solving training program. Explain that team leaders receive special training, enabling them to direct the efforts of a team without smothering the initiative, ideas, and talents of individual team members. Stress that there is no place on a team, either as a member or as a leader, for individuals with power-hungry egos.

Stage 3: Shared Feelings. Explain that, as individuals become more comfortable as team members, the fog about influence and power begins to clear. At this stage, the feelings of the members and of the group become more and more important. Point out that the team will soon be entering this stage of development. Suggest that, when the team arrives at this stage, members may find themselves asking the following types of questions:

- Can members freely express their feelings in this group, or do feelings get bottled up and explode at the wrong times?

- When we get bored, frustrated, or angry can we "lay the cards on the table" and work the situation out as a group?

- Do some members of this group wait until they get outside the door to tell other members or the team leader how they "really" feel about what the group is doing?

- When other members like an idea or a suggested course of action, do they actually let the team know?

- When members criticize ideas or express negative feelings, does the team see it as honest feedback that can help produce better results, or does the team see it as one personality against another?

- When members agree with others or express positive feelings, does the team see it as honest feedback that can help produce better results, or does the team see it as a way of patronizing members of the team?

Suggest that these are typical concerns that members may soon have about their own team. Point out that some of these concerns are addressed by the problem-solving training program. Explain that team leaders receive special training in recognizing behavior and situations that may threaten the success of the team. Stress, however, that it is really the responsibility of each team member to ensure that everyone feels free to participate. Stress the following points:

- Teams may fail quickly if individual members believe that their contributions are neither needed nor appreciated by the other members.

- If people's silence is taken as approval, something is wrong. Team members must feel free to openly express their approval or disapproval.

- If meetings turn into gripe sessions, the team has lost its sense of purpose, which is to identify and solve problems.

Point out that the third stage of development is often called the "honeymoon stage" because members have created a bond which holds the group together. Stress, however, that, for a team to develop further, members must not only value what they have in common, but must also develop a respect for differences.

Stage 4: Respect for Individual Differences Suggest that if enough trust develops within the group during the third stage of development, the team will become even more successful as members contribute their unique abilities and talents to the problem-solving effort. Stress that this will not happen until members of the team develop a respect for each other's individual differences.

Explain that, during the fourth stage of a team's development, team members come to value their differences more than their similarities. Suggest that the team benefits as members feel freer to contribute by drawing upon their own sets of knowledge, past experience, feelings, attitudes, and emotions. Point out that, at this stage of development, a new set of questions becomes important to the team. Some of these questions are:

- Do team members take the time and effort to learn about the knowledge, past experience, feelings, and attitudes of one another?

- In sharing ideas, do members look forward to the reactions of others and value their feedback?

- Do members let each other know that they appreciate each other's opinions and comments, even when they don't necessarily agree with them?

- Are team members willing to risk looking at old problems in new ways?

Suggest that, as a team enters the fourth stage of development, members must work to improve their listening and speaking skills. Stress that problem-solving teams work best when there is a conflict of ideas, not when there is a conflict of personalities. Suggest that personality conflicts can be avoided if members are able to speak freely and see criticism as honest feedback. Point out that if all members adopt this attitude without hurting anyone's feelings, the team is ready for the next stage of development.

Stage 5: Productive Teamwork Suggest that once a team begins to value the individual differences among its members, the team begins to work productively and creatively. Point out that productive teams are able to generate new ideas which none of the members would have thought of by themselves. Suggest that, at this stage of development, members ask questions such as:

- How much time and energy do we spend arguing about which ideas are "better" or "right," compared to the time we take to develop new ideas?

- Are we spending our time looking for the causes of problems, or are we just complaining about problems and talking them to death?

- When we identify problems, do we follow a process that analyzes them thoroughly, or do we jump at the first solution that comes along?

- Do we take the time and effort to seek the ideas, opinions, and reactions of everyone affected by the problem we are attempting to solve?

Suggest that one way by which members can control the course of their team's development is by learning how they can play positive roles during the team's problem-solving activities.

Roles Individuals Play in Groups

Suggest that the behavior of individuals within a group can be characterized in terms of positive and negative roles. Point out that when individuals play positive roles, their behavior increases the productivity of the group. Conversely, when individuals play negative roles, their behavior decreases the group's productivity and may even prevent the group from achieving its goals.

Positive Roles

List the following categories on the flip chart:

- The inquirer
- The contributor
- The elaborator
- The reviewer
- The evaluator
- The energizer

Explain that these categories are convenient labels for some of the positive roles that individuals may perform when acting in a group. Briefly explain these positive roles. Explanations may be as brief as the examples which follow.

The Inquirer. The inquirer is concerned with the raw materials of reasoning. This person focuses the group's attention on facts and figures, and on the methods which the group uses to interpret facts and figures. For example, an individual is performing in the role of an inquirer when he or she says, "Let's get down to cases. Just how many times a week does this problem occur?"

The Contributor. The contributor tries to provide the basis for sound group discussion by submitting factual information or considered opinions about facts already presented. For example, an individual acts as a contributor when he or she says, "Something must be going wrong here. Accounting reports indicate that breakage has increased by 13% since the new dishmachine was installed."

The Elaborator. The elaborator often performs an essential function by translating generalizations into concrete examples, or by projecting the effects of a proposed course of action. For example, an individual performs as an elaborator when he or she says, "Let's imagine what would happen if we applied that idea to our own situation."

The Reviewer. The reviewer tries to clarify relationships among the various ideas that the group is discussing, or attempts to redefine the group's position in terms of agreed-upon objectives. An individual acts as a reviewer when he or she says, "When we began this discussion we thought the problem was with the equipment, but now it appears that the problem may be with work methods."

The Evaluator. The evaluator observes the activity of the group and raises questions about facts, figures, or practical applications of a proposed solution. An individual acts as an evaluator when he or she says, "If we follow this plan of action, will we completely solve the problem?"

The Energizer. The energizer keeps the group's discussion moving by prodding members to settle on a specific course of action. An individual performs the role of an energizer when he or she says, "This discussion is very interesting, but is it really helping to solve our problem?"

Explain that by understanding the positive roles that individuals may play in group interaction, members can practice the types of behavior that contribute to a team's success. Point out that members may more easily recognize, appreciate, and encourage the positive roles played by other members of the team.

Negative Roles

List the following categories on the flip chart:

- The dominator

- The blocker
- The cynic
- The security seeker
- The lobbyist

Explain that these categories are convenient labels for some of the negative roles that individuals may perform when acting in a group. Briefly explain these negative roles. Explanations may be as brief as the examples which follow.

The Dominator. The dominator tries to run the show by asserting authority, demanding attention, interrupting others, making arbitrary decisions, or by insisting upon having the last word. An individual acts like a dominator when he or she says, "Now I've had some experience at this sort of thing, so let me tell you exactly what to do."

The Blocker. The blocker is often a frustrated dominator. When no one in the group acknowledges this person's claim to authority, or when members of the group seem to be moving away from his or her opinions, the frustrated dominator becomes stubborn and blocks the progress of the group at every possible opportunity. An individual acts like a blocker when he or she says, "That idea will never work; you might just as well throw it out right now and reconsider what I said earlier in the meeting."

The Cynic. The cynic refuses to identify with the group and belittles the efforts of the members to act as a team. This person may deliberately provoke conflict between members, or constantly annoy the group with an arrogant attitude of indifference. The cynic is likely to comment, "It's obvious that you people will never agree on anything, so let's call it quits."

The Security Seeker. The security seeker tries to get sympathy and attention from other group members by constantly focusing the discussion on his or her personal problems or unique experiences. An individual acts like a security seeker when he or she says, "Something just like that happened to me, only it was worse. What do you think I should have done?"

The Lobbyist. The lobbyist constantly pushes the special interests of other groups to which he or she belongs and never tires of plugging pet theories and ideas. A person acts like a lobbyist when he or she says, "Now you understand this makes no difference to me, but don't you think this is just another instance of being unfair to my co-workers in the kitchen?"

Explain that by understanding the negative roles that individuals may play in group interaction, members may be able to avoid the kinds of behavior that threaten the success of their team. Point out that members also may be able to more easily recognize and discourage the behavior of other members that prevents the team from reaching its goals.

Stress that these roles are not necessarily personality types. Point out that one individual could play several roles during a single problem-solving meeting.

Stimulate a discussion of these positive and negative roles by preparing flip chart sheets which list comments that individuals could make during actual problem-solving meetings. Exhibit 8.8 contains sample comments to use for this activity. Ask the team members to identify comments which indicate positive roles. Next, ask them to state how each of these comments may perform a useful function in a team's problem-solving efforts. It is not necessary to pinpoint the actual role indicated by each comment listed on the flip chart. The objective of the exercise is to ensure that the members can recognize positive contributions of individuals engaged in a problem-solving activity. After discussing the comments which indicate positive roles, direct a similar discussion of the negative roles.

Additional Training

In order to be able to function productively, problem-solving teams must also receive training in specific problem-solving techniques, in completing a cost/benefit analysis form, and in presenting management proposals. The best time to conduct this training is when a new team actually uses the process to solve its first problem. Chapter 9 examines these training topics as well as the type of training team leaders need in areas involving specific problem-solving procedures.

Exhibit 8.8 Roles Individuals Play in Groups

Positive Roles Individuals Play in Groups

The Inquirer

1. Is concerned with the basics of reasoning.
2. Focuses the group's attention on the facts of a situation.
3. Encourages the group to interpret the facts in different ways.

Typical Comments:

   ▸ "Just how many times does this happen?"
   ▸ "Does this happen with just certain people or does it apply to everyone in that department?"
   ▸ "Does the problem arise because of the worker or because of the work method?"
   ▸ "Whose responsibility is this?"

The Contributor

1. Submits factual information.
2. Attempts to build a basis for sound decision-making.
3. Offers considered opinions about facts.

Typical Comments:

   ▸ "I think our decision should be based on the figures Denise got from the accounting department."
   ▸ "Let's see if we can combine that idea with the feedback we received from the dining room manager."
   ▸ "I think that we should listen to the facts and discuss what we should do about this later."
   ▸ "Let me give you the feedback I got from maintenance and housekeeping."

The Elaborator

1. Translates generalizations into concrete examples.
2. Builds on the ideas of others.
3. Projects a picture of what might happen if a solution is implemented.

Typical Comments:

   ▸ "Let's imagine what it would be like if we tried that idea in my department."
   ▸ "What do you think other employees would say about that?"
   ▸ "How do you think that would work at the front desk?"
   ▸ "How would this affect our guests?"

Exhibit 8.8 (continued)

The Reviewer

1. Summarizes the progress of the group.
2. Clarifies relationships among the ideas that are being discussed.
3. Identifies points that the group agrees upon.

Typical Comments:

▸ "Let's recap what we've done so far."
▸ "Let me list the points that we seem to agree on."
▸ "Matt, let me try to rephrase what you just said and combine it with points that Andrew brought up at the last meeting."
▸ "So far we have identified five reasons why we need to do this. Let me list them and see if we all agree."

The Evaluator

1. Judges the group's thinking by its own standards.
2. Raises questions about facts and figures.
3. Explores the practical applications of proposed solutions.

Typical Comments:

▸ "Let's check these figures against the invoices in accounting."
▸ "Maybe we need a second and third opinion about this problem."
▸ "There could be another side to this story that we don't know about. We always try to get all of the information."
▸ "I think that we've tried things like this before and found out that we were on the wrong track."

The Energizer

1. Keeps the group's discussion moving along.
2. Stimulates new ideas that are pertinent to the topic.
3. Prods members to decide on a specific course of action.

Typical Comments:

▸ "Ok, we get the point, but what about this other idea?"
▸ "We're just spinning our wheels here. Let's move on to the next idea and come back to this later."
▸ "Let's wait on this point until we get the feedback we need from housekeeping. What's next?"
▸ "We've discussed this enough. Let's vote."

Exhibit 8.8 (continued)

Negative Roles Individuals Play in Groups

The Dominator

1. Demands attention and tries to run the show.
2. Constantly interrupts other people.
3. Imposes personal opinions on the group.

Typical Comments:

▶ "Now, I've had a lot more experience at this sort of thing, so let me tell you what to do."
▶ "The only way we're going to make progress here is by following up on my idea."
▶ "Hold everything, I know exactly what to do."
▶ "You're wasting everyone's time discussing these things; let's just do what I suggested earlier."

The Blocker

1. Is a frustrated dominator.
2. Repeats arguments and refuses to listen to anyone else's reasoning.
3. When ignored by the group, the person becomes stubborn and resists everything the group wants to do.

Typical Comments:

▶ "None of you really understands what I'm trying to say."
▶ "We went over that idea at the last meeting and I didn't like it then either."
▶ "Well, that's my opinion and I think its better than yours, so listen more carefully to me this time."
▶ "Why are we voting on this issue? There's a lot more I have to say."

The Cynic

1. Scoffs at the group's progress.
2. Tries to start conflicts and arguments among members of the group.
3. Is always negative.

Typical Comments:

▶ "I don't care what you do."
▶ "Do what you want, management won't approve it anyway."
▶ "You're just wasting your time if you're going to do that."
▶ "This whole thing is stupid; nobody cares what you guys think anyway."

Exhibit 8.8 (continued)

The Security Seeker

1. Wants sympathy or personal recognition.
2. Always had it worse than anyone else.
3. His or her personal experiences are always more important than anyone else's.

Typical Comments:

- ▶ "I wish somebody would have told me what to do when that happened to me."
- ▶ "I never know what to do when that happens in my department."
- ▶ "The situation is so bad in my department that even this solution won't work."
- ▶ "I always have so many things going on, I'll never have time to do that."

The Lobbyist

1. Always plugs pet theories.
2. Is only concerned with problems that involve his or her own department.
3. Will keep talking about his or her own ideas even though the group has decided to do something entirely different.

Typical Comments:

- ▶ "I've been pretty open-minded about this, but don't you think we're being unfair to the people in my department?"
- ▶ "That's okay if that's what you guys want to do, but I don't think you really understand my idea."
- ▶ "That's a good idea you have, but I think you forgot to consider the things that I said last week."
- ▶ "I agree with everything you say, but I just can't buy your conclusion."

9

Managing Problem-Solving Teams

As noted at the end of the previous chapter, members of problem-solving teams receive additional training as they solve their first problem. This additional training includes how to complete cost/benefit analysis forms and how to present effective solution proposals to management. Training in these areas is given only as needed. Members of teams do not have to become experts in problem-solving theory and techniques before they are able to function as effective problem-solvers. The more problems that a team attempts to solve, the more skilled the members become in using the tools of the problem-solving process. Team leaders, on the other hand, must be thoroughly skilled in each aspect of the problem-solving process. The success or failure of a new team greatly depends on its leader's ability to manage the team's activities.

The first sections of this chapter examine the role of the team leader and suggest criteria that can be used for selecting individuals to serve as leaders of problem-solving teams. The next sections examine the kind of training that team leaders must receive in order to effectively manage a team's problem-solving efforts. Team leaders go through the same training as team members, but they receive more in-depth training in the areas of interpersonal communications, group dynamics, cost/benefit analysis, and presenting proposals to management. In addition, team leaders receive special training in how to conduct productive meetings, and how to carry out their specific recordkeeping and reporting responsibilities.

The quality assurance manager is responsible for planning and conducting team leader training sessions. Upon completing the training program, leaders should still receive guidance from the quality assurance manager and their department manager, as they plan, organize, and coordinate their team's problem-solving efforts.

The final sections of this chapter show how quality assurance managers can monitor the progress of teams and measure the success of the problem-solving process at their hospitality organizations.

The Role of the Team Leader

The primary role of the team leader is to function as the servant, not the master, of the team. The leader must be able to avoid the temptation of imposing his or her will on the team's problem-solving efforts. This is not an easy role. Like everyone else, leaders like to do things that are their own ideas.

The leader's job is not to direct a team toward achieving goals which he or she thinks are in the best interest of the group. Rather, the leader's job is to see that the team reaches the goals that it sets for itself. Team goals should result from the decisions of the group, not from the needs, wants, or desires of the team leader.

A leader acts in the role of a servant as he or she assists the team throughout its problem-solving efforts. A leader keeps the team moving forward in the problem-solving process by interpreting, clarifying, and summarizing the thoughts and actions of members of the team. The leader's actions help a team to reach a group decision that all of the members understand and recognize as the will of the group.

When an individual sidetracks the team's discussions onto insignificant or irrelevant issues, the team leader acts in the role of a guide, pointing out the path which the team's discussion should take. A leader accomplishes this not by imposing his or her will on the team, but by stressing the primary goals of the group and imposing the will of the team on the member who is off the track. In some cases, the issues that a team member wishes to discuss may be held until near the end of the meeting or they may be put on a future agenda.

Individuals with power-hungry egos have no place in the problem-solving process, least of all in the position of team leader. A team leader must understand the basic conditions that define his or her role. A leader must understand that his or her power base is granted by the department manager. This power is not a right that is granted to an individual; it is a function of the role the individual performs, and is sustained only by the manner in which the individual carries out the specified duties and responsibilities.

Exhibit 9.1 lists some of the duties and responsibilities of team leaders. In order to effectively carry out these duties and responsibilities, a team leader must have a good general knowledge of how the team's department operates. Most important, a team leader must have the full support of the team's department manager. In some cases, the department manager's support may take the form of protecting the team leader when the findings or conclusions proposed by the team are at variance with thoughts or desires of the department manager's own peers or superiors.

Since department managers and supervisors must provide team

Exhibit 9.1 Sample Job List for Team Leaders

Duties and Responsibilities of a Team Leader

1. Participate in problem-solving team training sessions.

2. Participate in team leader training sessions.

3. Schedule team meetings.

4. Prepare an agenda for each team meeting, and distribute copies to members of the team before each meeting.

5. Prepare the meeting room.

6. Start meetings on time.

7. Rotate members of the team as recorders of the meeting's minutes.

8. Direct the team's activities according to procedures of the problem-solving process.

9. End meetings on time.

10. Maintain records of the team's activities, such as meeting agendas, meeting minutes, data collected, and materials used for management presentations.

11. Update the team's track record.

12. Distribute copies of the minutes of each meeting to: team members, the department manager, the quality assurance manager, and the general manager.

13. Report the team's progress to the department manager after each team meeting.

14. Seek guidance from the department manager whenever necessary.

15. Report the team's progress to the quality assurance manager after each team meeting.

16. Seek guidance from the quality assurance manager whenever necessary.

17. Assist the team in identifying problems to solve.

18. Assist the team in developing solutions to problems.

19. Assist the team in completing cost/benefit analysis forms.

20. Assist the team in preparing for management presentations.

leaders with essential support and necessary guidance, they should be actively involved in selecting the individual who will serve as the leader for their department's problem-solving team. Exhibit 9.2

Exhibit 9.2 Assessing the Leadership Potential of Individuals

Assessing Leadership Potential

Rating Scale

1   Demonstrates the behavior rarely
3   Demonstrates the behavior occasionally
5   Demonstrates the behavior consistently

1.	The individual is interested in and enthusiastic about the quality assurance problem-solving process.	1 2 3 4 5
2.	The individual's job performance demonstrates commitment, responsibility, and optimism.	1 2 3 4 5
3.	The individual is respected by peers and has established credibility in the organization.	1 2 3 4 5
4.	The individual demonstrates good judgment by being competent, thorough, objective, and open-minded on the job.	1 2 3 4 5
5.	The individual is cooperative, congenial, and relaxed in the work environment.	1 2 3 4 5
6.	The individual is a clear speaker and an active listener.	1 2 3 4 5
7.	The individual demonstrates leadership ability by planning, organizing, and coordinating job-related activities.	1 2 3 4 5
8.	The individual is experienced, knowledgeable, and suggests insightful improvements.	1 2 3 4 5
9.	The individual is an independent and innovative thinker.	1 2 3 4 5
10.	The individual is interested in self-development.	1 2 3 4 5
11.	The individual has an acceptable attendance record.	1 2 3 4 5
12.	The individual sets and achieves goals.	1 2 3 4 5

presents a form that can be used by department managers and supervisors to assess the leadership potential of individuals in their departments.

Team Leader Training

Team leaders should assist the quality assurance manager in training the members of their teams. Therefore, team leader training must begin before training sessions are conducted for their team's members.

Team leader training begins with the leaders receiving exactly the same training that their team members will receive. Although leaders attend the training sessions as participants, they also participate in their own training sessions in the role of assistant trainers.

In order to function in both roles, leaders must prepare for their first training session by studying the problem-solving process that is used at the property, and reviewing the detailed training plans developed by the quality assurance manager. If the quality assurance manager chooses to implement the process presented in this book, team leaders should prepare for their roles as assistant trainers by studying the steps in the problem-solving process which are examined in Chapter 7 and the contents of the training sessions which are suggested in Chapter 8.

By involving team leaders as assistants in conducting their own training sessions, the quality assurance manager can receive significant feedback about the effectiveness of the regular training program. In addition, team leaders may critique each other's presentations and gain valuable insight into their future roles as servants, not masters, of problem-solving teams.

At the first training session, each team leader should fill out a self-evaluation form similar to that shown in Exhibit 9.3. Leaders can use this first self-evaluation to determine important areas which need their attention during the training sessions. The evaluation forms should be filled out periodically as trainees fulfill their roles as team leaders. Team leaders can use their first self-evaluation as a benchmark against which to measure their progress as team leaders. The quality assurance manager can use the results of these periodic self-evaluations as a basis for planning further leader training in specific areas of the problem-solving process.

Interpersonal Communications

Leaders should be thoroughly familiar with the model of interpersonal communication that is presented in the regular training program. They should be able to use the model to explain that successful communication takes place when a message is received, understood, and acted upon by both the speaker and the listener.

The more familiar team leaders become with the model, the more sensitive they are likely to be in recognizing misunderstandings that may arise during the course of a team's problem-solving efforts. For example, when appropriate, leaders should be able to use the communications model to identify, explain, and clarify messages which are received but misunderstood by members of their teams.

Training sessions should present opportunities for team leaders to refine their speaking and listening skills. An effective exercise, which combines all of the facets of interpersonal communication covered in the regular training program, is to ask each team leader to break down a specific situation into the twenty steps of the interpersonal communications model. Other members of the leader training group

Exhibit 9.3 Team Leader Self-Evaluation Form

Think about your leadership experiences and rate yourself on each of the following skills or qualities. Evaluate your strengths and weaknesses as honestly as you can and chart your progress as a team leader. Use the following rating scale:

1 = Strong; 2 = Good; 3 = Unsure; 4 = Weak; 5 = Poor.

1. I can give a concise, clear description of the quality assurance problem-solving process.

2. When speaking before a group, I can project my voice and display enthusiasm.

3. While listening to a speaker, I am able to observe other people's behavior.

4. I am able to understand both spoken messages and non-verbal gestures.

5. I am able to ask open-ended questions which encourage others to share their ideas, feelings, or interests.

6. I can use effective openers to generate a lively group discussion.

7. I can focus a group's discussion by discriminating between significant and irrelevant information and comments.

8. I can restate or clarify another person's ideas.

9. I can take an unexpected incident or event and use it to teach a concept.

10. I am able to give constructive pointers to individuals in a non-judgmental manner.

11. When working with a group, I can share my own feelings about the topic under discussion.

12. I am able to elicit participation from most people in a group.

13. I have a sense of timing for pacing discussions and planning activities.

14. I can accept anger or criticism from a person or a group without becoming defensive.

15. I am able to help others comfortably display their emotions or relate their feelings.

16. I have a sense of humor and can laugh at myself.

critique the effectiveness of the speaker's delivery and the clarity of the breakdown.

Group Dynamics

Regular training sessions address the stages of a group's growth and development and identify the various types of questions that members may have at each stage. Leaders must be able to recognize the stage of their own team's development. They must create the conditions for further growth by making sure that the concerns of individual members are addressed. During training sessions, the quality assurance manager should discuss what actions leaders can take when certain members of a team hold unrealistic expectations in relation to the team's current stage of development.

While going through the regular training program, team leaders become familiar with the positive and negative roles that individuals may play in groups. Leader training sessions should focus on how leaders can recognize and encourage the positive roles played by individual members of the team, and how leaders can handle individuals who adopt negative roles that threaten the productivity of the team. In addition, team leaders should understand the positive roles that they themselves should perform while directing the efforts of a problem-solving team. These roles can be conveniently labeled as:

- The morale builder
- The conciliator
- The compromiser
- The expeditor
- The standard setter

The Morale Builder. The morale builder encourages individual contributors, creates a receptive atmosphere for new points of view, and provides positive reinforcement for team members. For example, a leader performs the role of a morale builder when he or she says, "That's an important fact to consider, Andrew."

The Conciliator. The conciliator recognizes differences of opinion, and tries to anticipate conflicts and relieve tensions by stressing common goals and emphasizing the cohesiveness of the team. A leader acts like a conciliator when he or she remarks, "Are we really as far apart as you seem to think, Matthew? After all, we do agree that . . . ."

The Compromiser. The compromiser reconciles conflicting views (even if it means modifying his or her own opinions), and seeks middle ground in the interests of team harmony. A leader performs the role of a compromiser when he or she comments, "I'll go halfway with you, Matthew, and agree that we . . . ."

The Expeditor. The expeditor helps the progress of the group by facilitating the contributions of others, especially when some members may be slowing up the problem-solving process. A leader acts in the role of an expeditor when he or she says, "Look, why don't we agree that each person can make a two-minute statement of his or her view on this point?"

The Standard Setter. The standard setter helps maintain a high level of group achievement in the quality of thinking and in solving the problems at hand. A leader acts like a standard setter when he or she says, "Can we really be satisfied with this analysis? I'm inclined to think that we've been too hasty."

The quality assurance manager should stress that these positive roles represent ways in which leaders can direct the efforts of a team without dominating the meetings, smothering the initiative of individual members, and stunting the growth and development of the team.

The quality assurance manager should define the role which he or she performs when attending team meetings. This role can be described as a process observer. As a process observer, the visiting quality assurance manager does not usually take an active part in a team's decision-making process. He or she sits on the sidelines, takes notes on the procedures, and may offer suggestions to the team near the end of a meeting or to the team leader after the meeting.

Cost/Benefit Analysis

Team leaders must receive appropriate training in completing the cost/benefit analysis forms which are used to translate the work of a team into the language that management understands best–dollars and cents. This training should focus on how to compute the annual cost of effects caused by a problem.

In order to effectively direct the early data-gathering and fact-finding efforts of a problem-solving team, a leader must be able to think ahead in terms of the facts and figures that will be needed when the team completes its cost/benefit analysis. For example, when a team identifies the effects which are caused by a problem, the team leader must structure the data-gathering and fact-finding activities of individual members according to useful categories. Two important categories in most cost/benefit analyses are wasted time and wasted materials.

During leader training sessions, the quality assurance manager should provide several examples which illustrate the calculations involved in computing wasted time and wasted materials. Quality assurance managers may wish to use the exhibits at the end of Chapter 7 as examples. Exhibits 7.17 through 7.22 are examples of cost of effect forms that compute the cost of wasted time. Exhibits 7.23, 7.24, and 7.25 are examples of cost of effect forms that compute the cost of wasted materials.

The more practical experience that leaders obtain in completing cost/benefit analyses, the better they will become at completing cost of effect forms. The quality assurance manager should coach and advise team leaders throughout the problem-solving process.

Management Proposals

After assisting the team in completing its cost/benefit analysis, the leader reviews the form with the department manager. After obtaining the department manager's approval of the solution, the leader helps the team to prepare for its presentation to management. Leader training in this area should present the following types of information:

- The kind of help which the leader can expect to receive from the department manager and from the quality assurance manager

- A recommended time limit for the presentation

- Procedures for evenly distributing presentation responsibilities among the members of the team

- The appropriate management representatives to invite to the presentation

- Types of visual aids (such as bar graphs, line graphs, pie charts, photographs, scale drawings, etc.) that may increase the effectiveness of the team's presentation

The quality assurance manager should provide a checklist for team leaders, identifying the procedures that must be followed before a team makes a solution proposal to management. Exhibit 9.4 presents a sample checklist.

Conducting Productive Meetings

Exhibit 9.5 presents a sample checklist to guide leaders in conducting productive team meetings. Quality assurance managers should develop similar checklists to guide leaders at their properties. The following sections examine practical techniques that will help leaders plan and conduct successful team meetings.

Prepare an Agenda for the Meeting

An agenda is a leader's plan for a successful team meeting. An agenda should list objectives and a time limit for completing each objective. The objectives should state the steps in the problem-solving process that the team should accomplish at the meeting. Time limits can be used to prevent members of the team from dwelling on insignificant issues.

Exhibit 9.4 Preparing for the Management Proposal: A Checklist

---

Management Proposal Checklist for Team Leaders

1. Has the quality assurance manager reviewed the cost/benefit analysis form?

2. Has the department manager reviewed the cost/benefit analysis form?

3. Have you reviewed key elements of the team's solution proposal with the ranking manager who will be attending the meeting?

4. Have you created an action plan for presenting information at the management proposal meeting?

5. Have team members collected the necessary information to be presented at the meeting?

6. Are presentation responsibilities evenly divided among the members of the team?

7. Does each member of the team know exactly what he or she will be expected to do at the presentation meeting?

8. Are visual aids to be used during the management presentation? If so, are they neat and free of misspelled words? Can they be read from the back of the meeting room?

9. Has the team rehearsed its presentation?

10. Have the appropriate managers been invited to the presentation meeting?

11. Are information packets ready for each manager who will be attending the presentation meeting?

When preparing an agenda, team leaders should carefully consider the sequence of activities that the group will perform in order to achieve the meeting's objectives. Generally, the first twenty minutes of a meeting are livelier and more creative than the last twenty minutes. Therefore, if items on the meeting's agenda require energy, bright ideas, and clear heads, it may be wise to list them at the top of the agenda. On the other hand, it is sometimes effective to save an important item until near the end of the meeting. This technique may keep members alert during the first half of the meeting as they gear up for the later activity.

Before distributing an agenda, the team leader should review the meeting plan with the department manager and the quality assurance manager. During these reviews, the team leader may receive tips and suggestions on how to conduct portions of the meeting, or the leader may receive advice that calls for changes in the meeting plan. After the

Exhibit 9.5 Checklist for Conducting Meetings

Before the Meeting

1. Schedule the meeting.
2. Write an agenda for the meeting.
3. Discuss the agenda with the department manager.
4. Discuss the agenda with the quality assurance manager.
5. Revise the agenda if necessary.
6. Distribute the agenda to members of the team before the meeting.
7. Remind members to confirm the time and place of the meeting if they have invited visitors.
8. Write the agenda on a flip chart sheet to be used at the meeting.
9. Review the problem-solving techniques to be used at the meeting.
10. Set up the meeting room and secure necessary supplies, such as flip charts, marking pens, visual aids, and handouts.

At the Meeting

1. Assign a member to record the minutes of the meeting.
2. Review the agenda listed on the flip chart.
3. Write the objective of the meeting on the flip chart.
4. Direct discussion and keep the team on track.
5. Use the appropriate problem-solving techniques to achieve the meeting's objective.
6. Ensure full participation of all members.
7. Summarize the meeting's accomplishments.
8. Ensure that members understand their assignments.
9. Provide an overview of events for the next meeting and remind members of any assignments that are due.
10. State the date and time of the next meeting.

After the Meeting

1. Record progress on the team's track record.
2. Distribute typed copies of the meeting minutes to team members, the department manager, the quality assurance manager, and the general manager.
3. Review the meeting's accomplishments with the department manager.
4. Review the meeting's accomplishments with the quality assurance manager.
5. Prepare for the next meeting.

agenda is finalized, the team leader is responsible for distributing copies to the team members and appropriate managers. Exhibit 9.6 presents a sample format for writing an agenda for team meetings.

Before the meeting, the leader should test the reactions of team members to items on the agenda. This enables the leader to find out

Exhibit 9.6 Sample Meeting Agenda

Meeting Agenda

Problem-Solving Team:
Meeting Number: Date:
Starting Time_____/Ending Time _____

Meeting Objectives	Time
Review: (by team leader)	
1.	
2.	
3.	
4.	
5.	
6.	
7.	
Summary: (by team leader)	

what to expect at the meeting. The leader should note any significant reactions of team members on his or her copy of the agenda. Before conducting the meeting, the leader should review the agenda and make any additional notes on it that will facilitate discussion at the meeting.

Rotate the Responsibility for Recording Minutes of the Meeting

The team leader is generally too busy conducting the meeting to record the meeting minutes. This responsibility can be rotated among the members of the team. Exhibit 9.7 presents a sample form that can be used to record the minutes.

The team name, meeting number, date, starting time and ending time, the names of the members present, and the names of late arrivals are essential data that must be included on every set of meeting minutes. The quality assurance manager uses this data to track the progress and success of the team.

The first item listed on the meeting's minutes should be the team leader's review of the previous meeting's accomplishments. Items listed as events are the discussions and decisions that took place at the meeting. Names of individuals do not appear in the events section. Events are feelings and decisions of the team; not of individuals.

Exhibit 9.7 Sample Format for Recording Meeting Minutes

Meeting Minutes

Problem-Solving Team:
Meeting Number: Date:
Starting Time_____/Ending Time _____

Members Present:

Late Arrivals:
Members Absent:
Non-Members Present:

Review: (by team leader)

Events:
      1.
      2.
      3.
      4.
      5.
      6.

Actions:
      1.
      2.
      3.
      4.
      5.
      6.

Summary: (by team leader)

Next Meeting Scheduled For: Date:
                                 Time:
                                 Room:

Actions are the steps that the team decided to take. Names of individual team members may be listed to indicate assignments and responsibilities.

After the meeting, the team leader is responsible for distributing typed copies of the minutes to each team member, the department manager, the quality assurance manager, and the general manager.

Keep the Meeting on Track

Team leaders should conduct the meetings by following the agendas which they have prepared. The only way to start a meeting on time is to start the meeting on time. If team leaders wait for everyone to get there, their meetings will always start late. By noting in the meeting's minutes those who arrive late or depart early, team leaders can encourage members to be on time and to participate in the entire meeting. The team leader and, if necessary, the department manager and the quality assurance manager should counsel team members who are repeated offenders. During the meeting, the team leader's primary responsibility is to see that all of the members of the team understand the issues and participate in the discussions.

In order to conduct a productive meeting, leaders must be able to control those members of the team who wish to do all the talking and monopolize the discussion. Some effective techniques by which to control these talkers are:

- Lean forward towards the person who is monopolizing the discussion.

- Fix your eyes on the speaker and raise your eyebrows.

- Nod quickly to indicate that the point is taken and understood.

- Interrupt the person and state, "We have to move on."

- Ask the person a closed question: a question requiring a simple "Yes" or "No" response.

Team leaders must also be able to draw out the silent members of the team. Silence may indicate a team member's hostility, shyness, lack of understanding, or indifference. Leaders must be able to determine the motive for the team member's silence. Some effective techniques by which to draw out the silent members are:

- Restate the purpose of the group.

- Ask for explanations or elaborations.

- Sit next to a quiet member and act like you're talking to him or her, one-on-one.

- Compliment normally quiet members each time they contribute to a discussion.

- Seek support from other members.

- Go around the table and ask each member what he or she thinks about the issue under discussion.

It is important for leaders to be sensitive to the body language of team members during the meeting. For example, when two team members look at each other and roll their eyes, the team leader needs to ask for their opinions.

Some team members may not feel confident enough to fully participate in the group. For example, young or new employees may be hesitant to express their opinions in the presence of older or more experienced employees. Leaders should ask new members for their opinions before asking for the opinions of the more experienced employees.

Side conversations at meetings can be disruptive to the progress of the group. Some effective techniques by which to control this situation are:

- Ask the members if they wish to share their conversation with the entire team.

- Discuss their behavior with them after the meeting.

- Casually stand behind them when they are whispering.

- Call on them by name and ask them an easy question or ask them to restate the last comment and give their opinion.

During team discussions, leaders should encourage a clash of ideas. This is the healthiest way to bring about a group decision. Examining the different sides of an issue generally produces the best solution. However, team leaders must moderate the discussion to ensure that the clash of ideas does not become a clash of personalities.

Sometimes, team leaders fail to stop a discussion soon enough. Leaders sometimes fail to realize that a group decision has been made and all are in agreement. Important points at which team leaders should stop the team's discussion include:

- When more facts are needed before a decision can be made

- When it is evident that expert opinions or technical advice must be obtained

- When team members need time to discuss an issue with their co-workers

- When events occurring outside the meeting will change or clarify the situation being discussed

- When there is not enough time to discuss the subject properly

- When it becomes clear that two or three team members can settle the issue outside the meeting and not waste other members' time

At the end of each meeting, the team leader should summarize what the group has accomplished, announce the time and place of the next meeting, and, if appropriate, remind team members of their assignments. As the team completes the various stages of the problem-solving process, the leader should update the team's track record. The track record provides the quality assurance manager with important data by which to measure the team's progress and to evaluate the success of the problem-solving process.

Measuring the Success of the Problem-Solving Process

As noted in Chapter 3, the overall progress of the quality assurance process can be measured by comparing the results of the original manager/supervisor surveys and employee surveys to the results of newly administered surveys. However, in order to maintain top management's constant support for the problem-solving process, the quality assurance manager should prepare periodic reports that summarize the progress of individual teams and measure the success of the problem-solving process. Training statistics, the minutes of team meetings, team track records, and completed cost/benefit analysis forms provide important data which can be summarized in informative reports to management. Significant training statistics include:

- The number of team leaders who have completed leader training
- The number of team members who have completed the regular training program
- The number of team leaders and team members currently being trained
- The number of new problem-solving teams created since the last report

Data gathered from the minutes of team meetings can be used to indicate the productivity of individual teams and provide statistics such as:

- The number of team meetings since the last report
- The number of times individuals have been absent from scheduled team meetings, which can also be expressed as a percentage.
- The number of times individuals have arrived late or have departed early from team meetings, which can also be expressed as a percentage.
- The number of meetings that started and ended on time, which can also be expressed as a percentage.
- The number of visits by managers, which can also be expressed as a percentage.

By reviewing the track records of teams, the quality assurance manager can evaluate the performance of problem-solving teams and measure the success of the problem-solving process. (Exhibit 7.5 in Chapter 7 shows a sample team track record.) If a team's track record shows that the team consistently fails to obtain management approval to implement solutions, one or more of the following conditions may exist:

- The team leader needs more training in directing the efforts of the group.

- The team leader and/or members of the team need more training in developing solutions.

- The team leader and/or members of the team need more training in completing a cost/benefit analysis.

- The quality assurance manager is not supplying sufficient guidance to the team leader.

- The team's department manager or supervisor or both are not supporting the problem-solving process.

- Top management is not fully supporting the problem-solving process.

If any of these conditions exists, the quality assurance manager must take the appropriate corrective actions.

Important statistics from team track records that can be summarized in reports for management include:

- The number of problems identified

- The number of solutions developed

- The number of cost/benefit analyses completed

- The number of management proposals presented

- The average length of time between the identification of a problem and the presentation of the solution to management

Reports to management can list these statistics for each problem-solving team and can also provide totals which summarize the progress of the entire problem-solving process.

The progress of individual teams and the success of the overall process can also be communicated to top management through a report that summarizes the anticipated annual savings of solutions which management has approved. These figures can be obtained from the completed cost/benefit analysis forms. A report can be prepared which lists figures for each problem-solving team and a total figure that measures the overall success of the problem-solving process.

Part IV
Performance Standards

10
Standards and Quality

Ask any manager of a professional baseball club what he must do to keep his job and he will probably answer, "Develop an excellent coaching staff and train the players on the team."

General managers of hospitality properties have much in common with the managers of professional baseball teams. Both types of managers keep their jobs by producing profits that provide owners with an adequate return on their investment. In baseball operations, the bottom line is directly related to paid attendance and revenue from media broadcasts; in hospitality operations, such as hotels and motels, the bottom line is geared to occupancy percentage. As paid attendances and media revenue consistently increase over time, the value of a baseball club goes up; as occupancy consistently increases over time, the hospitality business appreciates in value.

Baseball managers realize that their jobs depend on their ability to produce winning ball clubs. A team can play its home games in the most beautiful facility in the league and the back office can offer one special promotion after another; but, if the team constantly loses, fans will not pack the stadium, future revenue from media broadcasts will decrease, and the manager will be fired.

Successful managers in the hospitality industry also realize that their jobs depend on their ability to lead a winning team. A property can provide the finest of facilities and offer the most creative promotions; but, if guests receive inconsistent service from an obviously untrained and inconsiderate staff, they will not return and their negative word-of-mouth advertising will defeat even the best marketing efforts.

Obviously, the success of any manager is directly related to the success of the team. Baseball managers have developed sophisticated systems for measuring the performance of each player on their teams. Statistics are recorded and analyzed for almost every facet of the game. Managers use this information to determine the strengths and weaknesses of the players and to develop strategies for winning. The basic strategy used by most managers is twofold:

1. Build a foundation for success by structuring the team according to its strengths.

2. Build a winning team by developing weaknesses into strengths.

Effective managers build a foundation for the success of their organizations by structuring operations according to the strengths of individuals on the team. In baseball this generally means that a player with a high batting average bats first in the lineup, the player with the most home runs bats fourth, and so on. However, in order to develop weaknesses into strengths, baseball managers need much more specific information about their players than their batting averages and how many home runs they hit.

Assume that the manager of a baseball team judges a player's low batting average as a weakness that must be developed into a strength. The manager tells the batting coach to do something about it. In order to develop this weakness into a strength, the batting coach needs to know more about the player than simply his batting average. The fact that a player has a .157 batting average only tells the batting coach that, on the average, this player gets 157 hits for every 1,000 at-bats.

The batting coach needs to know if the player swings at low pitches or at high pitches; if the player always misses curve balls; if the batter panics when runners are on base; if the player hits better against right-handed pitchers than against left-handed pitchers. The coach also needs to check the player's batting stance, the weight of his bat, and so on. The coach examines this information and puts together an action plan by which the player can improve his performance. The improved performance creates a more successful team.

Performance statistics are just as important to managers of hospitality operations. In order to build a foundation for success, a manager needs to know the strengths of the players on the team. In addition, the manager needs to know the players' weaknesses. These weaknesses are opportunities by which to strengthen the organization and increase the bottom line. If weaknesses can be developed into strengths, the entire organization will benefit.

This chapter focuses on how top management can create a winning hospitality team by administering a process of developing, communicating, and managing performance standards. The chapter presents overviews of the management development program (discussed in Chapter 11) and the employee skills training program (discussed in Chapter 12), stresses the benefits of these programs, and points out barriers that must be overcome in order to build a winning team spirit.

Performance Standards

The primary objective of managing quality services is to ensure the consistent delivery of products and services to guests. The keys to consistency are the standards which a property develops, communicates, and manages.

Standards are required levels of performance. When performance standards are not properly developed, effectively communicated, and consistently managed, productivity suffers because people in the organization spend most of their time reacting to crises and putting out fires.

Standards are properly developed when the expectations of guests, management, and employees are coordinated into agreed-upon levels of performance for every position within the organization. The most important aspect of developing standards is gaining consensus on how jobs are to be performed.

Standards are communicated through management development and employee skills training programs. The most important aspect of communicating standards is top management's commitment to developing and training people in the organization.

Managing standards means ensuring conformity to the standards which have been developed on the basis of consensus and communicated through development and training programs. The most important aspect of managing standards is following up performance evaluations with specific coaching and retraining. This ensures that managers, supervisors, and employees throughout the organization consistently deliver quality services that conform to agreed-upon standards.

Management Development

An effective in-house management development program must focus on the specific performance standards for managers in the organization. Chapter 11 outlines an effective management development process which can be adapted to the unique needs and requirements of any hospitality business. The process begins with top management identifying fundamental management skills that all managers within the organization are expected to possess. These skills may include:

- Planning
- Organizing
- Coordinating
- Staffing
- Directing
- Controlling
- Evaluating

Defining and communicating what these skills involve to individual managers establishes a framework within which management development can take place.

After top management establishes the framework, individual managers write job breakdowns. They accomplish this by first preparing job lists which identify tasks that are specific to their positions. The managers then meet with their immediate supervisors, and together they categorize each task under *one* management skill area. After reaching a consensus, managers break down each task on their job lists. The breakdown specifies in simple, step-by-step form how each task should be performed. The end result is a single job breakdown for each manager in the organization. The job breakdown lists management skills, the tasks that correspond to each management skill, and a breakdown of each task.

The job breakdowns are used to conduct quarterly or monthly performance evaluations. The results of these evaluations indicate the strengths and weaknesses of each manager in the organization. Strengths form the basis for success; weaknesses indicate opportunities for creating a winning management team. The results of performance evaluations allow individual managers (and their immediate supervisors) to focus on developing specific management skills and allow top management to check that necessary managerial tasks are carried out correctly.

Employee Skills Training

An effective skills training program must focus on the specific performance standards for skilled positions in the organization. Chapter 12 outlines an effective skills training program which can be adapted to the unique needs and requirements of any hospitality business.

The process begins with department standards groups. These groups are responsible for preparing job breakdowns for all the skilled positions within their departments. Members of these groups should include:

- An organizer designated by top management
- The department manager (or supervisor)
- Several experienced employees of the department

Top management should set up the first standards groups in those departments with the greatest need for job breakdowns. These are the departments with the greatest number of service problems. Service problems generally indicate inadequate or disorganized training which results from a lack of well-defined performance standards. In less than a month, the concentrated effort of a standards group can produce a complete set of performance standards and training materials for a very complex department. In a smaller, less complicated operation, job breakdowns can be completed in less than a week.

Once standards have been developed and consensus reached, managers and supervisors communicate the standards to the employees within their departments. Therefore, managers and supervisors need special training as "trainers" so they will be able to effectively communicate the job tasks and standards. Chapter 12 presents a five-step training method for conducting effective training sessions.

It is important for employees to know the standards that will be used to measure their performance on the job. Therefore, it is important to break down the tasks and document those standards. A performance standard must be observable and measurable. A manager or supervisor conducting a quarterly performance evaluation should be able to simply check a box either in a "Yes" or "No" column: "Yes, the employee performed the task correctly," or "No, the employee failed to conform to the performance standard."

Benefits of Management Development and Skills Training

Management development and skills training programs benefit the guests, managers, supervisors, and employees. An organization that develops and trains its staff is constantly growing. There is excitement about the personal growth of everyone involved, and that excitement raises morale and motivates everyone to succeed in accomplishing the organization's objectives. Management development and skills training programs may reduce labor costs by increasing productivity and decreasing turnover. The following sections focus on some of the more important benefits of management development and skills training.

Organizational Stability. Managers, supervisors, and employees naturally become frustrated when they have difficulty performing their jobs. Without development or training programs, frustrations on the job increase and create stress which may threaten the stability of the organization.

Employees experiencing stress may exhibit poor attitudes toward management and co-workers. They may become careless, produce sloppy work, cause high breakage, and flagrantly violate company rules. As frustration rises, tardiness and absenteeism increase. This creates scheduling problems, and staffing duties begin to take up more and more of each manager's time. Soon, the managers become just as frustrated as the employees.

If the situation is not corrected, some managers and employees may resign or their employment may even be terminated. Those who remain in the organization build defenses against their frustrations on the job. These people become the "trainers" of the new employees entering the organization. The new employees learn not so much how to perform their jobs, but how to put up with the frustrations that come with their jobs.

Management development and employee skills training programs can put an end to this cycle of frustration, stress, and high turnover. As managers and supervisors develop and as employees receive training, the entire organization becomes more productive. Managers, supervisors, and employees tend to remain with organizations when they feel they are learning and growing. Their competence builds confidence in themselves and in the organization.

Increased Revenue through Guest Satisfaction. A competent staff produces satisfied guests; satisfied guests often mean repeat business and increased revenue. Guests recognize when a staff is well trained. They will comment to friends and associates about the competence of a trained staff, and few marketing plans can match the power of this word-of-mouth advertising. Guests also recognize untrained personnel. They *correctly* judge the competence of management by the performance of the staff. From the guest's point of view, employees are the "ambassadors" for the hospitality operation; they represent the organization and all that it stands for and is trying to accomplish. Therefore, employee attitudes and performance are critical to the success of a hospitality property. It is ironic that newly hired employees who occupy high guest-contact positions (such as housekeeping room attendants, front desk agents, and dining room servers) are often put on the job with minimal training.

Efficiency. When every employee knows his or her job and performs it efficiently, managers will find that they have more time for planning and other management responsibilities. If a staff is incompetent, much of the manager's time will be spent in close, direct supervision and in checking the work performed by employees. When employees have been trained to function as a skilled team, they will monitor their own performance and will accomplish their work, freeing managers for other activities.

Improved Relationships. When top management allocates the necessary funds and provides the appropriate resources for effective management development and employee skills training programs, the organization makes a serious investment in its people. Most managers, supervisors, and employees appreciate the opportunity to grow, to develop, and to achieve greater satisfaction in their work. This appreciation is the basis for improved management-employee relationships in which both strive toward common performance goals, and each benefits from the process.

Professionalism and Job Advancement. Development and training fosters professional pride. When managers, supervisors, and employees visit other hospitality properties on their days off and return to work talking about the obvious lack of training in those establishments, it shows appreciation for the professionalism behind their own property's performance standards. When employees within the organization can see the operation as guests see it, they realize that a trained staff does make a difference.

Some employees may be motivated by an opportunity for job advancement. Hospitality managers need to offer opportunities for advancement and show employees how training will help prepare them for these promotions. When upward advancement is limited because of the size of the operation, managers can show employees how they can advance laterally by cross-training. Generally, the more each employee knows how to do, the more productive the entire staff will be.

Training: Myths and Barriers

Management development and employee skills training programs help to ensure that managers, supervisors, and employees consistently carry out their jobs according to the agreed-upon performance standards. This is one of top management's most important responsibilities. When standards are not effectively communicated, the result is the inconsistent delivery of products and services to guests. This inconsistency leads to:

- Dissatisfied guests
- Low employee morale
- High employee turnover
- Loss of time and revenue
- High stress work situations
- Management "burn-out"

Failure to effectively communicate standards feeds the costly cycle of reactive management practices. In order to break out of this cycle, management must reject the common myths about training which pose barriers to effective management development and employee skills training programs.

Myths about training are barriers to the effective communication of performance standards. Many of these barriers are no more than misconceptions that are passed along to avoid facing the responsibility for training. These myths must be dispelled or managers and supervisors may not accept training for themselves or for their employees. The sections which follow examine some of the more common myths about training in the hospitality industry.

"Training Is Easy: Anybody Can Do It." A common myth about training is that it is so simple that no preparation is required. Managers or supervisors who have been promoted from the same job for which they are now training others may feel that they know "everything" about the job and that they can teach others spontaneously or as the need arises. This attitude produces a hit-and-miss training program whose results are almost always unsatisfactory. Training requires logical organization to be effective. The process of analyzing the tasks and skills of a position and arranging the training in a logical sequence (beginning with the simple and progressing to the more difficult) demands careful thought and preparation.

"Training Doesn't Pay." Some managers argue that it doesn't pay to train. They contend that trained employees are more difficult to manage because (a) they expect higher wages than the operation can afford, (b) they think they know more than management, and (c) they will be recruited away by competitors, thus increasing turnover. There are, no doubt, instances in which these and related problems have occurred, but they do not have to occur.

The important point to consider here is that decisions to train or not to train must be based on objective reasoning rather than on subjective attitudes and "second-hand" experiences. Training programs should be designed as a response to specific needs, not as a reaction to problems.

"Human Resources Takes Care of Training." Another mistaken belief is that training is not the responsibility of department managers. Some department managers try to avoid their training responsibilities with the attitude: "Isn't that why we have a human resources department?" The human resources department should assist managers in preparing to train. However, only in rare instances should training be conducted by representatives from the human resources department. Employees become loyal to those who train them. This loyalty is best directed toward their immediate supervisors. Therefore, department managers, not representatives from the human resources department, should be responsible for implementing training programs for employees.

"Experienced Workers Don't Need Training." Another misconception is that training will not be necessary if experienced applicants are hired. To some extent, this is true. There are basic similarities among segments of the hospitality industry. But there are just as many, if not more, differences. If management hires experienced applicants and does not conduct any training, job performance will be inconsistent.

Also, all experience is not necessarily good experience. Some experienced applicants may have been poorly trained and may have developed improper work habits. Retraining is often needed to overcome these poor habits.

Many managers are also aware that it is difficult to evaluate experience. The applicant with ten years of experience may in reality have "one year of experience repeated ten times." It is also very difficult to evaluate the extent to which prior experience will carry over to a new job.

"Training Is a Waste of Time." Some managers do not train because their egos get in the way. They think that their own skills are perfect, that no one will ever meet their standards of excellence, and that any attempt at training is a waste of their time. Or, they feel threatened that an employee will develop to a level of performance that surpasses their own.

Some managers may cling to this myth about training because, as they advanced through the ranks to management positions, they had to overcome the lack of training or the inadequate training which they received as line employees. Chances are that whatever "training" they did receive was poorly planned, poorly presented, and never followed up. It is unlikely that managers of this sort will be among those who survive and succeed unless their attitudes change and they come to the following realizations:

1. Employees must learn how to perform satisfactorily on the job. While not all employees can learn at the same rate, and not all employees can master the skills at the same level, all employees can learn.

2. Managers have a responsibility to provide employees with as many opportunities to learn as possible.

3. There will always be room for both managers and employees to improve their skills.

Lack of Commitment from Top Management. Top management is perhaps the greatest obstacle to effective management development and employee skills training programs in the hospitality industry. Many hospitality organizations, large and small, do not budget enough funds for development and training and only give "lip service" to its importance. Whenever profits decline, the few dollars that are allocated for development and training are usually among the first amounts cut from the budget. Unfortunately, top executives in many hospitality organizations are not convinced that development and training programs are cost-effective investments.

In some cases, the lack of top management commitment may arise because of past training experiences which were poorly planned and executed. In the past, top management emphasized the amount of time in training rather than the mastery of skills. Training was considered effective when it got the new manager or employee "on the floor" quickly. The new person was given "the basics" and was expected to pick up the rest through trial and error on the job.

Today, there is stiff competition among hospitality businesses, and guests are no longer willing to put up with the trials and errors of an untrained staff. Top management cannot afford to ignore development and training needs. Investment in people does not have to be risky. When management development and employee skills training programs are designed to achieve performance-based results, they can be effective and provide top management with a significant return on its investment.

Lack of Know-How. Another hindrance to training is lack of know-how within many hospitality organizations. Every year, more people without prior experience or training enter the hospitality industry as investors, owners, and operators. These individuals have, in many cases, experienced great success because of the overall growth of the industry; however, they often have great difficulty in establishing realistic performance standards for positions within their operations. Individuals with formal training and experience in the hospitality industry often join these organizations and help fill this void. Lack of know-how can, of course, result in a lack of standards and low productivity within an organization.

Lack of Resources. Development and training may also be hindered by an apparent lack of resources. Organizations that have clear standards generally develop good company manuals and operating procedures. These become the basis for designing training programs. On the other hand, organizations that lack management know-how often have no manuals or operating procedures. If managers cannot agree on how the jobs should ideally be performed, management will likely avoid writing the procedures. In their absence, training, when attempted, often becomes a futile effort.

There are many good training resources available to managers interested in developing and implementing training activities. These materials can be purchased and adapted for use within the organization. As time passes, experience and trial and error will refine the adaptations and provide the basis for tailor-made manuals and other company materials. In the meantime, training can be done quite effectively with generalized resources. In reality, then, there is no lack of resources; there is only a lack of willingness to use the many resources that exist.

Employee Resistance to Training. Employees may resist training, making it difficult for them to attain performance levels that meet standards. This is likely to happen when training is poorly presented. Likewise, when trainees are embarrassed, feel ridiculed, or fear the loss of jobs (when, for example, their post-training performance is judged unsatisfactory), they may resist training.

Employees are usually adults, and they expect to be treated as adults. Adults require clear logic and some self-direction in order to be receptive to learning. It is important to develop training techniques that take adult needs into consideration. Training that is designed to consider the employees' needs along with those of management is likely to be readily accepted and welcomed.

Disorganization. Finally, training will not be fully effective if it is poorly organized. When inadequate planning leads to operating problems and management institutes a "crash" training effort, such attempts are frequently too little and too late. Employees recognize the disorganization; they may lose interest and are not likely to take the training seriously. Training, to be fully effective, must be planned and executed on a systematic basis. This includes beginning training for new employees, continuing training for existing employees, and regular coaching for all employees.

Building a Team Spirit

Some professional baseball teams are overloaded with talented, expensive superstars. However, these teams rarely win their divisions. They are defeated by teams that have less talent but more spirit. A team's winning spirit takes its shape from the highest levels of the organization—from the philosophy of the owners and top managers. Team spirit grows best in an environment that is fair. Everyone makes mistakes, but no one needs to fail. When top management treats mistakes as opportunities for learning, trust develops throughout the organization.

It's also fair to be paid according to what you accomplish. When performance evaluations are conducted on the basis of job breakdowns, top management has the opportunity to pay managers, supervisors, and employees according to the degree to which they conform to established standards. If annual raises are tied to batting averages, employees who perform better are paid more than those who do not perform as well.

For example, a morning front office agent who averages 95% conformity to standards on a year's worth of performance evaluations may receive 95% of the raise for which he or she is eligible. Another front office agent who averages 87% may receive 87% of the raise for which he or she is eligible. This practice can create an environment of fairness, especially if employees are consistently retrained in the areas where their performance is weak. Pay according to skill provides an incentive to win.

The important point about team spirit is that standards alone do not ensure quality services; only the people within the organization can ensure the consistent delivery of products and services to guests. Standards make consistency possible for an organization, but only the people within the organization can make quality a reality by working together to develop, communicate, and manage standards.

This kind of cooperation becomes possible only when everyone within an organization absorbs a common language, a common set of values, and a common set of goals. Management development and employee skills training programs provide a common language of quality—consistency; a common set of values—performance standards; and a common set of goals—100% conformity to standards.

11
Management Development

Most hospitality organizations provide some kind of entry-level training for new managers. However, many of these programs only address essential administrative responsibilities for which all managers within the organization are held accountable. Some properties "develop managers" by sending them to seminars which exploit the latest management fads. In these cases, management development is a hit-or-miss affair rather than a planned sequence of ongoing activities that progressively refines crucial management skills.

This chapter outlines an effective management development process which can be adapted to the unique needs and requirements of any hospitality business. The process begins with top management identifying fundamental management skills which all managers within the organization are expected to possess. Communicating this information to individual managers establishes a framework within which management development can take place.

After top management establishes the framework, individual managers write job breakdowns for their positions within the organization. They accomplish this by first preparing job lists which identify tasks that are specific to their positions. The managers then meet with their immediate supervisors, and together they categorize each task under *one* management skill area. After reaching a consensus, managers break down each task on their job lists. The breakdown specifies in a simple, step-by-step form, how each task should be performed. The end result is a single job breakdown for each manager in the organization which lists management skills, the tasks which correspond to each management skill, and a breakdown of each task. The job breakdowns are used to conduct quarterly or monthly performance evaluations. The results of these evaluations form the basis for an effective management development system.

This chapter begins by proposing a practical definition of management and suggesting seven fundamental management skills which can apply to the management of any hospitality business. Subsequent sections of the chapter focus on how to develop job breakdowns for management positions, how to use the job breakdowns as the basis for evaluating the performance of managers, and how to use the results of performance evaluations as the basis for implementing a management development system.

Identifying Fundamental Management Skills

Before identifying fundamental management skills which all managers within an organization will be expected to possess, top management should agree on a basic definition of management. This may not be an easy task, because there are probably as many definitions of management as there are books on the subject. The important point to keep in mind is that the definition should be brief, practical, and apply to all management positions within the organization.

In essence, management is using what you've got to do what you have to do. A manager uses available resources to attain the organization's objectives. Resources available to managers in the hospitality industry include: people, money, time, work methods, materials, energy, and equipment. All of these resources are in limited supply. Most hospitality managers will readily admit that they rarely have all the people, money, time, and other resources that they would like to work with. Therefore, an important part of a manager's job is to determine how best to use the limited resources available to attain the organization's objectives.

Management skills are specific abilities that enable a manager to carry out the responsibilities of his or her position. Although specific management tasks vary from one management position to another, the same fundamental management skills are used. Examples of these management skills, in the approximate order in which they are used, are:

- Planning
- Organizing
- Coordinating
- Staffing
- Directing
- Controlling
- Evaluating

Exhibit 11.1 presents an overview of the management process and shows how each management skill is used in running a business. Top

Exhibit 11.1 Overview of the Management Process

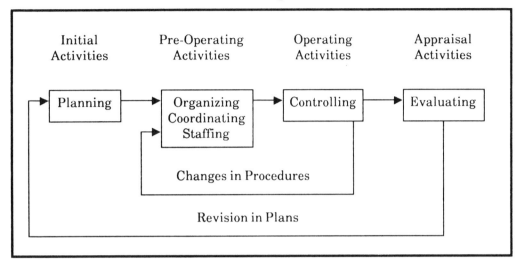

management must initially plan what the organization is to accomplish by defining its objectives. The desire to attain these objectives leads to organizing, coordinating, and staffing activities. Once personnel are selected, management can develop and implement control systems. It is as part of the control process that management typically learns if plans and pre-operating activities have succeeded or failed. An analysis of actual results may lead to changes in organizing, coordinating, or staffing procedures. Finally, management must evaluate the extent to which the objectives of the organization have been attained. As a result of evaluating all planning and operating activities, management may find that revisions to the organization's plans or objectives are needed.

The seven management skills are closely interrelated. The following sections briefly explain how each of these management skills is used in the process of managing a hospitality business. A more complete discussion of management functions can be found in Jack D. Ninemeier's *Supervision in the Hospitality Industry*, published by the Educational Institute.

Planning

Planning is probably the most important management skill that is used in running any type of business. Without competent planning, every day is filled with one crisis after another and productivity is low. The planning process begins with top management determining broad organizational objectives that will help managers focus on what the property is trying to accomplish. Organizational objectives state what the owners and top management officials of the operation wish to accomplish. These objectives indicate why the hospitality business exists and what it is trying to do. Without this kind of direction and focus, managers can easily become sidetracked, getting involved with tasks which are unimportant or unrelated to accomplishing the organization's objectives.

Planning continues with the formulation of operating objectives which become the specific responsibilities of department managers. For example, top management may plan an operating budget that specifies economic goals for the budget period. Managers of revenue-producing departments must then plan departmental budgets that will contribute to the economic goals of the property.

Managing daily department activities requires more specific types of plans. For example, personnel and equipment schedules must be developed. Plans must also be generated for special events, new training programs, and other activities.

The following principles of management indicate the importance of planning as a management skill:

- Planning should start at the top of the organization.

- Planning should be a formal process. It should be done as an integral part of every manager's job, not simply when time permits.

- Resources must be allocated for the planning task. That is, managers must be given the time to plan.

- Objectives must be established before plans can be developed; plans are then developed to attain the objectives.

- Long-range, strategic planning is just as important as short-range, daily planning activities.

- Planning should be done at the appropriate organizational level. For example, top management should not plan the employee schedules for operating departments. On the other hand, only top management can develop the strategic, long-range plans necessary for the strength and growth of the property.

- All pertinent information should be available for consideration at the time plans are developed. This means that department managers and supervisors should have available all information that concerns their areas of responsibility.

- Supervisors should be allowed to contribute to plans that affect their work. Likewise, employees should be allowed input to plans that affect their jobs.

- Planning should be flexible; it should recognize that situations change and that contingency plans must be considered.

- Plans must be implemented. While this is obvious, many managers fail to understand that, at the appropriate time, they must act with the best plan available.

Organizing

Organizing, as a management skill, is the ability to establish the flow of authority and communication between levels of the organization or between levels within a department. Organizing also specifies relationships between positions. An organization chart shows each position and how it relates to the others.

Using organizational objectives as a guide, managers exercise their organizing skill when they divide work in order to accomplish department goals. A manager must be able to divide up the work that is to be performed among members of his or her staff so that everyone gets a fair assignment and all work can be finished on time. Organizing includes determining in what order tasks are to be performed and when groups of tasks should be completed.

The following principles of management indicate the importance of organizing as a management skill:

- Authority should flow in an unbroken line from the top to the bottom of the organization. Someone, somewhere in the organization, must be able to make a decision. Likewise, someone must be held accountable for decisions which have been made and for actions which have been taken.

- Each employee should have only one immediate supervisor.

- Relationships between departments in the organization must be considered; what affects one department is likely to affect another.

- Similar activities should be grouped together to structure departments within the property and the work performed within each department.

- Similar tasks should be grouped together to structure positions within departments (a position is a group of tasks to be performed by one person; it is also referred to as a job).

- Organizational structure evolves through the life of a business. Changes in the management staff or changes in management positions may generate changes in the overall organizational structure. Organization charts and related documents must keep up with these changes.

Coordinating

The management skill of coordinating involves the ability to use various types and amounts of resources to attain the organization's objectives. A manager must be able to coordinate the efforts of many individuals who are all doing different sets of tasks within the same time frame.

Coordinating is much more than just standing around keeping an eye on the staff, and hoping that nothing goes wrong. A manager's ability to coordinate is closely related to other management skills, such as planning and organizing. It involves planning the overall work of the group and assigning duties so that the work is performed efficiently, effectively, and on time.

The following principles of management indicate the importance of coordinating as a management skill:

- Channels of communication must flow freely up and down the organizational structure. Top management must be able to communicate with lower-level staff members; conversely, lower-level staff members must be able to communicate with top management.

- Procedures for interdepartmental cooperation must be practiced in order to achieve harmonious working relationships.

- Effective managers interact with both formal and informal employee groups.

- Managers must have the authority (power) to enforce assignments, commands, and decisions. This authority should be delegated as necessary by top management.

- Responsibility (the need to account to someone for the use of formal power) cannot be delegated. For example, a department manager is responsible for aspects of the department's operating budget and cannot blame the staff if certain budget goals are not met.

- Generally, authority should be delegated to the lowest possible point in the organization. Staff members appreciate the opportunity to exercise the authority necessary to improve job performance.

Staffing

The management skill of staffing involves the ability to recruit applicants and select those best qualified for positions to be filled. Staffing also involves scheduling employees. Most hospitality operations employ some type of staffing guidelines. These guidelines are usually based on formulas which are used to calculate the number of skilled employees required to meet guest and operational needs under specified conditions. However, the management skill of staffing goes beyond simply mastering the mathematical system used for preparing base and variable staffing guides. Staffing is closely related to the other management skills of planning, organizing, and coordinating.

The following principles of management indicate the importance of staffing as a management skill:

- Jobs must be defined in terms of the specific tasks that must be performed. Personal qualities needed to adequately perform specific tasks must also be considered.

- All possible sources of job applicants should be considered.

- Screening devices should be used to assess applicants for positions. For example, selection tests might be used to assess performance and abilities of experienced applicants. Preliminary interviews and reference checks provide additional examples of screening devices.

- Employee orientation and training programs should be developed and implemented.

- Use of creative staffing patterns helps retain underemployed staff members. Ongoing employee development programs at all organizational levels are important.

- Decisions about transfers, promotions, and demotions are part of the staffing process.

Directing

For a department manager, the management skill of directing involves the ability to oversee, motivate, train, evaluate, and discipline people who work in the department.

Directing is a complicated management skill which is exercised in a wide variety of situations, and is closely related to other management skills such as organizing, coordinating, and staffing. For example, in order to be able to direct the work of other people, a manager must first be able to analyze the work that must be done, arrange the tasks in a logical order, and take into consideration the environment in which the tasks are to be performed. There are all kinds of distractions that can cause employees difficulty in carrying out assignments. As these hindrances arise, an effective manager directs the flow of activity around them so that objectives are accomplished on time.

The following principles of management indicate the importance of directing as a management skill:

- Leadership styles should vary according to employee needs. The attitudes of management affect the attitudes and subsequent performance of employees.

- Staff members must know what they are expected to do. Orders that are given should be reasonable, understood by employees, and compatible with the tasks to be performed.

- It is important to gain the cooperation of the people who are managed; managers should treat employees fairly and be honest with them.

- Managers should show their appreciation to employees who perform their jobs effectively.

- Ideas should be solicited from employees and, whenever possible, used. Organizational goals are easier to attain when they mesh with goals of staff members.

- Techniques of worker motivation can have positive results; the motivation process must be productive, comprehensive, and flexible.

Controlling

The management skill of controlling is the ability to see that operating procedures stay on the course of attaining the organization's objectives. Every hospitality operation has a system of internal controls for protecting the assets of the business. However, internal control systems work only when managers believe in their importance and follow the established procedures for their use.

The control process ensures that the actual results of operations closely match planned results. The following principles of management indicate the importance of controlling as a management skill:

- A manager must know how the operation is doing: whether, and to what extent, it is meeting its goals.

- Control procedures can determine whether delegated tasks are being carried out correctly.

- Through control procedures, managers can assess the effect of changes necessitated by the economy, market, and/or reactions to competition.

- Control procedures can identify problems early so they can be resolved before they turn into bigger problems.

- Control procedures can determine where problems are occurring.

- Control procedures help identify mistakes and lead to actions to correct these mistakes.

Evaluating

The management skill of evaluating is the ability to determine the extent to which organizational objectives are, in fact, attained. This

Exhibit 11.2 Developing Management Job Breakdowns

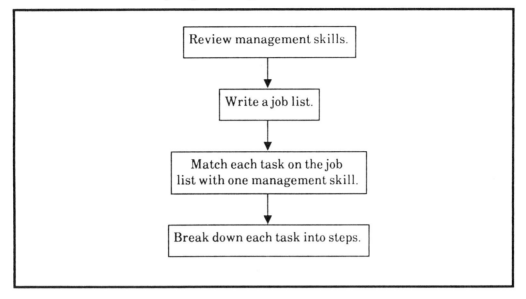

task is frequently overlooked in many properties, or it is done in a haphazard fashion. Evaluating is also the skill of reviewing organizational goals and providing input to the restatement of goals for future periods. The following principles of management indicate the importance of evaluating as a management skill:

- Evaluation helps managers determine how best to allocate resources in order to accomplish the organization's objectives.

- Evaluation tracks the effectiveness of training programs and helps to ensure that employees perform their jobs according to the property's standards.

- Evaluation helps to establish new and revised organizational objectives.

- Evaluation must be done on a timely basis, and it must be done objectively. Evaluation must be assigned a priority in the management of the operation; it cannot be left to do whenever there is time.

Developing Job Breakdowns for Management Positions

After defining management skills, the next step is to develop job breakdowns for all management positions in the organization. Exhibit 11.2 outlines the process of developing management job breakdowns.

The process begins with individual managers preparing job lists which identify tasks that are specific to their positions within the organization.

The tasks on a manager's job list should reflect the total job responsibility of the position. However, the list should *not* be a detailed breakdown of the steps that make up each task. The job list should simply state what the manager must be able to do in order to perform the job. Exhibit 11.3 shows a partial job list for a banquet manager's position.

After writing job lists, individual managers meet with their immediate supervisors, and together they categorize each task under *one* management skill area. Agreement between each manager and his or her immediate supervisor is essential, because the management skills are so closely interrelated that there is rarely an absolute correspondence between a particular management skill and a specific manager's task.

For example, preparing work schedules for employees seems to be a task that calls for skill in staffing. However, a closer look at what the task involves shows that there is a great deal of planning, organizing, coordinating, controlling, and even evaluating that must go into preparing practical and effective work schedules.

In the process of reaching consensus, each manager's job list may be revised. For example, administrative responsibilities may be added to the job list and placed under appropriate management skill categories. Every manager has paperwork to complete. The ability to complete all required administrative functions and accompanying paperwork (or computerized recordkeeping) accurately and on time is essential to the performance of every manager.

The next step is for individual managers to specify how each task on their job lists should be performed. The breakdowns use simple, step-by-step logic to specify how the manager is expected to perform each task. Exhibit 11.4 presents a sample job breakdown for the position of banquet manager. This sample form can be adapted to meet the needs and requirements of individual properties. Note that the job breakdown begins by listing reporting responsibilities, supervisory duties, and interdepartmental relationships. The job breakdown then categorizes the manager's tasks (and the breakdown of each task) under the appropriate management skill areas. The evaluation columns complete the job breakdown form.

Evaluating the Performance of Managers

The job breakdowns are used to evaluate the performance of managers. A manager meets with his or her immediate supervisor, and together they rate the manager's performance of each step of each task

Exhibit 11.3 Partial Job List for a Banquet Manager's Position

---

Date: xx/xx/xx

JOB LIST

Position: Banquet Manager

Tasks: Manager must be able to:

1. Plan goals for the department.

2. Prepare weekly work schedules for management and supervisors.

3. Prepare and coordinate work schedules for management and department employees.

4. Prepare an organization chart for the department.

5. Organize and conduct department meetings.

6. Establish communication within the banquet department and between other departments.

7. Interview and hire the best qualified applicants for available positions.

8. Staff according to budget projections.

9. Train and coach staff.

10. Coordinate individual and group goals to achieve the department's objectives.

11. Arrange continuing education for department staff.

12. Direct development of supervisors and employees.

13. Maintain key control.

14. Project labor needs from forecasts.

15. Evaluate job performance of supervisors and employees.

---

listed on the job breakdown. The sample job breakdown in Exhibit 11.4 uses a point value system for rating performance: three points indicate outstanding performance, two points indicate that the manager has met necessary requirements, and one point signals those areas in which the manager needs to improve. The manager receives a performance rating

Exhibit 11.4 Sample Job Breakdown: Banquet Manager

Position:	Banquet Manager
Name:	
Reports to:	Food and Beverage Director
Supervises:	Assistant Banquet Managers, Convention Floor Coordinator, Banquet Beverage Supervisor, Banquet Captains, Coffee Break Managers
Works with:	All Departments

	Outstanding (3 Points)	Meets Necessary Requirements (2 Points)	Needs Improvement (1 Point)

I. PLANNING

A. Complete administrative responsibilities.

1.	Plan to meet with team leader after each QA meeting.	2
2.	Plan performance evaluations and follow-up coaching on a monthly basis.	3
3.	Plan purchases requiring purchase orders in advance of when supplies are needed to ensure sufficient time for pricing and approval.	1
4.	Schedule one day each week to review and approve purchase orders at the accounting office.	1
5.	Plan to meet with supervisors and managers to review employee schedules. These schedules are to be turned into the payroll department on time.	3
6.	Plan time to review and approve time cards at the end of each pay period.	2

B. Plan department goals.

1.	Meet with management and supervisors.	2
2.	Brainstorm goals and set priorities.	2
3.	Plan programs to increase morale and ongoing motivation for team spirit.	2
4.	Communicate ongoing goals for upgrades in service.	1
5.	Plan methods and procedures for training.	1
6.	Update and revise job breakdowns as necessary.	1
7.	Establish policy and procedure manual.	1

C. Prepare work schedules for managers and supervisors.

1.	Plan work schedules according to weekly forecasts.	3
2.	Plan supervisor work schedules according to line employee work schedules.	3

Exhibit 11.4 Continued

D. Prepare and coordinate vacation schedules for banquet staff.

    1. Establish feasible vacation times. __1__

    2. Review vacation requests and, whenever possible, approve them. __1__

    3. Plan coverage for those with approved vacation times. __1__

E. Plan for rental or requisition of special equipment requested for banquet functions.

    1. Review in advance banquet equipment orders for details. __3__

    2. Confirm details with banquet coordinators. __2__

    3. Prepare/submit required purchase orders. __1__

    4. Consult/advise executive steward. __1__

F. Plan review of equipment pars and needs.

    1. Consult with executive steward. __1__

    2. Communicate needs for purchases. __1__

G. Plan for staffing needs.

    1. Assess needs for staffing levels. __3__

    2. Plan/prepare staff requisitions for human resources department. __3__

    3. Confer with human resources director for employment advertisements. __2__

H. Plan for department meetings.

    1. Plan weekly management meetings. __1__

    2. Plan monthly staff meeting. __2__

I. Plan to attend required meetings.

    1. Attend biweekly menu reading meetings. __2__

    2. Attend weekly F&B meetings. __2__

    3. Attend weekly meetings with executive steward and banquet chef. __1__

    4. Attend scheduled management training classes. __1__

    5. Attend scheduled pre-convention meetings to establish contact with meeting planner and review upcoming events. __3__

J. Plan cleaning/maintenance schedule.

    1. Educate staff on proper procedures for handling equipment. __2__

    2. Conduct regular inspections with department heads. __1__

    3. Determine frequency of cleaning needs. __2__

    4. Establish preventive maintenance program. __1__

Exhibit 11.4 Continued

    K. Plan and monitor labor/revenue budget.

        1. Establish labor projection from monthly forecast and set up daily monitoring form.   <u>2</u>
        2. Use computer printouts to calculate labor costs.   <u>2</u>
        3. Keep informed of revenue and labor percentages.   <u>2</u>
        4. Adjust staffing in response to revenue and guests' needs.   <u>3</u>

    L. Plan time to evaluate accounting reports.

        1. Use reports to identify trends.   <u>1</u>
        2. Use reports to monitor costs.   <u>2</u>
        3. Use reports to monitor areas that appear out of line.   <u>2</u>

II. Organizing

    A. Complete administrative responsibilities.

        1. Set times to meet with team leader after each QA meeting.   <u>2</u>
        2. Set times to conduct employee performance evaluations with trainer.   <u>2</u>
        3. Set up and maintain personnel files for each member of the banquet staff.   <u>2</u>
        4. Establish a file for tracking department purchase orders by month and account code.   <u>1</u>

    B. Prepare an organization chart for the department.

        1. Support the organization chart with job breakdowns.   <u>2</u>
        2. Work with the QA office.   <u>2</u>
        3. Work with department heads to monitor and revise job breakdowns and organization chart as necessary.   <u>1</u>

    C. Organize and conduct department meetings.

        1. Review department goals.   <u>2</u>
        2. Review upcoming business.   <u>2</u>
        3. Review notes from pertinent meetings with other departments.   <u>2</u>
        4. Update staff on procedures.   <u>2</u>
        5. Communicate concerns: guest feedback.   <u>1</u>
        6. Obtain feedback from staff.   <u>2</u>

    D. Organize special projects.   <u>2</u>

    E. Establish communication between departments.

        1. Organize a system by which banquet staff can communicate with other departments.   <u>1</u>

Exhibit 11.4 Continued

      2. Back up decisions on procedures with memo
documentation to relevant departments.   <u>1</u>

   F. Organize work areas.

      1. Establish productivity needs.   <u>2</u>
      2. Maintain organized work area and supplies.   <u>2</u>
      3. Use allotted storage space effectively.   <u>2</u>

   G. Organize inspections.

      1. Prepare cleaning lists.   <u>2</u>
      2. Prepare maintenance lists and work orders.   <u>1</u>
      3. Check condition of equipment.   <u>2</u>

   H. Organize training sessions.

      1. Determine training needs for new employees.   <u>3</u>
      2. Determine coaching needs for current employees.   <u>3</u>

III. Coordinating

   A. Complete administrative responsibilities.

      1. Coordinate work load with staffing to arrange time
for those members of the department who need to attend
QA meetings.   <u>2</u>
      2. Coordinate training of new employees, evaluating
performance, and coaching current staff.   <u>3</u>
      3. Coordinate submission of all personnel action request
forms to human resources/payroll departments.   <u>1</u>
      4. Coordinate training of supervisors and managers to
ensure compliance with accounting policies and procedures.   <u>1</u>
      5. Coordinate daily schedules of supervisors and managers
to allow time for daily review of time cards and approval
of overtime.   <u>3</u>

   B. Coordinate individual and group goals to achieve
department objectives.

      1. Establish the importance and value of participation in
QA problem-solving teams.   <u>2</u>
      2. Coordinate channels for improved communication.   <u>1</u>

   C. Coordinate purchases of needed supplies and equipment.

      1. Assess needs for supplies and equipment.   <u>1</u>
      2. Coordinate necessary purchase orders for pricing
and approval.   <u>1</u>

Exhibit 11.4 Continued

 D. Coordinate uniforms to maintain high standards of staff appearance.

  1. Research uniforms for image, durability, and availability. 2

  2. Propose uniform standards for approval of F&B director. 2

  3. Process necessary purchase orders for pricing and approval. 2

  4. Coordinate necessary standards and communicate to staff locations for purchasing uniforms. 2

  5. Coordinate orders for name tags with security. 2

  6. Coordinate communication with all managers and supervisors that name tags are required for all staff members. 2

 E. Coordinate communications.

  1. Coordinate all new/revised policies and procedures in manual. 1

  2. Coordinate business needs with executive steward and banquet chef on a daily basis. 2

  3. Keep staff informed about operating times of outlets so that, when occasions arise, they may promote other areas of the property to guests. 2

 F. Coordinate menu service by consulting with executive steward, banquet chef, service manager, and captains about upgrading menus. 2

 G. Coordinate with maintenance department necessary maintenance/repairs of convention area.

  1. Process proper work orders. 1

  2. Track completion of repairs/maintenance. 1

IV. Staffing

 A. Complete administrative responsibilities.

  1. Schedule members of QA teams to work on the day of their meetings whenever possible. 3

  2. Schedule time for training, coaching, and performance evaluations. 3

  3. Conduct employment reference checks on all applicants banquets recommends for hiring. 3

  4. Submit a staff requisition form to human resources whenever a new employee is required in banquets. 1

  5. Schedule time to be available to distribute paychecks on appropriate days of each month. 3

  6. Schedule time to review new/revised accounting policies and procedures and train department staff. 1

Exhibit 11.4 Continued

B. Interview and hire the best qualified applicants for available positions.

   1. Screen applicants. <u>3</u>
   2. Conduct interviews. <u>3</u>
   3. Verify references. <u>3</u>
   4. Confirm hiring with applicant. <u>3</u>
   5. Follow procedures and complete necessary forms for new hires. <u>2</u>

C. Staff according to budget projections.

   1. Establish staffing needs from forecasts. <u>3</u>
   2. Monitor labor costs in relation to revenue figures. <u>3</u>
   3. Staff according to people's strengths. <u>2</u>

D. Train and coach staff.

   1. Use job breakdowns. <u>3</u>
   2. Evaluate performance. <u>3</u>

E. Establish promotion path for staff. <u>1</u>

V. Directing

A. Complete administrative responsibilities.

   1. Direct QA team leader in efficient use of meeting time, but do not control the solution process. <u>2</u>
   2. Direct process of training, coaching, and conducting performance evaluations. <u>3</u>
   3. Any department manager considering the involuntary termination of an employee must review the reasons and facts involved with the human resources director before taking action. The exception is when an employee has violated a rule which has been declared grounds for immediate termination on the Rules of Conduct form. <u>2</u>
   4. Direct training of supervisors and managers to ensure compliance with accounting policies and procedures. <u>2</u>

B. Direct daily work productivity by ensuring that daily duties are being communicated to line employees. <u>3</u>

C. Direct paper flow.

   1. Review written communications. <u>2</u>
   2. File relevant paperwork. <u>2</u>

D. Discuss, determine, and distribute goals to managers and supervisors at weekly/monthly meetings. <u>3</u>

Exhibit 11.4 Continued

E. Direct employee concerns to appropriate management officials and departments.

    1. Follow organization chart.   3

    2. Develop good working relationships with other departments.   2

F. Ensure safe working conditions.

    1. Direct education of employees in safe working practices.   3

    2. Identify hazard areas.   3

    3. Establish policies to ensure safety.   3

G. Direct development of staff.

    1. Arrange meetings with representatives from other departments.   3

    2. Arrange for appropriate seminars.   2

    3. Develop motivational techniques.   3

    4. Train and coach employees.   3

    5. Establish a promotional path.   1

VI. Controlling

A. Complete administrative responsibilities.

    1. Control employee salary increases to ensure compliance with company guidelines and department budget.   3

    2. Establish a secure area for storing and distributing payroll checks, ensuring department manager access only.   3

    3. Review revenue and payroll reports issued by accounting and take appropriate action when necessary.   3

    4. Review "exception report" daily and identify employees who do not conform.   2

B. Evaluate the performance of department staff according to standards.   3

C. Control theft.

    1. Evaluate security of the department.   2

    2. Follow policies established by security department.   2

    3. Implement procedures established by security department.   2

    4. Communicate concerns to security department.   3

D. Maintain key control.

    1. Follow established policies and procedures.   3

    2. Educate staff about key control procedures, especially procedures for issuing keys.   3

Exhibit 11.4 Continued

E. Control breakage.

    1. Correct careless work practices.   3
    2. Educate staff about the cost of supplies.   2
    3. Train and coach staff in the proper procedures for
       handling supplies.   3
    4. Use breakage control sheets.   3
    5. Maintain secured areas for proper storage.   2

F. Take regular inventory and maintain par levels of equipment
   and supplies.   2

G. Control productivity by ensuring proper supervision of work
   assignments.   3

H. Control energy costs by following established guidelines
   on energy conservation.   3

I. Motivate staff.

    1. Instill a team spirit.   3
    2. Give credit where credit is due and coach as necessary.   3

VII. Evaluating

A. Complete administrative responsibilities.

    1. Evaluate QA team's track record with the team leader on
       a monthly basis.   2
    2. Evaluate performance of all employees according to the
       following schedule:
        ▸ 1 month
        ▸ 3 months
        ▸ 6 months
        ▸ 1 year   3
    3. Conduct performance appraisals for staff from monthly
       list provided by human resources department.   3
    4. Evaluate performance of all employees on the basis of
       the 90-day and annual review.   3

B. Evaluate labor costs by reviewing end-of-the-month labor
   figures and revenue dollars.   3

C. Evaluate labor needs by using forecasts and staffing accordingly.   3

D. Evaluate job performances.

    1. Review job descriptions and revise/update as necessary.   2

Exhibit 11.4 Continued

2.	Evaluate daily results of department and provide feedback to staff.	3
E.	Evaluate quality of service.	
	1. Review guest and staff comments.	2
	2. Provide input for upgrading standards.	2
	3. Ensure follow-through on training and coaching.	3
	4. Accommodate guests.	3
F.	Evaluate the competition.	
	1. Keep informed about competitors' products.	2
	2. Develop consistency in banquets' products.	2
G.	Anticipate guest needs.	
	1. Assess guest needs from banquet equipment orders and from communication with guests.	3
	2. Determine if present equipment can accommodate guest needs; if not, make appropriate arrangements.	3
H.	Evaluate department safety practices.	3
I.	Evaluate the effectiveness of training and, if necessary, revise training methods to improve communication and follow-through.	2

for each management skill area and a total performance rating. These ratings are computed by totaling the number of points possible and dividing that figure into the total actual points which the manager received. Exhibit 11.5 summarizes the banquet manager's performance ratings that appear in Exhibit 11.4.

When the manager's job breakdown is used to evaluate performance, the results indicate:

1. Strengths and weaknesses in management skill areas

2. Specific tasks which the manager must perform better

Exhibit 11.5 indicates that the banquet manager's strengths are staffing, controlling, directing, and evaluating. The manager's weaknesses are planning, coordinating, and organizing. The weaknesses indicate opportunities for strengthening not only the manager's skills, but also the overall management of the hospitality business.

Exhibit 11.5 Sample Summary of Performance Ratings

Position:	Banquet Manager		
Name:			
Reports to:	Food and Beverage Director		
Supervises:	Assistant Banquet Managers, Convention Floor Coordinator, Banquet Beverage Supervisor, Banquet Captains, Coffee Break Managers		
Works with:	All Departments		

	Possible Points	Actual Points	Percentage Rating
Planning	135	80	59
Organizing	72	44	61
Coordinating	63	36	57
Staffing	51	43	84
Directing	54	45	83
Controlling	63	56	89
Evaluating	54	47	87
Total Performance	492	351	71

In our example, the specific weaknesses seem to indicate that the banquet manager is performing more as the department's supervisor than as its manager. The manager excels at getting the function out and "handling the guests," but seems so busy doing this that other important management tasks (such as planning department goals, preparing and coordinating vacation schedules for staff, organizing department meetings, etc.) are put off as things that the manager "would like to do if there were time." If the food and beverage director (or some other manager) does not make up for the banquet manager's weaknesses, the success of the hospitality operation will be impaired. In addition, if the banquet manager's weaknesses are not developed into strengths, he or she will always be busy getting the functions out and "handling the guests," while some other manager picks up the slack.

Using job breakdowns to evaluate performance allows top management to tailor a management development program to the specific needs of each manager. In our example, it is now the food and beverage director's responsibility to help the banquet manager develop the weak management skill areas into strengths. If the director is a good planner, he or she becomes the banquet manager's planning coach. If other department managers are excellent planners, the director may solicit them to help also.

The strengths of a manager should not be ignored. In relation to our example, the banquet manager commands skills in the areas of controlling and evaluating. The food and beverage director should consider the banquet manager as a coach for other department managers whose performance evaluations reveal weaknesses in these areas.

Coaching managers in the development of management skills should be both an informal and a formal process. Informally, the manager's coach can provide useful tips and pointers that the developing manager can put to immediate use. Formally, the manager's coach should direct the development of specific management skills by implementing a structured plan. Steps that coaches may follow in creating a development plan are as follows:

1. Establish clear goals for what is to be accomplished.

2. Discuss the goals with the developing manager and document how achievement of the goals can be measured.

3. Make sure that the developing manager can explain in his or her own words the goals that are set, the steps to take in achieving the goals, and how achievement will be measured.

4. Collect and discuss all the necessary information about policies and procedures that may relate to the specified goals.

5. Set realistic completion dates.

6. Develop consensus checkpoints to review progress.

One of the important differences between the training of managers and the training of skilled employees is the degree of personal responsibility that must be assumed by the manager for his or her own development. Top managers may adapt the management development system presented in this chapter to the specific needs and requirements of their organizations and also provide other resources (such as training programs and specialized seminars), but the responsibility for development rests largely with the individual manager. The individual manager must recognize the need for development and demonstrate the personal desire to achieve a higher level of excellence.

12
Skills Training

One of the most important responsibilities of a department manager is to ensure that department employees receive proper training. This does not mean that a department manager must assume the duties and responsibilities of a trainer. The actual training functions may be delegated to supervisors or even to talented employees. However, department managers should be held accountable for ongoing training programs in their departments.

Many hospitality organizations have manuals that specify how to perform all of the tasks in their operations. However, few of these manuals are designed as complete training guides which include lesson plans for specific training sessions. The department manager is left with the responsibility for training employees, but without the necessary resources and tools to get the job done.

This chapter shows department managers how to use job lists and job breakdowns to develop an effective skills training program and an efficient system for evaluating employee performance. A job list for a skilled position is a list of tasks that must be performed by an employee in a specific department of the hospitality operation. A job breakdown specifies how each task on a job list should be performed.

The chapter explains how to set up department standards groups. These groups are responsible for preparing job breakdowns for all of the skilled positions within their departments. In less than a month, this concentrated effort can result in a complete set of performance standards and training materials for a very complex department. In a smaller, less complicated operation, job breakdowns can be completed in less than a week.

The chapter also instructs trainers how to develop a training program for new employees and for existing staff. A five-step training method is presented which shows trainers how to conduct effective training sessions. Additional information, such as principles of adult learning, factors which affect the learning process, and common training mistakes, is also presented. However, a complete discussion of the training function is beyond the scope of this book. More detail in this area can be found in Lewis C. Forrest's *Training for the Hospitality Industry*, published by the Educational Institute.

Job Lists and Job Breakdowns for Skilled Positions

A job list for a skilled position is a list of tasks that must be performed by an employee within a specific department of the hospitality operation. The tasks on the job list should reflect the total job responsibility of the employee. However, the list should *not* be a detailed breakdown of the steps that make up each task. The job list should simply state what the employee must be able to do in order to perform the job.

Exhibit 12.1 presents a sample job list for a morning shift housekeeping room attendant. Note that each line on the sample job list begins with a verb typed in capital letters. This format stresses action and clearly indicates to an employee what he or she will be responsible for *doing*. Whenever possible, tasks should be listed in an order that reflects the logical sequence of daily responsibilities.

Job breakdowns specify how each task on a job list should be performed. The format of job breakdowns can vary to suit the needs and requirements of individual properties. Exhibit 12.2 presents a sample job breakdown which is designed to serve not only as a training guide for newly hired housekeeping room attendants, but also as a tool for evaluating the performance of experienced room attendants.

The first column in Exhibit 12.2 shows tasks from the job list presented in Exhibit 12.1. The second column breaks down each task by identifying the specific, observable, measurable steps that an employee must take in order to accomplish the task shown in the first column. These steps are written as performance standards. They are lettered in sequence and begin with a verb that is typed in capital letters.

The third column presents additional information. Generally, this information explains *why* each step of the task is performed according to the standards listed in the second column. Note that the additional information column contains content information while the steps and procedures in the first two columns are the process elements of the job. The additional information column can also be used to stress the hospitality aspects of the job, such as desired attitudes. Additional information may also include hints, tips, or pointers which may help the employee to perform a task according to the property's standards.

The fourth column is set up as a checklist which is used to record quarterly performance evaluations. A performance evaluation identifies an employee's strengths and weaknesses. The weaknesses indicate specific training needs.

It is important for employees to know the standards that will be used to measure their performance on the job. Therefore, it is important to

Exhibit 12.1 Sample Job List: Morning Shift Room Attendant

Date : xx/xx/xx

JOB LIST

Position: Housekeeping Room Attendant

Tasks: Employee must be able to:

1.   PARK in designated area.
2.   WEAR proper uniform.
3.   PUNCH in.
4.   PICK up clipboard and keys.
5.   MEET with supervisor.
6.   OBTAIN supplies.
7.   PLAN your work.
8.   ENTER the room.
9.   PREPARE the room.
10.   MAKE the beds.
11.   GATHER cleaning supplies.
12.   CLEAN the bathroom.
13.   DUST the room.
14.   CHECK/REPLACE paper supplies and amenities.
15.   CLEAN windows.
16.   INSPECT your work.
17.   VACUUM the room.
18.   LOCK the door and mark your report.
19.   TAKE breaks at designated times.
20.   RETURN and restock cart.
21.   RETURN to housekeeping with clipboard and keys.
22.   PUNCH out.

break down the tasks and document those standards. In order to serve as a performance standard, each item in the second column of the job breakdown must be observable and measurable. A manager or supervisor conducting a quarterly performance evaluation should be able to simply check a box either in the "Yes" or the "No" column: "Yes, the employee performed the task correctly," or "No, the employee failed to conform to the performance standard."

Job breakdowns become useless when performance standards cannot be observed or measured. For example, a performance standard such as "BE happy" is useless when it comes to evaluating an employee's performance. One manager may think that an employee looks happy; another manager may think differently. A performance standard can state that an employee should "SMILE." A smile is an observable behavior; an employee is either smiling or not smiling, regardless of who is doing the observing.

Exhibit 12.2 Sample Job Breakdown as Performance Standard

POSITION: Housekeeping Room Attendant, morning shift

NAME:

SUPERVISOR:

JOB LIST	PERFORMANCE STANDARD	ADDITIONAL INFORMATION	1st Qtr. Yes/No	2nd Qtr. Yes/No	3rd Qtr. Yes/No	4th Qtr. Yes/No
7. PLAN YOUR WORK	A. STUDY your assignment sheet.	Early service requests, rush rooms, check-outs, V.I.P.'s and no-service requests will be noted on your chart.				
	B. CLEAN check-outs first, whenever possible.	Cleaning check-outs first gives the front desk rooms to sell.				
	C. CLEAN early service requests as noted on your report.					
	D. CLEAN V.I.P. rooms before lunch, whenever possible.	A V.I.P. is our most important guest.				
	E. LOCK your cart room door and proceed to your section.					
	F. HONOR "do not disturb" signs.	We must honor the privacy of guests. Many guests like to sleep in. Never knock on a door that has a "do not disturb" sign.				
	G. CHECK rooms marked c/o and then check the rooms which are circled on your report. These are rooms due to check out.	Rooms marked c/o have already checked out at the front desk. Check-out time is noon.				

Exhibit 12.2 Continued

JOB LIST	PERFORMANCE STANDARD	ADDITIONAL INFORMATION	1st Qtr. Yes/No	2nd Qtr. Yes/No	3rd Qtr. Yes/No	4th Qtr. Yes/No
7. Plan Your Work (continued)	H. PLAN your work around early service requests.	If you have early-service requests, be sure to clean these rooms at the proper time.				
8. ENTER THE ROOM	A. KNOCK on the door with your knuckles, while saying in a clear voice, "Housekeeping."	Do not knock with your keys; this chips the finish off the door and the sound can be unpleasant to guests within the room.				
	B. LISTEN for a response while waiting. If you do not get a response, knock again while saying in a clear voice, "Housekeeping."	If you receive no response, wait 10 to 15 seconds to knock again.				
	C. UNLOCK the door.					
	D. OPEN the door slowly.					
	E. ANNOUNCE yourself as you open the door by saying in a clear voice, "Housekeeping."	The guest may not have heard you the first time. You do not want to walk in and startle the guest. The guest may not have been able to answer your knock because he/she was sleeping, showering, or speaking on the telephone.				
	F. REMOVE the key and place it in your pocket.	Your key should be kept on your person at all times.				

Exhibit 12.2 Continued

JOB LIST	PERFORMANCE STANDARD	ADDITIONAL INFORMATION	1st Qtr. Yes/No	2nd Qtr. Yes/No	3rd Qtr. Yes/No	4th Qtr. Yes/No
8. Enter The Room (continued)	G. EXCUSE yourself from the room if the guest is not ready for you to clean the room.					
	H. SMILE at the guest saying, "Good Morning," or "Good Afternoon," as the case may be.	A proper greeting impresses the guest.				
	I. ASK the guest about the time he/she would like the room cleaned.					
	J. REPEAT the time the guest wants the room cleaned so that he/she knows you have understood.	Note service time in the comment section on your chart.				
	K. PROCEED to another room, if the guest prefers a later time.					
	L. TALK with your supervisor (or with the housekeeping office) if you can't get into any rooms in your section.	Your supervisor needs to know if your are having difficulties. If you can't get in to clean your rooms, you will be sent to another area.				
	M. POSITION your cart in front of the door.					
	N. ENTER the room carrying with you the vacuum, broom, and bed sheets.	Do not waste your steps. Every trip you make back and forth to your cart should be made for a purpose.				

Exhibit 12.2 Continued

JOB LIST	PERFORMANCE STANDARD	ADDITIONAL INFORMATION	1st Qtr. Yes/No	2nd Qtr. Yes/No	3rd Qtr. Yes/No	4th Qtr. Yes/No
9. PREPARE THE ROOM	A. OPEN the black-out drapes.	In stayover rooms, leave draperies the way you find them. The guest may wish them to remain that way.				
	B. CLOSE the sheers.					
	C. CHECK drapery pulls to make sure that they work properly.	Note any maintenance problems on your chart.				
	D. CHECK window panes, sills, and all corners for cracks and/or cobwebs.	Note any maintenance problems on your chart.				
	E. TURN off television and radio, if they were on when you entered the room. If the room is a c/o, set channel knob to station 2.	Televisions and radios are not to be on when you are cleaning rooms. Channel 2 is an in-house video channel which advertises the hotel.				
	F. REMOVE bedspreads, blankets, and pillows and place them on the unused bed or on a chair.	Do not throw linens on the floor because they will become soiled.				
	G. INSPECT bedspread, blanket, and pillows, as well as the bed pad.	Replacement bed pads and pillows are in your cart room.				
	H. STRIP the beds by undoing each end of the bed sheets.	Do not pull sheets off while standing at the foot of the bed. This could tear the bed linen.				
	I. REMOVE pillows from pillow cases.					

Exhibit 12.2 Continued

JOB LIST	PERFORMANCE STANDARD	ADDITIONAL INFORMATION	1st Qtr. Yes/No	2nd Qtr. Yes/No	3rd Qtr. Yes/No	4th Qtr. Yes/No
9. Prepare The Room (continued)	J. REMOVE used linens from bathroom area.					
	K. CHECK bath rug and shower curtain to see if they need to be replaced. If the room is a c/o, replace rug.	Make a mental note of how much terry linen you will need to pick up from your cart.				
	L. EMPTY dirty linen into laundry bag on your cart.	Place ripped or badly spotted linen into the box that is in your cart room.				
	M. REMOVE used water glasses, and place them on your cart.	Never wash a glass in a room. This is a serious violation of health codes. Dirty glasses should be removed from your cart and placed in your cart room.				
	N. EMPTY ashtrays into trash, making sure all cigarette butts are extinguished.	Check match books to see if they have been used; if so, replace them. Do not touch the guest's belongings, such as jewelry or loose change which are sometimes placed in ashtrays.				
	O. CHECK under beds, behind furniture and doors, and under cushions.	It's easier to look under beds when they are stripped.				
	P. REMOVE trash from these areas.					

Exhibit 12.2 Continued

JOB LIST	PERFORMANCE STANDARD	ADDITIONAL INFORMATION	1st Qtr. Yes/No	2nd Qtr. Yes/No	3rd Qtr. Yes/No	4th Qtr. Yes/No
9. Prepare The Room (continued)	Q. COLLECT all stray trash and waste from the room and place it in waste paper baskets, if the room is a c/o.					
	R. COLLECT only trash and waste placed in trash cans, if the room is a stayover.	In an occupied room, do not throw out anything that is not in the waste paper basket.				
	S. EMPTY trash into lined trash bag on your cart.	Do not put your hand directly into the trash that is in the waste paper basket.				
	T. WASH waste paper baskets inside and out.					
	U. WIPE waste paper baskets dry.					
	V. RETURN waste paper baskets to their proper places in the room.	Place the plastic waste paper basket in the bathroom; place metal waste paper baskets near the bar area.				
	W. REMOVE cobwebs in corners of the room.	Use your broom, if necessary.				
	X. CHECK rooms for lost and found items; open drawers and closets in c/o rooms to check for lost items.					
	Y. PLACE lost-and-found items in a bag.	Call housekeeping if the lost and found item is valuable.				

Exhibit 12.2 Continued

JOB LIST	PERFORMANCE STANDARD	ADDITIONAL INFORMATION	1st Qtr. Yes/No	2nd Qtr. Yes/No	3rd Qtr. Yes/No	4th Qtr. Yes/No
9. Prepare The Room (continued)	Z. WRITE on the bag: room number, date, and your full name. AA. POCKET room keys from c/o rooms. AB. CONTACT your supervisor (or the housekeeping office) if: • you have found an item for lost-and-found. • you have discovered damage to the room. • maintenance is needed for broken fixtures, etc. • linens or furniture are missing. AC. CLEAR any room service dishes, trays, etc. Set them outside the room and call extension 14 for tray pick-up.	Turn in lost-and-found items to your supervisor. Unclaimed articles are returned to the finder after 90 days. Never leave room keys on your cart. Turn in room keys to your supervisor. Dishes should be picked up promptly by room service.				

Developing Job Breakdowns for Skilled Positions

If one person in a hospitality operation is assigned the responsibility of writing every job breakdown, the job will never get done, unless the operation is very small with a limited number of tasks. The best job breakdowns are written by those who actually perform the tasks. Therefore, job breakdowns should be written by standards groups set up within each department. Members of these groups should include:

- An organizer designated by top management

- The department manager (or supervisor)

- Several experienced employees of the department

Management should set up the first standards groups in those departments with the greatest need for job breakdowns. These are the departments with the greatest number of service problems. Service problems generally indicate inadequate or disorganized training, which results from a lack of well-defined performance standards.

Most hospitality organizations have a policy and procedures manual. Although this manual rarely contains the detail necessary to set up effective training and evaluation programs, portions of it may be helpful to members of a standards group as they write job breakdowns for each position within their department. For example, if the procedure sections of the manual include job descriptions and detailed outlines of job responsibilities and duties, they may help a standards group in writing job lists and performance standards. The policy sections may be helpful sources of additional information which can be included in the job breakdowns.

The job breakdowns for tasks which involve the use of equipment may already be written in the operating manuals supplied by vendors. For example, a front office standards group should not have to write performance standards for operating computers at the front desk. Instead, the standards group may simply reference (or even attach) appropriate pages from the operating manual supplied by the vendor for in-house training.

Exhibit 12.3 outlines the steps for developing job breakdowns. The process begins with the organizer conducting a brainstorming session with a department's standards group. For each position within the department, the group brainstorms the tasks which must be performed. The tasks are then listed in an order that reflects the logical sequence of the position's daily responsibilities. This activity results in a job list for each position within the department.

Exhibit 12.3 Developing Job Breakdowns

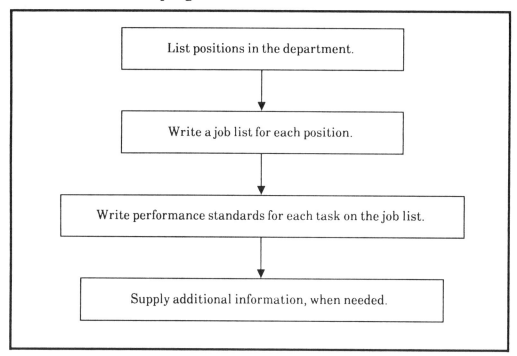

The next step is to break down each task by writing the performance standards which state the specific, observable, measurable steps that an employee must take in order to accomplish the task. The organizer assists the group in writing performance standards for at least two or three positions within the department. During this activity, the group provides any additional information that may be necessary to explain why certain steps of a task are performed according to the proposed standards. This additional information may stress the hospitality aspects of the job or may provide tips which help an employee to perform the task efficiently and effectively.

While assisting the group in writing performance standards, the organizer should stress that each performance standard must be observable and measurable. The value of each performance standard can be tested by asking whether or not a manager or supervisor can evaluate an employee's performance by simply checking a "Yes" or "No" box in the quarterly performance review column.

After the standards group has written job breakdowns for two or three tasks, the writing of job breakdowns for the other tasks in the department should be assigned to individual members of the group. Within two weeks, they should submit their work to the organizer, who then assembles the breakdowns, has them typed in the same format as shown in Exhibit 12.2, and provides copies to all of the members. A

Exhibit 12.4 Training with Job Breakdowns

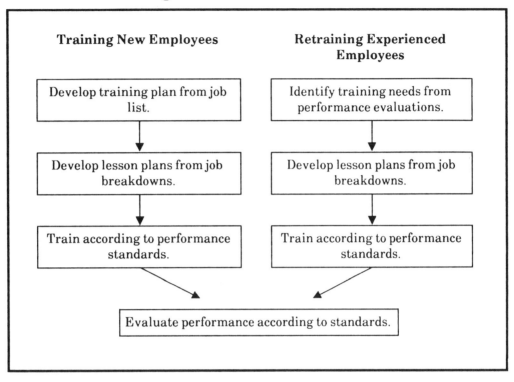

Training New Employees

Develop training plan from job list.

↓

Develop lesson plans from job breakdowns.

↓

Train according to performance standards.

Retraining Experienced Employees

Identify training needs from performance evaluations.

↓

Develop lesson plans from job breakdowns.

↓

Train according to performance standards.

Evaluate performance according to standards.

final meeting is held, and the group carefully analyzes the breakdowns, simplifies procedures, and reaches consensus on the job breakdowns for each position within the department.

After the job breakdowns of a department have been finalized, they should be used *immediately* to train the department's staff. If the job breakdowns are not used immediately, service problems will continue and department morale may sink to an all-time low. There is nothing more depressing to members of a standards group than to see the results of their efforts gathering dust on a manager's shelf. Also, word will spread quickly throughout the property, and the work of other standards groups will be affected. Few will take their work seriously when management sends a signal that their work is not important.

Training to Standards

Exhibit 12.4 shows how job breakdowns can be used to train employees to perform tasks according to established standards. The trainer must develop a comprehensive training plan for newly hired employees who have little or no experience in hospitality jobs. The plan can be developed from the job lists of the positions that the new employees will occupy.

For example, Exhibit 12.5 shows a sample five-day training plan developed from the sample job list in Exhibit 12.1. The trainee masters one group of related tasks at a time and must achieve 100% conformity to performance standards before progressing to the next group of related tasks listed on the training plan. Note that, except for task number seven, the training plan follows the same sequence of tasks which appear on the sample job list. It is not always possible (or desirable) to train employees in the same sequence within which tasks are actually performed on the job.

The trainer's primary function is to communicate performance standards to employees in the department. This can be accomplished by following a five-step training method, which can be used to train both newly hired employees and experienced employees. The five steps are:

1. Prepare to train
2. Conduct the training
3. Coach trial performances
4. Reverse roles (trainee trains the trainer)
5. Follow through

This training method can be adapted to the special needs and requirements of almost any hospitality operation. The method can be used for either individualized instruction or for group training programs.

The following sections briefly describe what each step of the training method involves. Exhibit 12.6 summarizes the five-step training method and may serve as a job list for trainers. For more detailed information about implementing training programs and conducting individual or group training sessions, see Lewis C. Forrest's *Training for the Hospitality Industry*, published by the Educational Institute.

Prepare to Train

Many managers and supervisors think they know the skills required of employees so well that they can teach them to others without any thought or preparation. However, it is easy to forget important details. Trainers need a written format to guide them while conducting training sessions. The following sections explain how trainers should prepare for training.

Write Training Objectives. Training objectives are the tasks which the trainee will be expected to demonstrate at the end of the training session. These tasks should already be listed in the first column of the job breakdown for the position for which the trainee is receiving training. In addition, training objectives should clearly state that the

Exhibit 12.5 Sample Five-Day Training Plan

Position: Housekeeping Room Attendant **Date Prepared:** xx/xx/xx

Tasks: Employee must be able to:

Employee: _____

<table>
<tr><td>Tasks</td><td>100% Conformity
to Standards</td></tr>
</table>

Day 1
1. PARK in designated area.
2. WEAR proper uniform.
3. PUNCH in.
4. PICK up clipboard and keys.
5. MEET with supervisor.
6. OBTAIN supplies.
8. ENTER the room.
9. PREPARE the room.

Day 2
10. MAKE the beds.
11. GATHER cleaning supplies.
12. CLEAN the bathroom.

Day 3
13. DUST the room.
14. CHECK/REPLACE paper supplies/amenities.
15. CLEAN windows.

Day 4
16. INSPECT your work.
17. VACUUM the room.
18. LOCK the door and mark your report.

Day 5
7. PLAN your work.
19. TAKE breaks at designated times.
20. RETURN and restock cart.
21. RETURN to housekeeping with clipboard and keys.
22. PUNCH out.

---

only acceptable performance is 100% conformity to standards. The training objectives should be communicated to the trainee at the start of the training session.

Develop Lesson Plans. Write step-by-step lesson plans for demonstrating the tasks which the trainee is expected to learn. It

Exhibit 12.6 Five-Step Training Method: A Job List for Trainers

Step 1:   PREPARE TO TRAIN

WRITE	training objectives.
DEVELOP	lesson plans.
DECIDE	on training methods.
ESTABLISH	a timetable.
SELECT	the training location.
ASSEMBLE	training materials/equipment.
SET UP	the work station.

STEP 2:   CONDUCT THE TRAINING

PREPARE	the trainee.
BEGIN	the training session.
DEMONSTRATE	the procedures.
AVOID	jargon.
TAKE	adequate time.
REPEAT	the sequence.

STEP 3:   COACH TRIAL PERFORMANCES

| ALLOW | the trainee to practice. |
| COACH | the trainee. |

STEP 4:   REVERSE ROLES (TRAINEE TRAINS THE TRAINER)

| BE TRAINED | by the trainee. |
| BE EVALUATED | by the trainee. |

STEP 5:   FOLLOW THROUGH

CONTINUE	positive reinforcement.
PROVIDE	constant feedback.
COACH	a few tasks each day.
EVALUATE	the trainee's progress.

should be easy to develop lesson plans directly from the performance standards shown in the second column of the job breakdown for tasks which the trainee is scheduled to learn. If the lesson plan involves a demonstration, make sure that the trainees' positions at the training location will enable them to view the demonstration from the actual position from which they will be performing the task(s).

Decide on Training Methods. When planning the training session, determine which teaching methods will be most appropriate for accomplishing the training objectives. Exhibit 12.7 presents several popular group training methods.

Establish a Timetable. Establish a timetable for instruction by: (1) deciding how long the training session will take, and (2) determining when the volume of business will be such that training can be conducted without interruption or distraction.

Select the Training Location. Job-related training should be conducted at the work station(s) where the work will be performed. Consider when the training can best occur without interfering with daily department functions. Make sure that the trainee's position at the training location will provide an uninterrupted view of the tasks which will be demonstrated. Also, the trainee should be able to see the demonstration from the actual position from which he or she will be performing the task(s). If a trainee is observing across the table from the trainer, then every movement will appear to be the reverse of the way it is to be actually performed. This may seem like a minor point, but it can become so frustrating that a trainee may develop a resistance to learning the task(s).

Assemble Training Materials/Equipment. Gather copies of the appropriate job list and job breakdowns. These are the most important materials needed for the training session. The job breakdowns should indicate other materials and/or equipment that will be needed for teaching a particular task. All these materials and the necessary equipment should be set up in the area where the training is to take place.

Set Up the Work Station. If a work station will be used as the training location, lay it out exactly the way it is usually stocked. Each piece of equipment should be positioned in the same way that the employee is expected to operate it and/or maintain it.

Conduct the Training

After the trainer has prepared for the training, the actual training session can begin. The following sections suggest guidelines for how to present the training.

Prepare the Trainee. Present an overview of the training session and help the trainee become motivated to learn. Explain the training objectives for the session and let the trainee know exactly what will be expected. Tell the trainee why the training is important, how it relates to the job, and how the trainee will benefit from the training. Help the trainee understand how the learning objectives relate to the total responsibilities of the job. Emphasize how the trainee can make immediate use of the skills that will be learned.

Begin the Training Session. Use the job breakdowns as a training guide. Encourage the trainee to study the job breakdowns so that he or

Exhibit 12.7 Popular Group Training Methods

GROUP TRAINING: WHAT'S IT ALL ABOUT?
I. Consider Training in Groups When: • several employees need training in the same task   • a large amount of information must be dispensed to several or more employees   • individualized training methods are not practical   **II. Popular Group Training Methods**

Method	Overview of Procedures	Advantages	Disadvantages
1. Lecture	Least effective method. One person does all the talking, may use handouts, visual aids, question/answer to supplement lecture.	Less time needed for trainer preparation than other methods; provides a lot of information quickly when retention of details is not important.	Does not actively involve trainees in training process; trainees forget much information when it is only presented orally.
2. Demonstration	Very effective for basic skills training. Trainer shows trainees how to do something; can include opportunity for trainees to also perform the task(s) being demonstrated.	Emphasizes trainee involvement; several senses (seeing, hearing, feeling) can be involved.	Requires a great deal of trainer preparation and planning.
3. Seminar	Good for experienced employees. Can use several group methods (lectures, discussions, conference) which require group participation.	Group members are involved in the training; can use many group methods (role playing, case study, etc.) as part of the seminar activity.	Planning is time-consuming; trainer(s) must have skill in conducting a seminar; much time is required for training experience.
4. Conference	Good problem-solving approach. Group approach to considering a specific problem or issue—and reaching agreement on statements or solution.	Much trainee participation; obtains trainee consensus; can use several methods (lecture, panel, seminar) to keep sessions interesting.	Group may be hard to control; group opinions generated at the conference may differ from manager's ideas; conflict can result.
5. Panel	Good when using outside resource people. Provides several points of view on topic in order to seek alternatives to the situation. Panel members may have differing views but also must have objective concerns for the purpose of the training.	Interesting to hear different points of view; process invites employees' opinions; employees are challenged to consider alternatives.	Requires a great deal of preparation; results of the method can be difficult to evaluate.
6. Role Playing	Good for guest relations training. Trainees pretend to be selected people in specific situations and have an opportunity to experiment with different approaches for dealing with the situation.	Trainees can learn possible results of certain behaviors in a classroom situation; skills in dealing with people can be practiced; alternative approaches can be analyzed and considered.	Much time is spent getting points across; trainers must be skillful and creative in helping the class learn from the situation.
7. Case Studies	Good for teaching situational analysis. The	Can present a real-life situation which enables	Cases are difficult to write and time-consuming to

Exhibit 12.7 Popular Group Training Methods (continued)

Method	Overview of Procedures	Advantages	Disadvantages
	case study is a description of a real or imagined situation which contains information that trainees can use to analyze what has occurred and why.	trainees to consider what they would do; can be used to teach a wide variety of skills in which application of information is important.	discuss; the trainer must be creative and skillful in leading discussions, making points, and keeping trainees on the track.
8. Simulations	Good for skill development. Trainees imitate actions required on the job (such as repeating the steps in a demonstration after it is presented).	Training becomes "real;" trainees are actively involved in the learning process; training has direct applicability to jobs to be performed after training.	Simulations are time-consuming; they require a skillful and creative trainer.
9. Projects	Good for experienced employees. Projects require the trainees to do something on the job which improves the operation as well as helps them learn about the topic of the training.	Projects can be selected which help resolve problems or otherwise improve the operation; trainees get first-hand experience in the topic of the training; little time is needed up front of the training experience.	Without proper introduction to the project and its purpose, trainees may think they are doing somebody else's work. Also, if they do not have an interest in the project—for example, there is no immediate impact on their own jobs—it will be difficult to obtain and maintain their interest.

she will know the standards by which performance will be evaluated. Stress that 100% conformity to standards is expected. Follow the sequence of each step in the performance standards column of the job breakdowns. Tell the trainee how to do each step and explain why each step is important.

Demonstrate the Procedures. As each step is reviewed, demonstrate how to do it. The trainee will understand and retain more by seeing a demonstration than by listening to a lecture. Encourage the trainee to ask questions at any point where he or she does not fully understand the demonstration or the explanation.

Avoid Jargon. Use words that the trainee can understand. Jargon and technical terms that may be familiar to other employees may seem like a foreign language to a person new to the job.

Take Adequate Time. Proceed slowly. Remember that the trainee is seeing and hearing many things for the first time. Carefully show and explain everything the trainee should know about the step. It is often difficult for many trainers to slow the pace of their instruction and maintain it at a level appropriate for the trainee. Try not to become frustrated if the trainee does not understand each step as well or as soon as expected.

Repeat the Sequence. Go through the entire sequence once and then a second time to ensure that the trainee knows the process thoroughly. Stress that 100% conformity to standards is expected. When going through the process for the second time, ask the trainee questions to check on his or her comprehension. Follow the job breakdowns and repeat the steps as often as necessary until the trainee knows the procedure.

Coach Trial Performances

After the trainer and the trainee agree that sufficient learning has occurred to make the trainee familiar with the job and enable him or her to complete the steps in an acceptable manner, the trainee should be allowed to try to perform the tasks alone.

Have the trainee demonstrate each step of the task presented during the training session. Then have the trainee explain each step while performing it. This, in addition to asking the trainee questions, will help check for comprehension.

Allow the Trainee to Practice. New skills which are properly demonstrated and explained, followed by immediate practice, result in good work habits. Help the trainee smooth out motions and strive to increase skill. Stress that 100% conformity to standards is expected.

Coach the Trainee. Help the trainee gain the skill and confidence necessary to perform the job. As a coach, compliment the trainee immediately after correct performance; correct the trainee immediately when problems are observed. If bad habits form at this stage of the training process, they will be very difficult to break in the future. Be sure that the trainee understands the "why" behind the "how to" of each step and that 100% conformity to standards is expected.

Reverse Roles (Trainee Trains the Trainer)

This step in the training method reverses the roles of the trainer and trainee: the trainee acts as a trainer and presents the training to the trainer, who assumes the role of a trainee.

After the trainee has mastered the responsibilities of the job (as specified in the performance standards of the job breakdowns), he or she should be given the opportunity to train the trainer. Most teachers will admit that they mastered the subject matter which they teach not when they were students learning the material, but when they actually taught the material to others. Training the trainer enables trainees to feel this same sense of mastery. Reversing roles also gives the trainer an opportunity to show confidence in the trainee's performance and to demonstrate respect for the trainee's abilities.

The last procedure in the training is for the trainee to evaluate the trainer. This important feedback can identify the trainer's strengths and weaknesses. The evaluation should be viewed as a tool by which a trainer can capitalize on current strengths, eliminate weaknesses, and become better at teaching and coaching. In addition, Exhibit 12.8 presents a list of questions that may guide a trainer's self-evaluation.

Follow Through

Once the trainee has been coached in trial performances of the job, he or she is ready to try it alone. However, the trainer's coaching responsibilities remain the same. The trainer must observe the trainee's work to ensure 100% conformity to performance standards.

The trainer should gradually reduce coaching as the trainee learns to perform according to standards set by the job breakdowns. However, the trainer should periodically check back on the employee and follow through.

Continue Positive Reinforcement. Reinforcement reminds the trainee what he or she has learned. It is important to recognize the difference between positive and negative reinforcement. Positive reinforcement acknowledges correct performance; negative reinforcement corrects incorrect performance. Reinforcement may take the form of verbal feedback during or after training.

When a trainee is on the job and strays from performance standards set by the job breakdowns, first compliment the person for performing some of the tasks correctly and then guide the trainee back to the correct procedures. This technique will result in improved employee performance and develop within the employee a positive attitude toward training.

Provide Constant Feedback. Feedback occurs when the trainer tells the trainee how he or she is performing throughout the training. The trainer should tell the trainee what is correct as well as what is incorrect about his or her performance. The amount of feedback given to a trainee is determined by the trainer's own judgment. However, feedback must be given to help the trainee reach the desired behavior as outlined in the training objectives.

A trainee will always have questions about new tasks which have been learned. The trainer should always encourage questions and discuss ways of improving performance and efficiency. A trainee also needs to know where to go for help when the trainer is not available.

Coach a Few Tasks Each Day. A trainee can only retain a limited amount of information at one time without becoming tired and frustrated. In one training session, teach what the trainee can reasonably be expected to master and allow time for practice. Then, teach more material in later sessions until all of the job responsibilities are covered.

Exhibit 12.8 Are You a Good Trainer?

1. Do you consider preparation to be the first step in instructing an employee?

2. Do you spend at least as much time getting things ready for training as you do in the actual training session?

3. Do you use the performance standards from job breakdowns as your lesson plans?

4. Do you list key points around which you will build the instruction?

5. Do you devote time to explaining to the employee how he or she will benefit from the training session?

6. Do you determine what the employee already knows about the job before you start training?

7. Do you set up a timetable showing the amount of time you plan to spend training employees, and when you expect their training to be completed?

8. Do you expect that there will be periods in the course of the training during which no observable progress will be made?

9. Do you expect some employees to learn two or three times faster than others?

10. Do you both tell and show the employee how to do the skill involved?

11. When an employee performs incorrectly during training, do you acknowledge correct performance before pointing out areas that need improvement?

12. Do you give instructions so clearly that no one can misunderstand them?

13. Do you ask the employee to try out the skill and to tell you how to do it?

14. Do you praise correct performance frequently?

15. Do you expect 100% conformity to standards?

(All of the questions should be answered "Yes.")

Evaluate the Trainee's Progress. Evaluation is the guideline that is most often forgotten in training. Training efforts should be evaluated in terms of whether or not the trainee accomplished the training objectives. Did the trainee actually demonstrate the behavior that the trainer specified before training began? If not, the trainer should provide additional guidance and practice until the trainee successfully masters the behavior specified in the training objectives. Evaluation should take place before, during, and at the completion of training, as well as periodically after training to ensure 100% conformity to performance standards.

The final sections of this chapter present helpful tips for beginning and experienced trainers which can help them better understand basic principles of adult learning and factors which affect the learning process. Portions of these sections appear in Lewis C. Forrest's *Training for the Hospitality Industry*, published by the Educational Institute.

Principles of Adult Learning

The following sections present what every trainer should know about teaching adults in order to conduct effective training sessions. Many of the methods used in the United States for educating children in the school system are rejected by adults. Not many adults are receptive to day-long lectures, "homework" composed of repetitive drills, or attending class five days a week for many consecutive weeks. Trainers need to know the basic learning principles which are useful in training adults. Each of the following concepts tells something about how adults learn.

The Desire to Learn. Adults must want to learn. Adults will usually resist learning anything merely because someone says they should. They learn most effectively when they have a strong inner motivation to develop a new skill or to acquire a particular type of knowledge. They must be *ready* to learn. It is seldom effective to force training upon adults without explaining, defending, and justifying the need for training and how it will benefit them. If the trainer demonstrates the benefits to be derived from training and if the training experiences are made interesting and challenging, the trainees' attitudes may be modified. This can result in a desire to learn that replaces a lack of interest in the training being presented.

The Need to Learn. Adults will learn only when they feel a need to learn. They are practical in their approach to learning. They want to know, "How is this going to help me right now?" Sometimes they can be persuaded to learn things that will help them in the clearly foreseeable future, such as when a promotion is imminent. However, adults learn best when they expect to get immediate benefits and when the knowledge or skills they are trying to acquire will be directly useful in meeting a present responsibility.

Adults expect results from the first class, lecture, or home assignment, and from each additional session of the course. They have little patience with a trainer (either in a formal program or in an informal coaching session) when the trainer insists on providing a lot of preliminary background, theory, or historical review. Adults want direct and concise instruction. They want the trainer to say, "This is what you do; this is how you do it; and this is why it works." If adult learners decide that the training has no relevance to their personal needs, they will probably become dropouts–physically if the training is voluntary, mentally if attendance is required.

Learning by Doing. Adults learn best by doing. They need to actively participate in the learning process. Adults will frequently forget much more of what they learn passively (by reading a book or by listening to a series of lectures) than of what they learn actively. Retention of new knowledge or skills is much higher when adults have immediate and repeated opportunities to participate in the learning process and practice or use what they learn.

A Realistic Focus. Adult learning must focus on realistic problems. Adults will learn best if training begins with specific problems drawn from business experiences, and if they are allowed to solve the problems and identify for themselves the principles they learned from the problem-solving exercise.

The importance of realism in adult training cannot be overemphasized. Many adults simply will not bother to figure out a problem which is clearly contrived for training purposes only. When any situation differs from their experience, they assume that it is a "pretend" situation which could not occur in the "real world." Adult interest in training increases when it is built around real, rather than "pretend," problems.

Relating Learning to Experience. Adult learning must be related to, and integrated with, the accumulated results of a lifetime of learning experiences. If the new knowledge does not fit in with what the adults already know (or think they know), the knowledge will probably be rejected. In fact, past experiences may actually prevent adults from absorbing the meaning of newly presented information or, at least, prevent them from perceiving it accurately.

The practical implication of this for trainers is that adults must be given every opportunity to interrupt, to ask questions, or to disagree with the trainer. Through a give-and- take exchange, the trainer can determine what the trainees' experience includes and what viewpoints they have acquired. Then the skillful trainer can present new ideas in such a way that the adults' experiences will reinforce, rather than contradict, the new information being presented.

An Informal Environment. Adults learn best in an informal environment. Adult learners may be as old as, or much older than, the trainer. Efforts by the trainer to treat trainees like children or to "manage the classroom" will be met with resistance. Adults want the classroom to be orderly, but they also appreciate an informal environment.

Trainers will find their leadership and training roles much easier and more pleasant if they deal with employees as professional colleagues rather than as subordinates. Staff members often act as they think their supervisor expects them to act. If they believe that they are expected to be immature and childish, then they may well act that way. Frequently, this response to expectations is not a conscious response. It just seems to happen. When trainers treat employees like colleagues and expect them to assume adult responsibilities, employees are more receptive to achieving organizational goals.

Guidance not Grades. Some adults are apprehensive about their learning capacity, since they have been out of school for some time. If they are confronted with tests, grades, and other devices for comparative evaluation of their progress, they may withdraw from the entire experience for fear of being humiliated.

At the same time, adult learners want to know how well they are doing. Before they continue learning, adults need to know whether they are learning correctly, if they are performing correctly, and how well they understand the basic ideas. Adults tend to set exacting goals for themselves; often they are impatient with their errors and become easily discouraged about their inability to learn. They need as much praise as the trainer can honestly give them. If it is absolutely necessary to criticize an adult learner, the criticism should be constructive and it should be given privately, in a pleasant manner.

Factors Affecting the Learning Process

People are individuals and, as such, they learn at different speeds, in different ways, and have different levels and types of abilities as well as different needs. Their backgrounds differ in terms of capabilities and life experiences.

Training programs and trainers must have the flexibility to deal with the individual differences of all the employees who need training. An important step toward dealing with individual differences is to be aware of basic factors that affect the learning process. Each is important and should be considered when making decisions about how to train employees.

Attention Span. People learn best, and remember longer, when the presentation or training activity does not exceed their span of attention. Therefore, as the length of training time increases, trainers must use a variety of techniques to keep renewing interest.

Spacing. People learn best when the training is spaced. For example, four one-hour sessions are usually better than one four-hour session. An exception to this principle is made when a specific learning objective requires intensive experience. Rest periods can be utilized to help refresh the trainee as training time increases.

Learning Speed. People learn at different rates of speed. When people are faced with a new task, they usually start by making rapid progress. Then there is a period when little or no progress is made. Sometimes learners actually regress during this leveling-off period. This is very common when trainees are learning tasks or a job. They may temporarily forget what was learned, or they may perform more slowly than when they first began.

Then they usually accelerate again and progress rapidly. During training it is advisable to have individuals compete against themselves to improve their speed rather than to compete against other trainees. Competition between trainees may lead to conflict and reduced learning.

Some trainees will learn faster than others. When a trainee is slow, the trainer should be patient and attempt to determine the cause. If the trainee suspects that the trainer is impatient or irritated, his or her confidence can be destroyed and progress will be slowed even more.

Right Way First. People remember best what they learn first. If errors are made in acquiring speed before accuracy, those habits may be difficult to break. Therefore, accuracy should be stressed before speed. An exception to this principle is made when a particular operation requires speed for competence.

Repetition. People learn information faster, and remember it longer, if it is repeated several times. For example, words, phrases, and symbols are repeated several times in advertising. Such repetition may seem annoying, but the slogans are not quickly forgotten. Even a good joke will not be remembered unless it is told several times soon after it is heard. Saying the same thing several different ways can serve to reinforce and review the most important aspects of content in a training session.

Motivation. People learn best when they want to learn. Learning is self-motivated. The trainer cannot motivate the trainee; only the trainee can motivate himself or herself. The trainer can help the trainee become motivated to learn by applying principles of adult learning as training is planned and conducted. The actual amount of learning that takes place, however, depends upon the trainee's interest in and immediate need for the training activity.

Participation. People learn and develop skills best by actually doing them. For example, a person who wants to learn how to prepare flambé dishes might read a book on tableside cookery and then watch a maitre d'hotel prepare a flaming dessert. However, the skill will not be developed until the person actually prepares a flambé dish and ignites the liqueur. When participation is not included in training, the result is often limited to "knowledge about" rather than the "ability to do" the task for which training is being offered.

Step-by-Step. People learn best when steps are presented in a consecutive manner. For example, front office agents should know about room types and rates before they learn how to register and room a guest or how to prepare folios. The trainer can ensure progress by making each step easy to master, easy to complete, and worthwhile.

It helps the learner when he or she is shown the whole job before it is broken down into its smaller parts. Elements of any job should be practiced separately only after the individual has a feel for the whole task. After showing the trainee the whole job, the trainer should then break it down and begin training with simple steps. The trainee should learn the basic steps before trying to learn the more complex variations.
Progress. Employees learn best when they can see progress being made. If what they learn proves to be useful on the job, this will provide a stimulus for further learning. Trainees gain satisfaction from feeling that they are progressing.

Common Training Mistakes

No trainer will ever be perfect. The ability to design and execute a training program is so involved that it becomes difficult to recall every principle and factor which affects the learning process. Training can be successful if trainers give their best effort, sincerely try to use as many of the principles of learning as possible, and avoid as many mistakes as they can. A brief description of common mistakes by trainers is presented here to help trainers know what to avoid. Each training mistake relates to a violation of a learning principle.

Training Too Much at One Time. Sometimes, trainers think they cannot afford to allocate time for training. When they do schedule a training session, they feel they have to cover everything in one session. After the session, they become frustrated because employees do not apply much of the material that was reviewed in training. One reason for the lack of application may be that too much was covered at one time. The training should be broken up into short sessions that focus on a few skill or knowledge areas. Then, the next training session can build on what was learned in the first session, and the employees can gain experience practicing what they have learned.

Training Too Quickly. Besides trying to teach too much at one session, a trainer can make the mistake of training too quickly. Learning takes time for many employees. Trainers sometimes fail to remember that employees may not have the same background, education, or experience that they do, and they attempt to train too fast. Allow employees time to grasp the concepts and skills before moving on. The time spent in training will be repaid many times when employee performance improves.

Ignoring the Trainee's Point of View. Peeling potatoes and cleaning out grease traps may seem like "easy jobs" to many trainers, but very few of them actually do these jobs themselves. Employees have to learn some undesirable tasks as well as those that are more pleasant. The trainer should consider the task that is being presented from the trainee's point of view. Whether the task is pleasant or unpleasant, simple or complex, it may be the first time that the trainee has been exposed to it. Trainees who are having difficulty learning a task or accepting the responsibility to perform an undesirable task do not want trainers to talk about how simple or easy it is. They appreciate empathy.

Losing Patience. Management should strive to be patient with slow learners, seemingly unmotivated trainees, and careless workers. These types of employees can be irritating, but if the trainer loses his or her temper and fails to cope with the situation, the training session will become completely worthless. Patience during training and coaching activities is always the best approach.

Ignoring Interest Factors. Another common training mistake is failing to judge the trainees' interest and responsiveness. A good trainer should pay close attention to the trainees. The trainer must watch and listen to the trainees and attempt to gauge their level of interest. If the trainees seem uninterested and bored, or if they reject the training, the trainer should attempt to regain interest by discussing the goals and objectives of the training.

Ignoring Individual Needs. Failure to recognize that different trainees need different amounts and kinds of training results in wasted time and money. Trainees reject training that does not meet their needs. Trainers should recognize this by developing training plans to meet specific needs. They should train employees in areas identified by performance evaluations.

Lack of Tact. Trainees learn best when the training enhances their self-images. If the trainer responds to questions without consideration for the trainee's feelings, the trainee may withdraw from the learning process. Tact, like patience, requires maturity on the part of the trainer. Trainees should be treated with the respect they deserve.

Child-like Treatment. Another common training mistake is trying to train adults like children. As children mature, they begin to require a reason for having to learn. Employees will not respond favorably to training if the only reason given is, "because the manager says you must." Adults, as well as children, demand a certain amount of independence in learning. They learn what makes sense to them, what they want and what they think they need to know.

Ignoring Backgrounds. Trainers should not ignore the individual differences of trainees. Good training builds on past experiences and, for this to occur, the trainer must have some understanding of each trainee's background. Past experiences can include employment, education, prior training, personal environment, goals, and ambitions.

Lack of Follow-up. Managers may take the attitude, "I showed them once and explained it to them completely. That should be enough for people who are serious about their jobs." The trainer may do everything right: plan the training based on a real need, present the training with an excellent demonstration and visual aids, allow trainees to demonstrate the skills, and answer questions to ensure understanding. Then the trainer ignores the trainees' performance until months later at performance evaluation time. The manager looks at each employee's performance and discovers that the procedures learned in training have not been followed since shortly after the training was concluded. There was no follow-up on the training to coach employees to apply what was learned and to maintain performance standards.

Inadequate Training Techniques. Trainers should recognize that a combination of audio and visual methods is much more effective than either training technique used alone. Lecturing used by itself may result in great recall shortly after training, but much less retention as time passes. The same general results occur when visual methods are used alone. However, when audio and visual methods are used together, results are much better; there is a greater amount of recall after training than when either method is used by itself.

No Opportunity for Trainees to Practice. Practicing some skills will cost money. For example, a chef might argue that he or she could not afford the luxury of trainees practicing because it would "upset the food cost." The chef could easily become frustrated over how to bridge the gap between his or her demonstration of the correct procedure and the trainees' mastery of the skill. It may not be possible to justify (in the chef's mind) wasting expensive ingredients that the trainees might ruin during the practice. As a result, the chef will be likely to have little success in developing a competent staff. Practice, then, may cost something, but it is essential in order for trainees to master skills.

Failure to Train in a Logical Sequence. Training materials must be sequenced in a logical order beginning with the first step in performing a job, moving on to the next logical step, and then on to another. Therefore, learning is arranged to begin with the simple steps and progress to the more difficult. When deciding which job to teach first, the same principles should apply.

Lack of Preparation by the Trainer. Perhaps the most common mistake made by managers who carry out their training responsibilities is the failure to prepare adequately for the training session. There is a common misconception among managers that, because they are knowledgeable about how to perform most of the skills required in their operations, they also know how to teach those skills to others. In order to ensure successful training, smart managers will learn as much as they can about how to prepare for training and about how people learn.

The Educational Institute Board of Trustees

The Educational Institute of the American Hotel & Motel Association is fortunate to have both industry and academic leaders, as well as allied members, on its Board of Trustees. Individually and collectively, the following persons play leading roles in supporting the Institute and determining the direction of its programs.

Caroline A. Cooper, CHA
Department Chair
Hospitality/Tourism
Johnson & Wales University
Providence, Rhode Island

Arnold J. Hewes
Executive Vice President
Minnesota Hotel & Lodging Association
St. Paul, Minnesota

Edouard P.O. Dandrieux, CHA
Director
H.I.M., Hotel Institute Montreux
Montreux, Switzerland

Howard P. "Bud" James, CHA
Hotel Consultant
Steamboat, Colorado

Robert S. DeMone, CHA
President, Chairman & CEO
Canadian Pacific Hotels & Resorts
Toronto, Ontario
Canada

Richard M. Kelleher, CHA
President & CEO
Guest Quarters Suite Hotels
Boston, Massachusetts

Ronald A. Evans, CHA
President & CEO
Best Western International, Inc.
Phoenix, Arizona

Donald J. Landry, CHA
President
Manor Care Hotel Division
Silver Spring, Maryland

Robert C. Hazard, Jr., CHA
Chairman & CEO
Choice Hotels International, Inc.
Silver Spring, Maryland

Bryan D. Langton, CBE
Chairman & CEO
Holiday Inn Worldwide
Atlanta, Georgia

Lawrence B. Magnan, CHA
President & CEO
Select Asset Management
Mercer Island, Washington

Gene Rupnik, CHA
General Manager/Partner
Days Inn
Springfield, Illinois

Jerry R. Manion, CHA
Executive Vice President - Operations
Motel 6
Dallas, Texas

Charlotte St. Martin
Executive Vice President
Operations & Marketing
Loews Hotels
New York, New York

John A. Norlander, CHA
President
Radisson Hotel Corporation
Minneapolis, Minnesota

William J. Sheehan, CHA
Vice Chairman
Omni Hotels
Hampton, New Hampshire

Michael B. Peceri, CHA
Chairman
Marquis Hotels & Resorts
Fort Meyers, Florida

William R. Tiefel
President
Marriott Lodging Group
Washington, D.C.

Philip Pistilli, CHA
Chairman
Raphael Hotel Group
Kansas City, Missouri

Paul E. Wise, CHA
Director
Hotel, Restaurant
    & Institutional Management
University of Delaware
Newark, Delaware